D0231259

LEEDS BECKETT UNIVERSITY
LIBRARY

DISCARDED

Leeds Metropolitan University

17 0110609 1

The Spectre of Capitalism

WITCH!

By the same author

Mrs Thatcher's Economic Experiment
Mr Lawson's Gamble
Britain Without Oil
Who Runs the Economy? (with R. Pennant-Rea)

THE SPECTRE
OF
CAPITALISM

THE FUTURE OF THE WORLD ECONOMY AFTER
THE FALL OF COMMUNISM

William Keegan

RADIUS
London

© William Keegan 1992

The right of William Keegan to be
identified as Author of this work has been asserted
by William Keegan in accordance with the
Copyright, Designs and Patents Act, 1988

All rights reserved

This edition first published in 1992 by
Radius

Reprinted 1992

Random House UK Limited
20 Vauxhall Bridge Road, London SW1V 2SA

Random House Australia (Pty) Ltd
20 Alfred Street, Milsons Point, Sydney, NSW 2061, Australia

Random House New Zealand Ltd
10 Poland Road, Glenfield, Auckland 10, New Zealand

Random House South Africa (Pty) Ltd
PO Box 337, Bergvlei, 2012, South Africa

A CIP catalogue record for this book
is available from the British Library

ISBN 0 09 174596 9

Typeset by Raven Typesetters, Ellesmere Port
Printed and bound in Great Britain by
Mackays of Chatham PLC, Chatham, Kent

LEEDS BECKETT UNIVERSITY
LIBRARY

LEEDS METROPOLITAN
UNIVERSITY LIBRARY
DISCARDED

1701010804
B32Hv
750x 6.2 95
23.3 90
330.15 KEE

Contents

For Hilary

I should like to thank everyone who has helped in the writing of this book. Sir Ian Gilmour, Adrian Hamilton, Anthony Howard, Richard Youard and Dr Ray Richardson read the manuscript and made invaluable comments. Mark Frankland and Dr John Steadman read sections and gave valuable advice. Bartholomew Keegan also assisted at a vital stage. Jeffrey Care, the *Observer*'s librarian, answered many a query. Ruth Fisher typed and helped with research. And my thanks are also owed to Donald Trelford, editor of *The Observer*, and to Neil Belton and Karen Holden, of Radius.

Preface

Communism has failed, but capitalism has not succeeded. Communism was an imposed system, willed upon hundreds of millions of people against the grain of human nature. Capitalism evolved: it is not so much a system, as a way of conducting governmental, industrial and business affairs that can take many different forms. One of the ironies of the 1980s was that communism itself ran into terminal trouble at the same time as the leading capitalist and "market" economies were finding the going much tougher. Although it may not have felt like it at the time, the period 1950–73 was something of a golden age of capitalism – at least for the richest fifth of the world.

Since then successive oil crises, problems with inflation, and an excessively free market approach have all contributed to a deterioration in capitalism's performance and slower economic growth. The hopes of visionaries who a generation ago thought enlightened capitalism would by now have solved most of mankind's material needs have been sadly disappointed. In this moment of triumphalism, capitalism faces many unresolved problems.

One of the developments widely considered to have enfeebled the US economy is the growth of its budget deficit. Yet it was the defence programme associated with the deficit that proved the final straw for communism. The USSR recognised that it could no longer even pretend to compete with the capitalist economies. And, as events unfolded, it became clear that there had never been a serious contest.

The threat from communism was a factor leading to co-operation between capitalist countries on a level never experienced during the inter-war years. But when dissatisfaction with the performance of the market economies became widespread in the 1970s, an opportunity for the New Right and extreme free marketeers to gain the ascendancy arose. Their ideas, or prejudices, not only led to the wild embrace of "deregulation" in the 1980s, but also had a pernicious influence on attitudes towards third world aid and shaped the kind of "big bang", radical economic reform which risks economic and social chaos in Eastern Europe and the former Soviet Union now.

The reason for the East down fall.

Paradoxically, it is Anglo-Saxon theories of capitalism and the free market which are promulgated in Eastern Europe, yet it is the more interventionist and consensus-seeking Japanese economy whose performance is generally respected. Similarly, despite its recent problems with the financing of reunification, the pragmatic German approach to economic policy has been more successful in the long run than the ideological swings of its Anglo-Saxon rivals.

The following pages attempt to explain some of the background to the evolution of modern capitalism, to delineate the different approaches of the various models, and to come to grips with such important questions as: why communism failed as an economic system, and why the Japanese economy has become the envy of the Western world. The consensus-seeking, centrist approach of Germany and (especially) Japan is seen to hold lessons for the rest of the world. But it also emerges that, with growing threats from environmental and migration problems, capitalism may indeed have to start planning its future – at just the moment when the collapse of communism had made the concept of planning anathema.

Capitalism needs to take stock of its differing patterns around the world, and to develop a wider view of economic man than that promoted by the obsession with narrow self-interest that was so fashionable in the 1980s. In the end, the self-interest of the "market economies" is likely to force a wider view upon them.

Introduction

The collapse of communism was seized upon in the West as heralding the final victory of capitalism. In the UK, in particular, it was regarded by the former Prime Minister Margaret Thatcher as the ultimate vindication of her Government's policies during the 1980s. In the US, one researcher attached to the State Department even asked whether events in Eastern Europe signified "The End of History?"[1]

Since there seem to have been quite a number of historic events in the past few years, the author of "The End of History?" has been subjected to considerable derision. In his defence, Francis Fukuyama has tried to point out that all he meant was history in a Hegelian sense – "the history of thought about first principles, including those governing political and social organisation".

Thus, for Fukuyama, "the end of history" means "not the end of events, but the end of the evolution of human thought about such first principles". According to Fukuyama, Hegel was correct in seeing the liberal-democratic states created by the French and American revolutions as "the end of history" (in this narrow sense); Marx devoted most of his life to proving Hegel wrong; and "the total and manifest failure of communism forces us to ask whether Marx's entire experiment was not a 150-year detour."[2]

It was an expensive detour, both in terms of the tens of millions of lives lost to the perpetuation of Stalinist and other regimes, and in terms of the feeble economic performance of communism. But it was not obvious that it was a detour until the momentous events symbolised by the demolition of the Berlin Wall. Whatever one thought of communism, until relatively recently it was a rival ideology and economic system, apparently competing for supremacy with something called "capitalism".

The Berlin Wall came to symbolise the fact that, in the last analysis, most people living under communist regimes wanted to leave, whereas defectors from the West were few and far between. Whatever one thought of the defects of capitalism, communism was infinitely worse. George Blake, one of the British spies who defected, told of how, after he married a Soviet woman, the woman's friends used to ask him why he had come to Russia voluntarily – most of them were trying to get out.[3]

The evidence of repression in the Soviet bloc was available to the West for many years. The failure of communism as an economic system took longer to become widely accepted; certainly, in the public mind there were the stories of jeans and sweaters being demanded in Red Square from Western visitors; but there was also the Sputnik, Russia's achievement in putting the first man into space, and, earlier than that, the massive Soviet war effort in 1939–45. Western consumers understandably tended to take more note of the handful of East European items that sold well in the West, than of the thousands of consumer goods that were simply not available in the East.

When the Wall came down, it gradually became apparent that the performance of the Soviet and East European economies was far worse than most Western experts had imagined. Even in East Germany, the East European "showpiece" once estimated by the World Bank to have "overtaken" some key Western economies, the economy turned out to be in a shambles. (The rescue of the East German economy was not assisted by the exchange rate at which monetary union was effected.)

The victory of capitalism appeared to be complete when the more adventurous spirits of the reform movement in Eastern Europe began to sound like "pure capitalists", with a faith in privatisation and market forces calculated to warm the hearts of the most Conservative of Westerners. The name of Margaret Thatcher, for instance, was frequently invoked by certain Hungarian and Czecho-slovak Ministers – and of course Mrs Thatcher herself made the maximum advantage out of her relationship with Mikhail Gorbachev.

As it turned out, the West was rather misled by the Russian word it got to know so well – namely "perestroika", or "restructuring". For most of us, the word first came into our ken after April 1985, when Mikhail Gorbachev, General Secretary of the Central Committee of the Communist Party of the Soviet Union, unveiled what his adviser Abel Aganbegyan called "the new economic strategy of development for our country"[4] (as opposed to Lenin's ill-fated "New Economic Policy" of the 1920s). The new "political concepts" were "uskorenie" (acceleration), "perestroika" (restructuring) and "glasnost" (openness). Perestroika and glasnost became household words in the West, but uskorenie somehow got lost – perhaps reflecting the fact that, as far as the economy was concerned, the only acceleration during the subsequent six years was in the wrong direction.

It was not until 9 November 1989 that the Berlin Wall came down. When writing about "perestroika" in October 1989, the Professor of Russian History at Berkeley, Martin Malia, rather dramatically opted for the pseudonym "Z". He subsequently explained this resort to anonymity by pointing out that at the time his article could have appeared as "provocatively anti-perestroika" – which it was: Malia's whole point was that the West had mis-interpreted perestroika, and made too many allowances for Gorbachev. The Russians were trying to restructure communism, whereas Malia's argument was that "for structural reasons going back to 1917, communism was irreformable; it had to be wholly dismantled if the nations it ruined were to survive. Mikhail Gorbachev's 'half measures' thus encouraged the illusion of reformability and put off the moment of truth."[5]

Malia had been worried about compromising the reformers if his name appeared. As recently as October 1989 the Communist Party was sacred, the dramatic resignations from the Party of figures such as Boris Yeltsin and Gavriil Popov had yet to take place, and the market economy was a taboo topic in Russia. These reformers did not request the mere restructuring of communism, but wanted to abandon it in favour of "pluralistic democracy, private property, the market and a negotiated federation, even republic independence". But the reformers were still worried about *in*formers. Then came the historic "springtime" of November 1989 in Leipzig, Berlin and Prague, and the election of reformers as members of the democratic opposition in the USSR in 1990.

Since the autumnal "spring" of 1989 and the initial euphoria surrounding Eastern Europe's bid for freedom (which was most obviously successful in Poland, Hungary and Czechoslovakia) the former totalitarian economies have been struggling to come to grips with reality. When I visited Russia in the early summer of 1990, the enthusiasm of many officials, politicians and academics for "market economies" was infectious – but there was also a strong element of naivety about the means to this end, and the likely duration of the transition.

By contrast to Gorbachev's early reluctance to embrace anything other than half measures to reform the economic system, elsewhere in Eastern Europe we have heard a Hungarian Prime Minister and a Czechoslovak finance minister sound even more devoted to "free market" ideas than Ronald Reagan and Mrs Thatcher in their heyday. Advising Eastern Europe has offered a field day for economists who, after the disappointments of the 1980s, might be considered a little too extreme in their views in the West. (These economists are sometimes referred to in Eastern Europe as "suitcase economists" because of the speed with which they fly into town, deliver their nostrums, and zoom out again.)

One argument central to this book is that it is a mistake to interpret the collapse of communism as the triumph of the kind of capitalism that reigned supreme in the US and UK during the 1980s – even though it is probably fair to attribute to the prime exponents of that capitalism, Ronald Reagan and Mrs Margaret Thatcher, a share in the political developments which contributed to communism's final collapse.

Throughout the 1980s, the industrial economy most feared by the US and UK was Japan, which operates a high degree of long term planning in its industrial sector. And, while the "Thatcher Experiment" in disengaging from public sector activity was taking place, Continental Europe continued with traditional "mixed economy" ideals, and aspirations for a "Social Charter". Fukuyama refers to the triumph of "liberal democratic" states, but there is a marked difference between the economic and social policies of Continental Europe and the US, or Mrs Thatcher's attempt to emulate the US.

The US system is sometimes referred to as "liberal capitalism", or "democratic capitalism" and the German as the "social market economy", for which I offer the alternative term "social capitalism".[6] There are significant differences between the two approaches: once Mrs Thatcher had been forced to resign, the British Conservative Party was free, under the influence of John Major and the then Party chairman Chris Patten, to be drawn towards the German model, through growing links with the German Christian Democrats. This would not have been a popular move with the right wing of the Conservative Party, which had shared Mrs Thatcher's hostility towards Europe, and set up the "Bruges Group" to resist such heretical tendencies. In the event, at the Maastricht Summit of the European Council in December 1991, the Major Government declined to sign the Social Charter, and there was little sign that the Conservatives wished to be more Christian Democratic.

The US and UK are frequently bracketed together as the two leading "Anglo-Saxon" economies. But, to British eyes, the US looks a tougher, rougher economic environment altogether. "Market forces" appear to be given freer rein; free enterprise is worshipped; the labour force is less unionised and more willing (or at least more prepared) to accept low wages. Economists and a certain type of politician in Britain have for years wanted to see greater evidence of mobility and entrepreneurship – the average Briton has a tiresome disinclination to behave like part of a textbook equation. By contrast the US seems to be an economy imbued with the spirit of the frontier. There used to be apocryphal stories about Americans visiting London and being gullible enough to buy Tower Bridge from a passer-by; if anything, this fantasy served to reassure the British, who think of America as a nation of salesmen.

But even as Mrs Thatcher's eyes regarded the putative flexibility of the US economic system, close students of that system were increasingly concerned that the US was losing out to competition (fair or unfair – mainly, it was agreed, the latter) from Japan. In the world of "capitalism" or "market economies" it is Japan and Germany who have most disturbed competitor countries in recent years; indeed, for much of the time one of the principal themes of international economic meetings was the attempt to persuade the Japanese and Germans to "play fair" and take measures to reduce their enormous balance of payments surpluses. (The main step in this direction taken by West Germany in the end was to effect a monetary and economic union with East Germany. Absorbing the latter's problems actually eliminated the mighty German surplus in the early months of 1991.)

Those more familiar with the US scene than Mrs Thatcher might observe that the way in which Congress operates is a far cry from her ideal of minimum public spending. One of the many ironies of the Reagan period was that instead of being eliminated, as had been promised, an unbalanced budget was built into the system. Much of this, however, reflected higher defence spending; and, although public expenditure rose during the Reagan Presidency as a proportion of gross domestic product, it was still considerably lower than in Europe. The Scandinavian economies, with their extremely high levels of social spending, may have run into trouble in the early 1990s. But there remained an outstanding difference between the approach to, and level of public provision in Western Europe, and that of the United States. Mrs Thatcher's seeming disregard for Professor Galbraith's famous warning about "private affluence amid public squalor"[7] played an important role in her downfall. The proximate causes of Thatcher's dismissal were the ignominious failure of the "poll tax" and her increasingly intransigent anti-Europeanism. But backbench Conservative members of Parliament were also receiving the message that people were losing patience with the squalor of the public sector services. Thatcher had always favoured tax cuts rather than social spending; "Thatcherism" had put the Conservative Party way behind in the opinion polls, even before the events of the autumn of 1990, when Mrs Thatcher was succeeded by John Major.

Much international discussion of economies is of the "grass is greener" variety. For communists, or ex-communists, there was little question that the grass was greener on the capitalist side of the Wall. For Britons, who have patently lacked economic self-confidence in recent decades, the grass is now greener on mainland Europe, whose economic successes became more widely appreciated as the British travelled more in the 1980s and early 1990s.

Almost everybody envies the Japanese their economic performances, if not their life-style – the remark by a European Commissioner that the Japanese were "a nation of workaholics living in rabbit hutches" rankled when it was made in the late 1970s, and still rankles now. The pace at which Japan earned foreign exchange surpluses during the 1980s, and used the proceeds to expand its direct investments abroad, led some observers to express the fear that Japan, having been one of the losers in the Second World War, was about to conquer the world with finance – by simply buying up other countries.

While capitalism was winning the battle against communism, it was also "deregulating" itself. But the capitalist, or market economies, that were most envied – namely Japan and Germany – were also among those economies that were sluggish in removing regulations, possessed financial systems which favoured the "long term" view in dealing with industry, and – especially in Germany's case – favoured relatively high public spending and a decent "welfare state". They were very different from the Reagan/Thatcher prototype.

Before the fall of the Wall, the debate in the West seemed to be between those who thought capitalism was wonderful, and those who thought it could do a lot better. The first impression one tends to have on seeing the Russian or East European economies at close hand is one of horror, followed by a feeling that at least exposure to the economic ravages of communism puts the problems of capitalism in perspective. But it is not long, after returning home, before one is immersed once again in all the familiar debates about what is wrong with the US, the UK or wherever.

It took hundreds of years for the leading "market economies" of the West (and, of course, Japan in the east) to achieve the average standard of living which is the envy of Eastern Europe. That average standard conceals marked variations, and within countries there remain disturbingly large pockets of poverty. The disappointing performance of so many developing countries since 1945 is also a reminder of how long it can take to transform textbook theories into reality.

The stark contrast between capitalism and communism may be something of a false dichotomy. Communism, which means collective ownership, is a system which was *willed* and had to be enforced; "Communist economics is about what the Party wants, and depends essentially on denying the economic facts of life," in the words of one lifelong observer. Capitalism – private ownership based on legal property rights – is the way societies seem to have naturally evolved if communism has not been forced upon them. "Central planning" was an essential part of the communist system; and the market economy is also a system, requiring laws to ensure that contracts are carried out (or redress is available) and rules and policing so that the public's gains from competition and the profit motive are not threatened or restricted by the natural tendency of big business towards monopoly.

The human tendency to search for panaceas and magic solutions is well represented among politicians and economists. If central planning is a god that has failed, the perfect competition and harmonious equilibrium of the economist's textbook diagrams is seldom achieved. But the pursuit of the Holy Grail goes on. In practice politicians and officials try to impose order on an inherently messy world. And in their way both planners and extreme free marketeers are seeking to tidy up a world that does not always conform to a blueprint.

Although there was much huffing and puffing on Labour's left in favour of more central planning, there soon emerged a basic consensus between the Conservative and Labour Parties after 1945 on a mixed economy and a welfare state. There were differences at the margins, and some industries, such as steel, became political footballs, being kicked in and out of the public and private sectors. Britain spent much of the post-1945 period adjusting to the end of empire – which had given it captive markets and supplies of raw materials – but was not sufficiently adjusted to feel it necessary to catch the European Community bus when it started off in the 1950s. After the brief flirtation with Mrs Thatcher's mixture of nationalism and transatlanticism, and after Labour's traditional suspicion of Europe had been impressively overcome, the leadership of both major British parties was avowedly pro-European by 1991.

It was evident at the beginning of the 1990s that governments, businessmen and the financial markets thought and behaved increasingly as though the advanced industrialised world was divided into three trading blocs – centred on the US, the European Community and Japan. These accounted respectively for 36 per cent, 34 per cent and 19 per cent of the total output of the 24 member Organisation for Economic Co-operation and Development (OECD) club of "market economies". Germany dominated the EC, accounting for 9 per cent of OECD output, against 7 per cent for France, 6 per cent for Italy and only 5 and a half per cent for the UK.

The European Economic Community had been born out of the political desire to learn the lessons of history by tying Germany down in a united Europe which would never again go to war against itself. "Nothing," said Winston Churchill, "but the dread of Stalinized Russia could have brought the conception of united Europe from dreamland into the forefront of modern thought."[8] European integration was in fact urged by the US, and it became clear that, with occasional exceptions such as the close relationship between President Reagan and Mrs Thatcher (and, later, during the Gulf War of January 1991), the US saw Britain's role as being within the EC, and encouraged a closer relationship.

These were days when more and more of the British people were either taking their holidays in Continental Europe, or doing business there, or both. An American diplomatist commented: "What we are trying to get across to Mrs Thatcher is that 'Yes, we like the British and have an affinity with them, but the fact of the matter is that most of our relations are now with Bonn and Brussels, and it is better for Britain to assume its proper place in Europe.'"

Although the Thatcherite rump of the Conservative Party continued to hanker after a golden age of the "special relationship" with the US, even elements of the Labour Left were converted to a pro-European stance during the second half of the 1980s. It was a sign of the times when M. Jacques Delors, President of the European Commission, was invited to a TUC Conference and given a rapturous welcome. Against the background of the grinding down they endured under Mrs Thatcher's Government, the left saw a better chance of achieving their goals under the EC "Social Charter' and the generally more socially conscious policies of Continental Europe.

It soon became obvious that the countries of Eastern Europe that had rejected communism wanted associate status of the EC, and, eventually, full membership. The collapse of the communist economic system coincided with the moves in Western Europe first, towards the "Single Market" of 1992, and second, towards wider economic and monetary union. The Single Market initiative sprang from the fact that, while having a common external tariff, negotiating as a trading bloc, and imposing minimal tariff barriers on trade between EC countries, the EC in the 1980s still had many non-tariff barriers to its internal trade, exchange controls, and widespread restrictions on trade in services. It conducted trade negotiations as if it were one vast country, yet it was in fact a collection of nation states, with much less mobility of labour and capital within the EC than the US or Japan. The idea of encouraging trans-national mergers between companies, and generally removing "structural rigidities" to economic performance, was seen as a way of arresting the so-called "Eurosclerosis" by which the EC was allegedly afflicted in the early 1980s. The Reagan administration had actually preached the virtues of such a move for doctrinal reasons, although subsequently the US – increasingly concerned about the quality of its own economic performance – began to show concern about the possible damage that a "Fortress Europe" could do to its own trade.

The 1980s was a period when the capitalist or market economies themselves tried to reassert their belief in market forces and in a smaller role for the public sector. Privatisation and de-regulation had been all the rage. But in capitalism's finest hour – the manifest collapse of communism – the "club" of market economies faced a number of threats to their own success. Were these countries which avowed such firm faith in the virtue of the free market going to allow the trading frictions between the major blocks to develop into a trade war? Had deregulation of the financial system produced such chaos, in both the banking system and the fluctuating foreign exchange markets, that financial market forces were impeding the ability of the real market economy to deliver? And, in their enthusiasm for market forces and the private sector, were the major market economies neglecting the basic infrastructure which all market economies ultimately needed, and, indeed, risking destruction of the environment on which the future of the entire planet depended?

All these questions involved re-examination of the appropriate role of Government, or the state; of the balance between the public and the private sectors of the economy; of the question "when is Government intervention necessary and when are things best left to 'the market'?" And, perhaps most of all, it was necessary to scrutinise the "rules of the game" for the conduct of economic and trading relations between nation states and trading blocs. Countries or trading blocs which "do their own thing", and fail to co-ordinate sufficiently, may be threatening the future of that very "capitalism" which is celebrating its triumph over communism.

1

The Rescue of Capitalism

One of the first intentions of Soviet Communists after the October 1917 Revolution was to abolish the use of money for most purposes.[1] Private property was by definition anathema to the Revolution. By contrast, a leading Western thinker wrote that "the essential characteristic of capitalism [is] the dependence upon an intense appeal to the money-making and money-loving instincts of individuals as the main motive force of the economic machine."[2] The same writer, after a visit to Russia in 1925, wrote "People in Russia, if only because of their poverty, are very greedy for money – at least as greedy as elsewhere. But money-making and money-accumulating cannot enter into the life-calculations of a rational man who accepts the Soviet rule in the way in which they enter into ours."[3] Making his distaste for the regime abundantly clear, the writer went on: "If one is to make any generalisation in present conditions, it must be this – that at a low level of efficiency the system does function and possesses elements of permanence."[4] Leninism was "at the same time a persecuting and missionary religion and an experimental economic technique".[5] The economic technique held no attractions – being based on "an obsolete economic textbook which I know to be not only scientifically erroneous but without interest or application for the modern world".[6]

But the ruthlessness of the regime, and its missionary zeal, were more disturbing: "For modern capitalism is absolutely irreligious, without internal union, without much public spirit, often, though not always, a mere congeries of possessors and pursuers. Such a system has to be immensely, not merely moderately, successful to survive. In the nineteenth century it was in a certain sense idealistic; at any rate it was a united and self-confident system. It was not only immensely successful, but held out hopes of a continuing crescendo of prospective successes. Today it is only moderately successful. If irreligious capitalism is ultimately to defeat religious Communism it is not enough that it should be economically more efficient – it must be many times as efficient."[7]

From 1985 on, Mr Gorbachev's attempts at perestroika – even

though the initial aim was to reconstruct communism rather than to abolish it – were a clear sign to the whole world that communism had failed; the events of 1989 in Eastern Europe followed from perestroika. To turn round the prophetic words of that visitor to Russia in 1925, it had been established that "religious Communism" was many more times *in*efficient than "irreligious capitalism".

That visitor was, in fact, the British economist John Maynard Keynes. Keynes has a claim to have been the one person who, above all others, endeavoured to make capitalism less "irreligious", in the sense of trying to make it function more efficiently, and to embody a greater sense of social justice. For Keynes the obsession of private capitalists with money was the opposite extreme of the original Soviet attempt to abolish it. The political problem of mankind was how to combine economic efficiency, social justice and individual liberty. "In the economic field," he argued, "we must find new policies and new instruments to adapt and control the working of economic forces, so that they do not intolerably interfere with contemporary ideas as to what is fit and proper in the interests of social stability and social justice."[8] In an age when "almost alone among men, the City editors, all bloody and blindfolded, still piteously bow down [before] the free play of economic forces", Keynes warned that "the transition from economic anarchy to a regime which deliberately aims at controlling and directing economic forces in the interests of social justice and social stability, will present enormous difficulties, both technical and political."[9]

Keynes thought "capitalism, wisely managed, can probably be made more efficient for attaining economic ends than any alternative system yet in sight, but [that] in itself it is in many ways extremely objectionable."[10] The cure for unemployment, and for great in-equalities of wealth, lay outside the operations of individuals or the doctrine of *laissez-faire*. To Keynes the "moral problem of our age is concerned with the love of money . . ."[11]

Keynes devoted many years to the propagation of his economic ideas. Ironically, it was *after* these seeds of his thought began to grow that the capitalist world suffered the devastation of the slump of the late 1920s and early 1930s. It was against the background of Depression and high unemployment that Hitler came to power in Germany, democratically elected (with a little help from coercion) in January 1933, on 37 per cent of the popular vote, with the overwhelming majority against him, but fatally divided. Millions of unemployed had turned in desperation to the Communists or the Nazis, and, as William L. Shirer writes, "The Communists, at the behest of Moscow, were committed to the last to the silly idea of first destroying the Social Democrats, the Socialist trade unions and what middle-class democratic forces there were, on the dubious theory that although this would lead to a Nazi regime it would be only temporary and would bring inevitably the collapse of capitalism, after which the Communists would take over and establish the dictatorship of the proletariat."[12]

The theory was not so dubious with regard to the future of East Germany, and, of course, the rise and fall of Hitler ultimately led to the "dictatorship of the proletariat" for almost half a century throughout Eastern Europe. But the route may not have been quite what the Bolshevik/Marxists had in mind in 1932/33, and the proletariat was dictated *to* rather than doing the dictating itself. Indeed, according to Bullock, the Russians were not really serious about "exporting the revolution"; it was only after the repulsion of Hitler's invasion of Russia that communism in Europe became a serious possibility, which Stalin grasped at Yalta.[13]

Another irony was that it was Hitler's Germany which saw the most dramatic economic growth during the 1930s, and proved an early exponent of the kind of expansionist measures and use of public works urged by Keynes to reduce unemployment. Between 1932 and 1939 the gross domestic product of Germany grew by almost 80 per cent, compared to 26 per cent in the UK. In the US, where Keynesian-style policies were associated with Roosevelt's New Deal, gross domestic product rose by 41 per cent over the same period.

The Communists had opted for central planning of the economy. Keynes urged "collective action" to reduce uncertainty by collecting and disseminating helpful information for businessmen, while leaving "private initiative and enterprise unhindered."[14] The great effort to collect economic data and to build up accounts of national income and expenditure was made on both sides of the Atlantic during the Second World War (1939–45). The war necessarily involved a heavy degree of central planning – a "command economy" in several senses. The emphasis after the war was on ensuring, in the US, UK and elsewhere, that "capitalism" continued to function, but in a mixed economy, with an appropriate role for the public sector, and with government willing and prepared to intervene to promote employment in a way that was absent from most of the inter-war period. However, the formal commitment to full employment and to Keynes was stronger in the UK than the US, where the role of the public sector was always lower, and where the word "full" was dropped from official policy aims for employment as a result of pressure from the Right.[15]

A number of writers have questioned the received wisdom about the "wartime spirit" of the 1939–45 period, and the widespread view that differences were buried and nations such as Britain "pulled together"; nevertheless, there was sufficient sense of this for the emphasis of post-war policy to be on a greater feeling for social stability and social justice – although the concept of the "welfare state" was much more widely accepted and acted upon in Europe than in the US.[16] Despite the experience of the Depression, Americans remained more at home with the spirit of "raw capitalism" than did Europeans.

One does not wish to exaggerate the significance of Keynes. There were millions of others who wanted to preserve capitalism in a more enlightened, humane and managed form. His economic ideas were very similar to those of the contemporary Polish economist Kalecki; and there were many economists, such as Richard Kahn of Cambridge, and Alvin Hansen in the US, who contributed to the development of "Keynes's" economics. (There were many more who contributed to "Keynesian" economics after his death.)

Keynesian economics were a boost to capitalism, and helped it to make the most of the scientific and technological progress which capitalism thrives on. But Keynes was not the originator of the visionary plan conceived after the war according to which the United States, mindful of the damage wrought by reparations and misguided economic policies following the 1914–18 war, underwrote economic reconstruction in Western Europe. The author of that plan was General Marshall, in a speech at Harvard in 1947.

But the Keynesian message spread. As J. K. Galbraith points out, by the time the US economist Simon Kuznets had constructed a system of Keynesian national accounts for the US in the early 1940s, "the statistics, in their powerful practical impact, made Keynes inescapable."[17] Similarly Robert Marjolin, who worked on the French Plan of Modernisation and Equipment (1946–48) speaks in his memoirs about how he too was influenced by meeting and reading Keynes when it came to the challenge of ensuring that post-1945 economic policies differed from those of the 1920s.

Marjolin had been in the US during the Great Depression. He was also, in common with many members of his generation, so appalled by the defects of capitalism that he flirted with Marxism and Communism. In Britain Denis Healey, subsequently to be Labour Chancellor of the Exchequer and a great champion of the mixed economy, was one of many who actually joined the Communist Party during the 1930s in their youth.

"Almost any undergraduate who wanted to stop Hitler was then easy game for the Communists" Healey has observed.[18]

Marjolin's memoir of the 1930s provides an interesting indication of the view at the time that the answer lay in a more enlightened capitalism: "The United States in 1932–33 was a picture of desolation, but despite the plunge in output and the relentless rise in unemployment one could not help feeling the power of this industrial giant and acquiring the conviction that relatively little was needed to put it back on its feet."[19]

This was not the kind of thing one heard about the problems of the USSR in the early 1990s. Marjolin continues: "A modicum of experience and some knowledge of history were enough to cast doubt on the (Marxist) theory of an inevitable decline of capitalism owing to a falling rate of profit. How could one regard as irreversible and leading up to a complete economic and social transformation an experience that was no more than two or three years old, when the United States ... had previously known long decades of un-precedented prosperity? A moment's thought, and the idea that the world's working classes were condemned to 'increasing misery' stood revealed as having absolutely no foundation in history."[20] (He presumably did not have the Third World in mind in this context.)

Marjolin said that, with the arrival of Roosevelt and the New Deal "I became progressively convinced that even though the capitalist system was imperfect, vulnerable and unstable, it could be made to work better ... That men could destroy it through their ignorance, their errors and their folly was another matter; to me this seemed possible, if not probable."[21]

The "ignorance" of capitalists ran deep. The most minor social and welfare measures to alleviate the plight of the poor have often been resisted as "socialism" or "communism". As Keynes himself observed: "The Conservative Party ought to be concerning itself with evolving a version of individualistic capitalism adapted to the progressive change of circumstances. The difficulty is that the capitalist leaders in the City and in Parliament are incapable of distinguishing novel measures for safeguarding capitalism from what they call Bolshevism."[22]

Keynes's message was that economic, or "market" forces, were patently incapable of guaranteeing full employment, and that this required Government intervention. The kind of "micro-economics" approach which was appropriate to the firm or industry was inadequate for the economy at large. The question was: what determined the level of output in the economy?

Classical economists were obsessed with a theoretical world based on assumptions, such as "perfect competition" and extreme flexi-bility of wages and prices, which led to "equilibrium". Keynes argued that in the real world such equilibrium was a fantasy, and that, even if equilibrium were indeed achieved, there was no reason why this should be at full employment. What made sense at the "micro" level – saving for a rainy day – did not make sense at the macro level if there was too much saving and not enough spending. Keynesian economics became associated with the view that Governments could intervene to increase purchasing power through public works, tax cuts and so on, but Keynes's original emphasis was on the importance of investment in buildings, plant, machinery and public works. This did not necessarily rise if interest rates fell – everything depended on the prospective level of effective demand for goods and services, which it was within the power of government to influence if it so chose.

Roosevelt's "New Deal" in 1933–37 involved public sector investment and "pump priming" from "Keynesian" Budget deficits. Keynes's "General Theory", written largely to persuade fellow economists of his ideas, was not published until 1936. Keynes met Roosevelt before then, and preached his ideas in the US. But he was only one of many economists – such as Jacob Viner of Chicago – preaching "expansionist" ideas, and thought journalists over-estimated his influence on the New Deal.[23] Economists and officials preparing for the post-war world, and not wanting to repeat the economic disasters of the inter-war period, were increasingly won over to the Keynesian view that Government intervention was necessary to achieve full employment in the capitalist economies. And, in the UK, much work was done on the Beveridge Report (1942) and after to ensure that the post-war economy would offer a better welfare and education system for all, and a social security safety net for the old, the sick, and the unemployed.

Two economists opposed to Keynes in the 1930s were Lionel Robbins, of the London School of Economics, and the Austrian Friedrich von Hayek. An example of how firmly Keynesian economics had taken root in the post-war world was provided by a retraction Robbins made in his memoirs in 1971: "I shall always regard this aspect of my dispute with Keynes as the greatest mistake of my professional career, and the book, *The Great Depression*, which I subsequently wrote, as something which I would willingly see forgotten . . . I was not blind to the facts of deflation. But I missed the main cause thereof." Again: "fluctuations of aggregate demand must not be left to look after themselves . . . it is an important function of government, national or international, to pay attention to such matters."[24] Similarly, a submission about Hayek to the Nobel Prize Committee in the early 1970s stated "after several years of the Great Depression, it had become clear that Hayek's pre-scription of 'waiting it out' was inopportune . . . In those years of 'secular' stagnation and unemployment, a model for which full employment was the starting assumption could not compete with one that was based on unemployment equilibrium."[25]

The Keynesian influence on economics was not confined to domestic economic policy. The preponderant theme of the international discussions that led up to the Bretton Woods conference of 1944, and the subsequent formation of such international institutions as the International Monetary Fund, the World Bank, the Organisation for Economic Co-operation and Development and the General Agreement on Tariffs and Trade was the belief that enlightened co-operation *between* capitalist countries was also necessary.

After the 1914–18 war the main capitalist countries had started off on the wrong foot and had then fallen over. Reparations had been self-defeating, as had France's desire not to assist in the recovery of the German economy. "Each country sought to resolve its difficulties as if it were the only country in the world" . . . wrote Marjolin, "the international implications of the decisions taken by each country were seldom weighed realistically. The possible 'boomerang effect' was seldom foreseen, and if foreseen it was ignored."[26]

After the 1939–45 war, the "right foot" was provided by Marshall Aid, which was administered by the OECD's precursor, the Organisation for European Economic Co-operation, whose first head was in fact Robert Marjolin. Right from the start it was clear that the Americans wanted Europe to behave, as Marjolin put it, "as a unit". This was even before the setting up of the European Economic Community. One way of preserving capitalism was to try so to arrange things that Germany was tied down in a prosperous Western Europe. And France recognised this time that a flourishing German market would be in its own economic interests.

As George Marshall, the US Secretary of State, put it when foreshadowing what became known as the "Marshall Plan", on 5 June 1947, "It is logical that the USA should do whatever it is able to do to assist in the return of normal economic health in the world, without which there can be no political stability and no assured peace." Marshall promised support for a programme to put Europe on its feet economically, but said it was the business of the Europeans to draw up the programme.[27] (The British Embassy in Washington did not think the speech worthy of a telegram, and US officials had to draw British attention to the significance of what was being said.)

Keynes himself had a major role in the preparations for the setting up of the IMF. To avoid the autarchy of the 1920s and 1930s, the IMF was specifically charged with aiming "to facilitate the expansion and balanced growth of international trade, and to contribute thereby to the promotion and maintenance of high levels of employment and real income and to the development of the productive resources of all members as primary objectives of economic policy."[28]

During the four year period of the Marshall Plan, the US provided aid equivalent to an average of 1.2 per cent of its gross domestic product for each of the years 1948–51, equivalent to a total of nearly $250 bn now.[29] Marshall's speech had stated that "our policy is directed not against any country or doctrine but against hunger, poverty, desperation and chaos."[30]

Was this pure altruism? Participants at the time make the usual distinction between the US Administration and Congress. Some thought Marshall Aid stemmed from a genuine act of goodwill on the US administration's part, irrespective of the fight against communism, and of fears that the Iron Curtain might move further west. Dean Acheson, Marshall's successor as Secretary of State, stated in his memoirs that Marshall was "wholly right" in stating that the fight against "hunger, poverty, desperation and chaos" was the American *governmental* purpose; but Acheson added: "I have probably made as many speeches and answered as many questions about the Marshall Plan as any man alive . . . and what citizens and the representatives in Congress alike always wanted to learn in the last analysis was how Marshall Aid operated to block the extension of Soviet power and the acceptance (by Europe) of Communist economic and political organisation and alignment."[31]

One of the interesting things about Marshall Aid – which might be relevant to Eastern Europe – is that the European Recovery Programme (to give it its official title) was not launched immediately after the end of the war, but two years later. By this time it had become clear that attempts at long run structural reform were being frustrated. The European economies were having their work cut out to supply people with basic necessities after the severe winter of 1946–47. The idea behind the Marshall Plan was to break the vicious circle. As the Economic Commission for Europe has put it: "Marshall emphasised that United States assistance was meant to provide a cure, not a palliative."[32] Another aspect of Marshall Aid was that it showed what could be achieved by a confident economy, in a basically expansionary atmosphere: the US was even prepared effectively to tolerate discrimination by Europe against its own exports until the Western European economy had found its feet.

But the Marshall Plan did not come easily, and there is a precedent for the sluggish response of the West in 1991–92 to Russian requests for help in the trouble Western Europeans had in convincing the US of the seriousness of their situation in 1945–47. Keynes himself,

working at the UK Treasury, had swiftly come to the conclusion in
1945 that Britain's balance of payments problems in rebuilding a
market economy would be daunting without further financial aid
from the US. With the cessation of the wartime "Lend-Lease"
arrangements, Keynes advocated a $6 bn. grant from the US to the
UK, but got short shrift from the US Secretary to the Treasury, F. M.
Vinson, who said the money was "only peanuts", the problem was
the mood of Congress and the American public. The British
eventually received a $4.4 bn. loan, but only after months of
acrimonious debate in Congress, and it was contingent on the
convertibility of the pound a year later (mid-1947), a move which
went disastrously wrong, and which had to be suspended within a
month.[33]

It became apparent that there was a severe dollar shortage in
Europe in 1947, and the entire economic recovery of the UK and
Western Europe from the war was at risk. "Europe will never
become independent of American aid (with all the Congressional
uncertainties and political implications of this) unless there is
substantial modification of its industrial and agricultural structure"
states one Whitehall memorandum.[34] There were anxious moments
when the Europeans wondered whether Marshall Aid would
actually be got through Congress. (This took until July 1948.) And
the European Recovery Programme laid the emphasis heavily on
ensuring that, by the end of the period, Europe would be well on the
way to standing on its own feet, rather than economically and
politically prostrate, begging an unpredictable Congress for more.
"Failure of Europe to recover spells communism" states a minute of
a UK Treasury and Foreign Office meeting of 5 January 1949.[35]

The *sine qua non* of European economic recovery in those years
was the correction of Western Europe's balance of payments deficit
with the Western hemisphere. This was the background to the
Marshall Plan and to the preparations which led to the setting up of
the European Economic Community. While there are many obvious
differences, the fact that Western Europe required assistance on the
scale of the Marshall Plan to recover from its own (albeit relatively
brief) experience of a wartime command economy is manifestly
pertinent to the much greater transitional problems facing the
former Soviet Union and Eastern Europe in the 1990s.

The catalyst for General Marshall's speech appears to have been a
visit to Europe by William L. Clayton, US Assistant Secretary for
Economic Affairs, in spring 1947, leading to a memorandum stating
that Europe was "steadily deteriorating" and fears in Washington
that there was "an impending collapse of European capitalism".[36]
According to Lord Franks, who became chairman of the Committee

of European Economic Co-operation after Marshall's speech "in the spring of 1947 the economic and social state of Western Europe was far graver than in the thirties."[37]

Some 45 years later the reports of economic chaos in the former Soviet Union were plentiful, and throughout 1991 and early 1992 dire warnings could be heard about the prospects for war, anarchy and nuclear chaos in the former Soviet Union if larger-scale assistance was not forthcoming from the West. For a long time the reaction in Washington was similar to the negative political mood as judged by the US Treasury Secretary Vinson in regard to the UK's pleas in 1945–46. The British Chancellor of the Exchequer, Norman Lamont, took up the case for major G7 assistance for the former Soviet Union in January 1992, and the cause was espoused by, among others, Michel Camdessus, Managing Director of the International Monetary Fund, and Jacques Attali, of the European Bank for Reconstruction and Development.

What finally prodded the Bush administration into serious consideration of large scale balance of payments assistance (a $24 bn. package was proposed for the former Soviet Union during 1992) was an almost simultaneous (but unco-ordinated) assault by Presidential Democratic candidate Bill Clinton and ex-President Richard Nixon. The Bush administration was concerned about being upstaged by the Democrats during election year. But Nixon's warning of a missed historical opportunity, after all the years fighting communism, appears to have had the most powerful impact.

With the considerable help of the European Recovery Programme, the second half of the 1940s was a period of economic reconstruction. The post-war "golden age" is generally dated from 1950, and to have lasted until 1973. In his study, "The World Economy in the 20th Century", Angus Maddison distinguishes four phases: first, "the liberal, market oriented order' which ended in 1914; second, the long period of "conflict and autarky" of 1913 to 1950; then the 1950–73 "golden age"; and later, "slower growth and accelerated inflation" from 1973 onwards. Economic growth per capita in 16 leading member nations of the OECD averaged 1.6 per cent a year in 1900–13, followed by only 1.2 per cent a year in 1913–50, which contained two world wars and the Great Depression. In the "golden" period of 1950–73 per capita growth was over double anything previously achieved this century, at 3.8 per cent a year; it then halved to 1.9 per cent a year in the period 1973–87.[38]

As Maddison wrote of the "golden age": "There was a successful dismantling of trade barriers, an unprecedentedly fast growth of international trade, a restoration of private international capital flows, and the inauguration of large scale official aid programmes."[39] For a long time, until the Organisation of Petroleum Exporting Countries (OPEC) flexed its muscles, the capitalist industrial countries also enjoyed what they regarded as "favourable" commodity and basic material prices, but what critics interpreted as the ability to exploit the less developed countries. This had also occurred during the inter-war period. The difference, as Maddison stresses, was: "The fundamental innovation in post-war policy in the OECD countries was the commitment to full use of resources through activist real output management."[40] Italy, France and Japan, in particular, were happy to use government intervention whenever necessary to strengthen their own fundamentally capitalist economies – the feature of capitalism being "predominantly private ownership of the means of production". Full, or high, employment was a goal of economic policy in the US, UK, Canada, and Scandinavia.[41]

Looked at from the point of view of Keynes' criteria in 1925 – efficiency, social justice and liberty – policy makers during the "golden age" can at least be said to have had a good try. The more liberal international order was very much in accord with traditional capitalist or market principles, but also contributed to greater economic efficiency. The achievement of reasonably full employment for most of the period was unprecedented in modern times, and made for greater social justice than in 1914–39. The rise from 27 per cent of GDP to 37 per cent in government spending within the OECD between 1950 and 1973 was due largely to "increases in social security and spending on merit wants such as education and health";[42] this, too, made for a less harsh climate than pre-war capitalism. Within the overall trend there were obvious differences, the US being at the lower end of the scale in welfare spending, Scandinavia at the top, and countries such as the UK in the middle. Average living standards in the capitalist countries doubled over this period.

Throughout the capitalist "golden age", the principal communist economy was not exactly standing still. The recorded per capita growth rate of 3.6 per cent a year for the USSR between 1950 and 1973 was just over one and a half times faster than in 1913–73, compared with the threefold increases in the growth rate of the OECD countries.[43] These were years when there was still supposed to be some kind of competition between capitalism and communism, before the latter system threw in the towel. As we shall see in more detail later, however, the quality of the statistical measurements being applied to economic development in the eastern bloc proved questionable – to say nothing of the quality of what actually did take place, symbolised years later on television for a startled world in the pictures of the Chernobyl disaster, and the way in which sub-standard housing gave way so easily to earth tremors in Azerbaijan.

One of the developments that greatly improved the lot of capitalist consumers was the dramatic improvement in the speed and quality of freight transport, including the widespread use of refrigeration. Equally, it could be said that this greatly increased the North's ability to tap the resources of the South.

The point about the "golden age" is that, although all the elements of capitalism had been there before, it was only the combination of the Keynesian approach to policy, and the spirit of international co-operation that brought out the best in the system. One often hears hymns of praise to the various characteristics of capitalism, but most of these characteristics were there during the good and the bad periods – private property, the exchange economy, capital and labour markets, the incentive of profit and the safety net of limited liability. And those institutions which the British right wing finds so offensive to liberty and decency, namely the trades unions, existed both during the inter-war years and the subsequent golden age.

The remarkable thing about the poorer performance of the "enlightened" capitalist system after 1973, however, was that it ushered in a breed of economic and political evangelicals on both sides of the Atlantic who wished to turn the clock back to the pre-Keynesian era, and in large measure they succeeded. Whether they embarked on this course through a genuine belief that they had a better answer, or because (in a truly old-fashioned capitalist sense) there was more money in it for them, is an open question. Many were going to profit from the new turn of events; many more were not.

2

Capitalism, Markets and the Keynesian Standard

The British apostle of pure, undiluted capitalism, Arthur Seldon, goes so far as to claim that "the role of the law on property was probably more important in stimulating economic growth than the technical advances of the Industrial Revolution."[1] This is an ambitious assertion. The USSR and Eastern Europe achieved economic growth in the absence of property rights, a western law of contract, or a capitalist financial system. Their problem, in this respect, was that they did not do nearly as well as the capitalist economies. What capitalism seems to have proved is that greater economic satisfaction, for a larger number of citizens, can be achieved through a combination of scientific and technological progress, *and* a capitalist system of property rights and "market economy". Whether extreme flexibility in financial markets can actually impede the efficiency of the rest of a market economy is an open question. But 20th century experience suggests that it is possible to add a third dimension to technological progress and the capitalist/market system – namely an enlightened way of harnessing the two together on Keynesian lines, nationally and internationally.

It was the harnessing of capitalism and technological progress on enlightened principles that took the sting out of much of the criticism of earlier capitalism. Crude capitalism was modified principally as a result of pragmatic and self-interested adjustment to the potentially revolutionary threat from below. As Reinhold Niebuhr observed, "there are definite limits in the capacity of ordinary mortals which make it impossible for them to grant to others what they claim for themselves."[2]

One thing highlighted by the collapse of communism is that capitalism in fact takes various forms. What we may term "primitive capitalism" is capitalism in a state of nature, red in tooth and claw – a situation where those employers whose ideal would be mastery over slaves, find they can rub along by paying minimum wages, applying negligible safety standards, and displaying scant regard for the welfare of their labour force – other than to keep them working until they drop. That kind of capitalist was still to be found in the British Empire and Commonwealth until relatively recently, and may well linger on in the outposts even now. Certainly, working conditions in South Africa in the early 1970s provoked an international outcry.[3] (By "capitalist" in this connection, we understand both the direct employer of the capital, and the lender of funds for such purposes, usually described in traditional textbooks as "the rentier", and often, in recent years, the manager of pension and insurance funds on behalf of mild progressives who might not approve if they knew what was providing them with investment, or "unearned", income.)

Although the "paternal" capitalist traditionally makes spontaneous improvements in the lot of his workforce, it is through the democratic process that capitalism has been humanised. Once they had won the vote, the vast majority of people, who were "non-capitalists", wanted reforms – indeed, it was the need for reforms which made them agitate for the vote in the first place.

Such reforms have taken place, during the 19th and 20th centuries, in most of the leading industrial countries. Thus, when one identifies various forms of capitalism, one is doing so at a much higher level of social and legal reform, and of citizen's rights, than would have been the case a hundred years ago.

This said, one can distinguish three basic standards of capitalism in the developed world: first, American capitalism – sometimes called "democratic capitalism" or "liberal capitalism"; second Continental European Capitalism, sometimes called "Social Market" (after German experience) or Corporatist (to describe the active role of Government, and the embrace of key interest groups – or "social partners" – in a combined effort to run the economy and implement social legislation); and Japanese Capitalism, which has elements of "corporatism", but which could also be called "Industrial Capitalism", because of the strong focus of Government and all elements of society on industrial and, in particular, manufacturing success. Another useful distinction is that between the "consumer-directed" market economy (the US) and the "administratively guided" market economy (Japan).[4]

Within these categories there are clear overlaps: all the major capitalist countries are also democracies – some more mature than others. All have large industrial sectors. All have some level of collective social provision. The differences are differences of perception and emphasis, but also of performance. Americans will tend to offer more hymns of praise to "the free enterprise system" than Continental Europeans. The need for Government to play an active role in industrial and social policy is more recognised outside the US than within it. The United States has a relatively low level of social provision – but increased the share of GDP devoted to welfare spending by a half under the Great Society programme of the 1960s.[5] Japan is the envy of the rest of the world for its trading performance, but does not strike the visitor, or the resident, as being as well off as the statistician suggests.

The belief that the "grass is greener" in the way people think of other, more successful economies, has already been mentioned. In Japan's case, it is a question of whether there is not even a shortage of green grass for the residents of cities. Thus the OECD estimates that "park area" is a mere 2.5 square metres per capita in Tokyo, compared with 12.2 in Paris, 30.4 in London, 37.4 in Bonn and 45.7 in Washington D.C. Again, comparisons of the ratio of the population with access to sewerage services indicates only 44 per cent in Japan, compared with 64 per cent in France, 73 per cent in the US and 91 and 95 per cent respectively in Germany and the UK.[6]

Government "intervention" in the economy or in social policy is not automatically assumed to be a bad thing in Continental Europe. And, although "Government" is almost a swear-word in many political debates in the US, the truth is that many a big corporation depends on Government or state contracts, and the defence industry, in particular, was closely linked to Government funding for research and development throughout the period of the Cold War. In practice, while being "anti-Government", the US administration contrived to run vast Budget deficits during the 1980s.

Another distinction can be made between Anglo-Saxon Capitalism and the rest, in that it is widely recognised that the emphasis in US and British capitalism is very much on short term performance ("getting rich quick') when financial judgements are made by the stock market and banking system. Partly for historical reasons, partly out of choice, German and Japanese capitalism places more emphasis on savings and investment, long term planning and on long term relationships between the financial and industrial sectors, *and* between employers and employees. In the US, individualism is an obsession, whereas in Japan and Continental Europe the concept of "community" is not considered inimical to creativity or to the "incentive to work". Again, this is not to say there are not considerable exceptions, but these are not propositions on which most observers would be likely to disagree.

Britain, characteristically, has one foot in Anglo-Saxon capitalism and another in Continental Europe. It was observation principally of British capitalism that provided Adam Smith, the classical economists and Karl Marx with much of their raw material. It was Britain that started the economist's ball rolling with theoretical *laissez-faire* models (of perfect competition and the like) which have had a protracted life-span, but which bear little relation to the complex world of capitalism and technology as we know it. But it was also Britain that, along with Germany and Scandinavia, led the way in the provision of a higher level of social welfare than is the case in the US and Japan.

As dreams, and the reality, of empire faded – for years Britain effectively enjoyed captive markets, and captive sources of basic materials around the world – Britain was inevitably dragged closer to Continental Europe. It was both the welfare and European aspects of British capitalism which Mrs Thatcher spent a decade trying to resist. During this time she and her closest colleagues frequently invoked models of economic life – "Victorian Values" and assertions that "There is no such thing as society" – which indicated a desire to turn the clock back. Mrs Thatcher was against public spending in general (with notable exceptions such as defence, law and order and the requirements of her private office at No 10 Downing Street) and against welfare spending in particular. She glanced with envious eyes across the Atlantic at the American version of Anglo-Saxon capital-ism – at about the same time that feeling was growing *within* the United States that the public squalor diagnosed years earlier by J. K. Galbraith was in fact getting out of hand, that the public education system was a national disgrace – and a drag on the economy – and that perhaps some sort of industrial policy might not also be necessary. In fairness to Mrs Thatcher it has to be emphasised that, at least while in office, she would have enjoyed a Hollywood studio fantasy about the realisation of the American Dream, and not been subjected to the filth, squalor and degradation of American cities that confronts even the most casual visitor from Europe.

That very same California which manufactures Hollywood fantasies had benefited much from "New Deal" expenditure in the 1930s. And during the 1970s and 1980s the "high tech" industries of California and the sun-belt generally were no mean recipients of the largesse provided by government contracts and high defence spending. Conversely, by the early 1990s California was suffering above average unemployment during the recession, as a result of the immediate impact of the Peace Dividend on public sector defence contracts. It was estimated, for example, that nearly half the 545,000 jobs in the aerospace industry would have disappeared by the end of the 1990s.[7] California, the mecca for so many successful Western capitalists, has an economy that is more dependent on a judicious mixture of public and private sector than some evangelists of the right would have one believe – so much so that, having experienced extreme degrees of dependence on private sector transport, as opposed to public, and severe atmospheric pollution, the Californian public authorities are now criticised by business for being in the vanguard of the anti-pollution and "regulation" movement.[8]

Throughout the Cold War, comparisons were made of the virtues and vices of the capitalist and communist "systems", and it is difficult to eschew such short-hand phrases. However, it is one of the contentions of this book that communism was more of a system – an imposed, or "willed", system – than capitalism, which, although it takes various forms, is really a stage we have arrived at in historical development. It is difficult to deny that capitalism, in one shape or form, and "market economies", are common to the more prosperous economies. Nor to deny that governments, and public sectors – national, regional, local – have a prominent presence in such capitalist societies, with varying degrees of belief about the extent to which they can or should lean on, or intervene in, the activities of the private or capitalist sector in the public interest.

Capitalism has been "tamed" to some extent by the democratic process and by the legal, regulatory and general institutional structure that has grown up around it. Motivation, in capitalist and market economies, is not just the desire to make money: pride in achievement, the desire to build something, the social prestige and recognition accorded to captains of industry and the financially successful – all play their part in motivation. One interesting phenomenon is that of the "capitalist" who thrives best at having an idea, building up and running a small business, and who, later, having been bought out and made his fortune, prefers to build up something new all over again, rather than to "enjoy" the power and perquisites of running a large, bureaucratic organisation. (Sometimes, however, such entrepreneurs do not leave voluntarily, having been perceived by other shareholders to have outlived their usefulness in the enterprise they created.)

But greed and the desire to make a fast buck do not necessarily lead to benefits for society. The early examples of capitalism in the former USSR and Eastern Europe seem to be heavily biased in favour of mafioso-style gangs, and racketeers who may well be making money, but are not necessarily passing much in the way of conceivable benefits on to the consumer. In Russia, for example, the food distribution system in 1990–91 appeared to be a highly corrupt friendly society for criminals.

Most people have a deep-seated resentment against profiteering, as opposed to the making of due profits which go partly towards reinvestment for the future and partly as a reasonable reward for money employed, and for the taking of risk. This is not a distinction that the more free-market economists find easy to perceive.

The truth is that there is much in the capitalist spirit that is enterprising, socially productive and laudable, and much that is immoral, socially damaging and reprehensible. It is one of the tasks of democratic governments to try to get the balance right. And, given the obvious dangers to the global environment from the pursuit of economic development which ignores social costs – development either by capitalists qua capitalists, or capitalist nations competing with one another – we soon arrive, paradoxically, at the need to devise a system for controlling capitalism at about the time the communist system has been rendered defunct, and "planning" has become a dirty word.

During the decade that saw the final collapse of Leninist communism, the values of the virtually unrestricted "market" were praised to the skies. But the "market" is, at one level, no more than the free-play of competitive forces and anarchic tendencies, and, at another level, what people, or "consumers" want. Thus, when economists and right wing politicians say "the market knows best", they mean that the allocative system of the market is the best means we have for uniting willing sellers and eager buyers – for people getting what they want.

But a moment's reflection indicates that many of the ethical and behavioural problems of life are related to the manifest difficulties of allowing people to have exactly "what they want". Much of human upbringing is an exercise in being taught precisely that one cannot necessarily have what one wants – life is more complicated than that. The "free play of market forces" produces chaos, and too many victims. It also brings out the worst in human characteristics and behaviour. The interesting question is the degree to which "market forces" have to be controlled.

Socialism and communism were invented because naked capitalism was so offensive. The fact that communism has failed does not make it any the less necessary to beware of the many unpleasant facets of what we call capitalism, and to try to modify them in the interests of the nobler goals of society. At the very least, even if nobler goals are easier to aspire to than to reach, the question of the basic efficiency of capitalism is one that commands attention at a time when the leading market economies, for all their regular "summit conferences", seem to be turning inwards on themselves.

One of the fundamental concepts of economics is that of "diminishing marginal utility" – that, the more one has of something, the less pressing the need for further increments. In the 1970s a kind of "satiation thesis" was invoked in international economic meetings. The German delegation would say: Why do we need to expand demand when so many of our citizens have such a good standard of living already? It is easy to underestimate people's demands, or need, for more; but if one thing is certain about the contemporary capitalist world, it is that about four fifths of the globe still has plenty of needs, as does a sizable proportion of the populations of even the most advanced and successful capitalist economies. Germany, for one, has found some 17½m people with needs in Eastern Germany. And the reaction of Western Germans towards the prospect of helping their "eastern brothers and sisters" suggests that they themselves feel far from satiated.

Although the French Revolution's route to democracy was hardly without blemish, it gave mankind the goals of liberty, equality, fraternity. The Nobel prizewinning poet Octavio Paz, writing in the light of the collapse of communism, says: "As I see it, the central word of the triad is *fraternity*."

"Liberty can exist without equality, and equality without liberty," writes Paz. "Liberty, in isolation, makes inequalities more profound and provokes tyrannies; equality oppresses liberty and in the end destroys it. But fraternity is the nexus that connects them, the virtue that humanizes and harmonises them."[9] "Given the natural differences between human beings, equality is an ethical aspiration that cannot be realised without recourse either to despotism or to an act of fraternity." (The French Revolution preceded the Feminist Revolution, but we can no doubt take "fraternity" to embrace "sorority.")

Soviet communism managed to achieve despotism, lack of liberty, equality – but not for all – at a low level, and an absence of fraternity. Orwell's "some are more equal than others" was absolutely right. And one of the hardest things for the left in the West to swallow, as news gathers of the real goings on under the old system, is that most of the jibes and cheap cracks about privileges and special shops for the Party were only too well founded. The hypocritical standard of communism was remarkably high.

Meanwhile, in Latin American countries such as Chile and Argentina, capitalism has gone through notorious phases of practising repression under the guise of liberal economics. The association of the Chicago school of monetarism with the repressive Pinochet regime during the 1970s has been a source of embarrassment and shame to the entire economics profession. The problem for critics of capitalism in more enlightened societies than Latin American dictatorships is not only that there is a great difference between "freedom from" and "freedom to" (the Isaiah Berlin distinction), but that "freedom to" is very much prescribed by economic circumstances. Even left wing critics are prepared to concede some things to capitalism – for example: "At the heart of capitalism is a competitive economic struggle, from which all citizens may gain in the long term as the whole system moves upwards."[10]

But, of course, rights and freedoms are all relative – "Freedom to purchase an education or to migrate have a different meaning for an unemployed worker than for a rich company director. Freedom of speech will mean different things for an international media tycoon than for an ordinary citizen."[11]

These are familiar problems. They have not disappeared simply because of events in Eastern Europe. It is easy to poke fun at Paz's emphasis on "fraternity." In Britain the very word "brothers", in a political context, evokes memories of satires on the worst aspects of trades union excesses in the 1960s and 1970s. Nevertheless, fraternity (of both sexes . . .) conjures up the sense of fairness and feeling that "things have gone too far", that were evoked in Mrs Thatcher's Britain when the poll tax was levied, at the same flat rate, on rich and poor alike – provoking even Mr Donald Trump to appear on the BBC saying Mrs Thatcher had overstepped the mark. A similar feeling of revulsion appears to have been caused by other aspects of Britain's attempt to move back to "Victorian" capitalism in the 1980s, so that opinion polls in the early 1990s consistently produced the remarkable results that the vast majority of the population would prefer better public services, and more public spending to help the poor, to further tax cuts. But there were limits. Although the British were happy for Mrs Thatcher to resign, they could not contemplate voting for the tax *increases* offered by the Labour Party in April 1992.

Even if it is being sorely tested by the difficult process of absorbing Eastern Germany, a sense of "fraternity" is very apparent in the capitalist country whose economic performance most other European ones seem to want to emulate, namely Germany. There is fraternity and balance between central government and the Länder, including constitutional provisions that actively prevent some Länder from becoming "more equal" than others. There is the strong social "safety net", where the traditions of social democracy and Christian Democracy meet. And there is even, among other EC countries, the concern that Germany bends over backwards to assist its less efficient industries, such as coal.

The generous way of looking at it is to argue that the very achievements of "enlightened" capitalism make the sores stand out. But what was so deeply offensive, reprehensible and unnecessary under the phase of "Greed Capitalism" during the 1980s was the deliberate attempt, certainly in the US and UK, to reverse the trend towards enlightened capitalism. The official justification was that this was in the interest of economic efficiency; but both the statistics, and the manifest level of dissatisfaction within the US and UK about recent economic performance, belie the claim.

This was the decade of "market values" being inflated out of all sense of proportion. Apart from the obscenity of government acquiescence in urban decay, poor state schools, and a proliferation of beggars on the streets, it is not very satisfying to the sovereign "consumer" in capitalist societies to develop such large areas where people are too embarrassed, or terrified, to tread. It is precisely because the innocent passer-by has neither the time nor the knowledge to determine whether a beggar is in genuine need or merely "trying it on" that the social welfare net was woven in the first place. And such uncaring capitalism is not even efficient – as was once observed: "Pauperism presents a danger to the market process."[12]

Some of the more wishy-washy aspirations for equality tradition-ally voiced by critics of capitalism have been dulled not merely by the cynicism of the Soviet experience but also by hard appreciation of the difficulties. The actual process of embourgeoisement has been a bitter pill for some idealists to swallow. Nevertheless, the sight of Anglo-Saxon governments deliberately embarking on a policy of making society more unequal has produced a reaction in public feeling, and truly offended people's sense of justice, equity and "fraternity".

Enlightened capitalists do not deliberately foment confrontation and tension between government and industry, or within industry, between employers and employees. (Nor between themselves and their fellow men and women whom they occasionally have to encounter in the streets.) Such confrontation was very much a part of the Thatcher Anglo-Saxon vision in the 1980s. More impressive in its results is the Continental tradition of Christian Democracy, where consultation and discussion over economic and industrial problems are taken for granted: "They can serve to spread under-standing of an economic situation, or of the policy of a government or management, or to create that more general, informal agreement on which informal authority rests."[13] Instead of the "individualist" view of capitalism, the Christian Democrat view is better understood by the epithet "personalist."[14]

Government, and the running of an economy are a judicious mixture of competition and co-operation. They also involve important choices about the exercise of power and the control over power, the encouragement of individualism and its restraint. Variations on such themes have been the stuff of political theory throughout the ages; what seems to be little disputed in the 1990s is that the economies where the consensual and the consultative are regarded as the right approach – indeed, where the mere suggestion that this should not be the case raises eyebrows – are those where the appropriate balance between competition and co-operation appears to have been achieved – namely Germany and Japan. By contrast the recent history of the British economy has been one in which management and workforce seem to be competing with one another, rather than co-operating in the common competitive trading struggle.

The German "social market economy" arose against the background not only of wartime devastation but of memories of the centralisation of power under the Nazis in the 1930s. The desire of the Allied powers to balance political power within Germany was accompanied by the wish of the Germans for a balance of economic power within the country. As Hans Otto Lenel has written: "A basic advantage of market economies is that they tend to guard against the accretion of power by separating the political and the economic spheres. This advantage is, however, in danger when private economic power grows too large – in the words of Wilhelm Ropke, when the 'torrent of personal interest' is directed over the 'turbines of the economy', but not dammed by competition. The 'invisible hand' does not create 'harmony' just like that."[15]

The originator of the term "social market economy" (Soziale Marktwirtschaft) was Alfred Muller-Armack, an official and close adviser of Ludwig Erhard, the German Economics Minister from 1949–63, and subsequently Federal Chancellor. Erhard is the man credited with the German post-war "economic miracle", and although free market economists have naturally tended to associate that miracle with the abolition of "controls", the controls that were abolished were essentially wartime ones; there was not a sudden drive towards the state of nature much favoured by Chicago economists. Indeed, the economist Fritz Schumacher, subsequently famous for the book "Small is Beautiful", recalled being in an Allied delegation which had to convince a sceptical and nervous Erhard that it was time to abandon controls. Erhard feared a social explosion.[16]

"The idea behind the social market economy," Muller-Armack wrote in 1956, "is that market freedom is combined with social balance . . . a successful economic policy needs a co-ordinating principle . . ." He emphasised that "while the functional importance of competition was recognised under the 'Old Liberalism', nevertheless insufficient attention was paid to social and sociological problems." The problem with socialism, Muller-Armack foresaw, was that "there is good reason to doubt whether a central control system, once created, would be able to resist the temptation to intervene in free consumer choice and free choice of jobs." He went on: "The concept of a social market economy may therefore be defined as a regulative policy which aims to combine, on the basis of a competitive economy, free initiative and social progress." This allowed, for instance, for "a complex and complete system of social security". Indeed, Muller-Armack had an engaging way of putting his case. The market mechanism was best for consumers, because it enabled *them* to "control what is produced in the economy." Again "The pricing system is an indispensable instrument of co-ordination and search which reconciles the consumers' innumerable and diversified individual *plans* (my italics) and permits them to take effect." A system of central control tended to produce goods "which do not accord with consumers' wishes" but the social market economy's orientation to consumption "represents what might be called a *social service*" (my italics).

The tone of the father of the "social market economy" writing in 1956 could hardly be more different from the throwback to 19th century capitalist values witnessed during the Reagan/Thatcher era. "Income creation . . . provides a solid basis for the redistribution of income by the state. Income redistribution is brought about through welfare benefits, equalisation of pensions and compensation payments, housing grants, subsidies et cetera. To disregard this process of redistribution, in assessing the social dimension of the market process which sustains it, would be to fail to appreciate the social content of the social market economy."[17]

Many contemporaries were involved in the development of these ideas. In addition to concern for the less fortunate, which is implicit in the above account, social marketeers emphasised "morality in all business dealings."[18]

It was on such foundations that the post-war German economy evolved into a position where it became the envy of the rest of Europe – west and east. US, German and Japanese capitalism all shared a belief in the virtues of competitive capitalism; but the social side of capitalism was more developed in Germany than in the US and Japan (and for that matter, it was more developed in the UK), whereas the competitive capitalism aspect – competition leading to innovation and further productivity increases – appears to have reached its apotheosis in the performance of the Japanese economy.

The social market ideas, as indeed most theories of capitalism, were developed well before concerns about the global environment and "limits to growth" appeared on the horizon. For the moment, however, it is sufficient to note that from the experience of post-war

Germany one can see it is possible to balance the economic potential of capitalism with wider social needs – not necessarily recognised by crude capitalists. If we are alert to the broader concerns about the global environment, and the threatened breakdown of the co-ordination of the world trading process, we see the need for combining the achievements and goals of competitive capitalism, and the social market economy in what may usefully be termed "Social Capitalism".

Economic welfare in any meaningful sense does not thrive under autocracy of either the Stalinist or the Pinochet kind. Communist and extreme right wing authoritarian regimes can preside over economic growth via what is known as "extensive development" (for example by directing agricultural labour into basic industries, and increasing use of capital, labour and raw materials). Totalitarianism is not so good at industrial innovation and adaptation to consumer demand.

It has been pointed out however that "it was extremely difficult to reconcile democracy with economic growth when the process was initiated from a very backward position."[19] And there are many who wonder how the democratic chaos which has accompanied liberalisation in the former Soviet Union can possibly be combined with a successful move to a market economy.

Eastern Europe and the former Soviet Union are where they are, however, and liberalisation and the desire for a market economy have so far gone hand in hand – although at the time of writing severe doubts remain about Russia's commitment. Although Parliament preceded industrial capitalism in Britain, what we know as true Parliamentary democracy – one person, one vote – in fact followed capitalism. That was the way things evolved. It was the excesses of raw capitalism, and the threat to the ruling classes if they did not bow to reformist pressures, that slowly, reluctantly but inexorably allowed democracy as we know it to take root in the pioneering capitalist countries.

In recent years democracy and reasonable economic performance have gone hand in hand in the market economies of Spain, Portugal and Greece. These were never so enfeebled of entrepreneurial spirit as Eastern Europe under communism; and Greece, of course, gave us the word "market" some 2,500 years ago. But, at a time of fledgling, fragile democracy in Eastern Europe, this experience must offer some hope. Indeed, it can reasonably be averred that, if the examples of Germany and Japan are taken, capitalism can work best when linked to as much democracy and consultation as possible.

Nevertheless, the route to such a position is a long and hazardous one. The dilemma of Liberalizers was stated by none other than Karl Marx in 1851: democracy is acceptable if it keeps them in power, but not so attractive when it rejects them. Schumpeter defined democracy as a system under which rival parties competed for the people's vote: a contemporary writer has noted: "The problem that thrusts itself to the centre of the political agenda once a dictatorship breaks down is whether any institutions that will allow open-ended, even if limited, contestation will be accepted by the relevant political forces."[20] As the OECD has drily observed: "In countries with newly elected democratic governments, the authorities have to contend with the unrealistic expectation of their populations that throwing off the yoke of a command society would yield immediate economic improvements; in all transition economics there is a lack of public understanding of the unavoidable costs of systemic changes." Indeed: it does not take long for the average visitor to Eastern Europe to come across the proverbial resident who says "we were better off under the old system".

While the initial horrors of the gap between the collapse of a command economy and the building of a democratic market economy are soon manifest, the advantages – apart from the important one of political freedom itself – are long delayed. Meanwhile, those missing advantages are all too readily available to see on television screens – or in reality, for the minority of the populations in the former Soviet bloc that can afford holidays in the West. This serves to increase the risks of democracy turning sour, especially in Russia itself, where, as Mark Frankland has observed: " 'Re-joining Europe', an enchanting prospect to Poles, Czechs and Hungarians, sounds very different to Russians who are not (and seldom have been) sure they really belong to Europe or wish to share its political, cultural and moral values." Indeed, Frankland maintains that Yeltsin's reformist Ministers, who offered their resignations in April 1992, were nervous because they knew that "by driving the country towards the market and private property, they are going against what many of their fellow-countrymen believe to be the Russian grain."[21]

It has been well noted that in the West capitalism has been associated with the growth of Parliamentary democracy and Parliamentary democracy has itself contributed to capitalist development. But "after two centuries of capitalist development, democracy is still the exception not the rule."[22] With few exceptions, until recent events in Eastern Europe, Parliamentary democracies tended to be found in developed capitalist countries. In general, dictatorship and corruption were all too characteristic of the post-colonial, underdeveloped third world, whether capitalist or communist.

For many years the advanced market economies, through the World Bank and IMF, were perfectly content to assist right wing dictatorships around the world, and notably in Latin America. At the very least they connived at their activities; but in the eyes of many observers, and not just the Marxist left, Washington was content actively to encourage such regimes, occasionally, via the CIA, actually setting them up. In the fight against the encroachment of communism, even democracy was a casualty: the only democracy that seemed to matter in the end was that of the United States itself.

It is, as the vulgar expression has it, "no coincidence" that democracy and human rights have only risen to the forefront of World Bank and IMF lending criteria since the collapse of the Berlin Wall. Democracy can now be encouraged in countries where previously dictatorial capitalism was preferred to even the mere threat of communism (in some instances a threat detected in mildly left-wing parties whose main emphasis was on democracy and human rights).

For a long time the advanced capitalist countries could pretend to themselves (or at least to their critics) that what were euphemistically known as "co-ercive" governments assisted economic development. But as a relatively recent arrival on the international financial scene has declared: "Such doctrines have not stood the test of time. Dictatorial regimes corrupt innovation . . . strong democratic states have a leading role to play in the creation of institutions that enable the growth of the private sector, that curb black market activity, that prevent corruption and violence from creeping into a competitive economy."[23]

Hayek and his New Right supporters followed a long tradition in seeing capitalism as a necessary basis for democracy. But, well before the collapse of communism, the New Right saw a threat to liberty – particularly the liberty of markets – in too much democracy. Thus excessive public expenditure, "welfare-ism" and the "industrial democracy" movement were seen as inhibiting the magic manipulations of the invisible hand. "Pork barrel" politics, interest groups indulging in a kind of orgiastic democracy, trades unions and left wing parties generally – all were seen as restraining the freedom of market forces in the name of democracy. In the 1970s democracy, for the New Right, was something of a sitting target; why, the great enemy of the time – inflation – was itself a manifestation of democratic pressures. The protection of the market's abstract "consumer" became, as it were, a consuming obsession. Thus the Western Right welcomed democratic movements in the East after having shown increasing distaste for the economic fruits of "excessive" democracy in the West. Monetarism, the cry for independent central banks, the desire to hand economic power back from politicians and the people to the marketplace – these made up the prevailing mood of the 1980s in advance of the collapse of communism.

As he watched his beloved, old-style Conservative Party hijacked by the New Right, Sir Ian Gilmour, the guardian of the Party's conscience, warned: "Untrammelled market forces are likely to lead to the destruction of the market."[24] The "market-led" decade of the 1980s, during which international economic policy co-ordination was for long periods left to the vagaries of these mysterious "market forces" produced a capitalist world by the early 1990s where unemployment was high, and trade disputes rife: indeed, the leading participants did not exactly rush to obey their own advice about "opening up markets" in order that the former Soviet bloc could benefit from the free trade in which capitalist and market economies purported to believe.

Markets work best when they are regulated. The tidy-minded bureaucrat can never for long impose a blueprint on society (even the communists gave up), but a sensible regime of rules and regulations can limit the damage of market excesses – just as the police never expect to eliminate crime, or a regulator in the City of London to stamp out fraud, or crooked bankers: the most they can achieve in this imperfect world is "an acceptable minimum" of rotten apples.

The natural instinct of the marketplace is that of the herd. The textbook case of the purity of the marketplace is the street market where the price of (good) apples seldom deviates for long from one stall to another; another classic example is the way bookmakers on a race-course keep an eye on one another's boards and continually adjust their odds in accordance with the market.

Similarly, in the financial markets which have been allowed to exercise so much sway over national and economic life in recent years (markets which consist largely of handlers of "other people's money") the intermediaries between savers and borrowers do not like to be out of line with the rest of "the market" for very long. Thus they will drive a country's exchange rate too high, by comparison with what might be justified by "economic fundamentals", or too low, but seldom achieve the "equilibrium" of the textbooks.

Although the USSR and its satellites had trading and banking links with the West for most of the communist period, the COMECON bloc was to all intents and purposes a "closed system". As long as it was a closed system, it was producing goods, even if these were often of an inferior kind. It did not place great demands on capitalism, other than the obvious threat it was thought to pose to the very survival of capitalism.

The collapse of communism and the arrival of democracy place great demands on the West – demands that coincide with a crisis of confidence within the very capitalist world that has won the Cold War. There is a demand for capital, a demand for technological and institutional advice, a general cry for help. The OECD economies after the Second World War, and the newly industrialised countries of South East Asia, built or rebuilt their market economies against an auspicious background of declining trade barriers; by contrast, as the OECD has pointed out, "the transition economies are facing an environment of growing protectionism and the strengthening of trade blocs, from which so far they are excluded."[25] Again, the earlier successes were assisted by low interest rates and plentiful flows of international capital, whereas "the transition economies are facing a world saturated with foreign debt, a growing shortage of capital, and a rising real rate of interest, for which a partial responsibility rests with the policies of some of the OECD countries."

During the Civil War "Putney Debates" of 1647, Colonel Thomas Rainsborough said: "Either poverty must use democracy to destroy the power of property, or property in fear of poverty will destroy democracy." The world has seen many in-between stages of these extremes since then. A top-level official conference on the problems posed by capitalism's "victory" over communism found some participants, looking at the bleak prospects facing the former Soviet bloc in the short term, predicting mass emigration, while another contributor said the choice boiled down to "Marshall Plan or martial law".[26]

In addition to his division of the 20th century world, Angus Maddison has made a brave attempt at sweeping perspective by dividing the economic "performance characteristics" of Four Epochs. Taking the years 500 AD to 1500 AD he puts them into the category of "Agrarianism", during which nothing resembling economic growth occurred at all. The years 1500–1700 are described "Advancing Agrarianism" when there was negligible economic growth – and none, according to the French economic historians Le Roy Ladurie and F. P. Braudel.[27] "Merchant Capitalism" – 1700–1820 – was the world captured by Adam Smith in the "Wealth of Nations" (1776). This was the era of monopolistic trading companies, when technological progress was seen principally in navigation and armaments. It was partly this era that Marx

himself drew on when talking about European capitalist exploitation of the rest of the world as being a necessary feature of
capitalism. Economic historians have detected *some* growth in
average per capita incomes during that period (as opposed to the
growth of the incomes of the merchant capitalists themselves), but
Maddison puts it at a mere 0.2 per cent a year.

While the former Soviet Union still struggles with its agricultural
problems, it is interesting to recall that the Industrial Revolution in
England was assisted by an agricultural revolution in the 18th
century. Based on primogeniture and large land-holdings, the
agricultural revolution enabled the aristocracy to invest their profits
in canals, turnpikes, and technical advances as they came along.
There was a ready supply of savings – and of cheap labour migrating
from country to town.

The Free Trade and *laissez-faire* so beloved of the New Right in
recent times were actually late developments in the original British
industrial and capitalist revolutions. For Britain trade followed the
flag, and was accompanied by guns. Britain developed its capitalism
and market economy against the background of an industrial
revolution which was closely linked with its empire, shipping routes,
and control of markets that its pre-eminent position made possible.
There were echoes of imperial capitalism in Japan's ventures of the
1930s, and there are still such echoes in the United States'
relationships with Saudi Arabia and the Gulf.

Although the Industrial Revolution began in England at about the
time Adam Smith was writing, it was obviously too early for Smith to
see the true potential of scientific and technological progress. He
drew attention to the possibilities offered by specialisation and
greater efficiency of existing processes, rather than the coming
spectacular wave of new products and new processes characteristic
of 19th and 20th century capitalism. Smith talks of the refinement
and the improvement of manufactures, and is inclined to give credit
to the workers, as well as to the capitalists, for improved techniques
– "A great part of the machines made use of in those manufactures in
which labour is most subdivided, were originally the inventions of
common workmen, who being each of them employed in some very
simple operation, naturally turned their thoughts towards finding
out easier and readier methods of performing it."[28] It is true that
Smith also credits "speculators" with the ingenuity of improving
machines, but these were speculators in the old fashioned sense –
"philosophers or men of speculation, whose trade it is not to do
anything, but to observe everything; and who, upon that account,
are often capable of combining together the powers of the most
distant and dissimilar objects."[29]

Smith could be forgiven for not having foreseen the enormous acceleration in the rate of scientific and technological progress which was to come. As Maddison has pointed out, although economies of scale and specialisation continued to be a source of productivity growth, their relative contribution to economic progress was smaller under capitalism than during the merchant capitalist period (when technical progress was much slower).[30]

Nor did Smith foresee the great potential of the joint stock company. "The only trades which it seems possible for a joint-stock company to carry on successfully, without an exclusive privilege, are those of which all the operations are capable of being reduced to what is called a routine, or to such a uniformity of method as admits of little or no variation" (by which he instanced banking, insurance, canals and water supply).[31] According to Seldon, it was the sluggish arrival of that great capitalist device, limited liability, that also limited the pace of economic growth in the 19th century. The early inventions of the Industrial Revolution, from, say, 1760 onwards, were developed by business enterprises and partnerships financed by family, friends, neighbours and banks – but not through the all-embracing net of strangers attracted by the limit to their liability. Shortages of finance, according to this view, were a severe constraint on development, until limited liability was introduced in 1862.

On the other hand, it is also true that the systematic application of science to industry came late. As Rosenberg and Birdzell have suggested: "When Karl Marx was writing in the mid-19th century, the 'colossal productive forces' he saw at work had been created primarily by people working in industry, with little contribution from people whom we would call scientists today . . . Since about 1880, however, industrial technology has come to owe a more substantial debt to scientific sources outside industry."[32]

Marx and Engels produced the Communist Manifesto in 1848 after a period of unbridled *laissez-faire*, when prevailing economic theory tried to justify slave wages and child labour. After showing contempt for the Benthamite justification – "the greatest good of the greatest number" – the Marxist historian Eric Hobsbawm empha-sises the familiar horrors of the effects of the Industrial Revolution in the first half of the 19th century. "In the 1830s," Hobsbawm wrote, "even the crudest accountant's criterion of economic progress, real income per head (which must not be confused with the average standard of living), was actually – and for the first time since 1700 – falling. If nothing was done, would not the capitalist economy break down? And might not, as observers increasingly began to fear around 1840 all over Europe, the impoverished, disinherited masses of the labouring poor revolt? As Marx and Engels said in 1848 "a spectre haunts Europe – the spectre of communism."[33]

But, after the "Hungry Forties", living standards rose and unemployment fell, even though the conditions of employment may frequently have been atrocious. "No subsequent cyclical depression was even faintly as catastrophic as the slump of 1841-42", according to Hobsbawm. "And above all, the sense of imminent social explosion, which had been present in England almost without interruption since the end of the Napoleonic Wars . . . disappeared. Britons ceased to be revolutionary."[34]

There are many historians who disagree with Hobsbawm. But, certainly, conditions in "capitalist" England during the first half of the 19th century were one of the principal inspirations of the Communist Manifesto in 1848. Schumpeter notes that, according to Engels, Marx adopted the term "communism" in preference to "socialism" because "socialism had by that time acquired a flavour of bourgeois respectability".[35] "Communism" came to mean the complete abolition of private property; "socialism" the public ownership of the means of production.[36] (Perhaps it was because they led such a bourgeois life in private that the party elite in the twentieth century stuck so often to the epithet "socialist" . . .) The reports of Parliamentary Committees were a rich source of evidence for Marx and Engels of the appalling condition of so many of the people under early British capitalism.

English law developed a body of case-law against contracts which were "in restraint of trade" and monopolies required patents from the Crown. Polanyi has demonstrated how "there was nothing natural about *laissez-faire*", which was enforced by the state.[37] "The thirties and forties saw not only an outburst of legislation repealing restrictive regulations, but also an enormous increase in the administrative functions of the state, which was now being endowed with a central bureaucracy able to fulfil the task set by the adherents of (economic) liberalism."[38]

Much of the social and political history of the 19th and 20th centuries was dominated by the reaction in many countries to the effects of *laissez-faire* or economic liberalism on the people. Under *laissez-faire*, the market economy reigned supreme, labour was a mere factor of production, the cheaper the better, and all was allegedly justified by classical economics. *Laissez-faire* had been the intellectual product of the merging strands of the 18th century thought of Locke, Hume and others, which stressed individualism, and the economics which taught that enlightened self interest would also serve the general interest. They also serve who only stand and watch others amassing the greater good. But, whatever the "intellectual" justification or rationalisation for *laissez-faire*, it was also the practical policy of most employers.

Keynes pointed out that the phrase *laissez-faire* does not actually appear in Adam Smith or Ricardo or Malthus: coined by the Marquis d'Argenson in 1736 ("To govern better, one must govern less") it was taken up by Jeremy Bentham and the Utilitarians, as *laissez nous faire* (a somewhat elitist version), and subsequently popularised.[39] *Laissez-faire* was no doubt helped along by the experience of corrupt governments in the 18th century and by the fact that the Industrial Revolution itself had sprung spontaneously from what is now known as the private sector of the economy.

One of the tasks of government is to manage change; but in Britain industrialisation, the move from the land to the towns, and the general social upheaval of the early 19th century which produced the social hardship and chaos documented by historians and novelists such as Dickens and Mrs Gaskell, was hardly "managed" at all. The conditions produced by the Industrial Revolution, and by the *laissez-faire* reluctance to do more than the minimum to alleviate them, led to the rise of socialism. For Marx and Engels in 1848 there was a "spectre haunting Europe – the spectre of communism." The 18th century thinkers had emphasised property rights as part of their individualist philosophy. These had turned out to be property rights for the minority.

During the next nearly 100 years the capitalist economies embarked on intermittent programmes of social reform in order to ward off the revolution which would remove private property and "capitalistic production". As the American economist Taussig put it: "There is a vast difference between the mitigation of present inequalities and the complete removal of the causes which led to the inequality characteristic of the existing regime."[40] Social reform was not socialism. Poor laws, workmen's compensation acts, sickness insurance, old-age pensions, factory regulations, minimum wages – these were often called "socialist". "But ... they leave private property, capitalistic production, the competitive wage system, the leisure class, rent, interest, as elements of the economic order, essentially untouched. At the most, they somewhat restrict the field of competition and fix the plane upon which competition shall operate; the thing itself remains."[41]

Germany became one of the leading countries where the growth of a social democratic party proved a bulwark against socialism or communism itself. The Social Democratic Party (1875) anticipated the formation of the British Labour Party by over 25 years. "The policy which Bismarck brought to bear was two-fold," wrote Ogg.[42] "1. relentless repression of socialist agitation, and 2. legislation for the amelioration of those conditions in consequence of which the working-classes were induced to lend socialism their support." Bismarckian social insurance was much criticised abroad for being "socialistic" – and then much emulated abroad for saving capitalism from socialism at a relatively low price.

Dicey set out to look for the "collectivist" trend in British public opinion and could not find it. Instead all he could find were the so-called "collectivist" acts themselves. "The upshot of his penetrating enquiry," declared Polanyi, "was that there had been complete absence of any deliberate intention to extend the functions of the state, or to restrict the freedom of the individual . . . the legislative spearhead of the countermovement against a self-regulating market as it developed in the half century following 1850 turned out to be spontaneous . . . and actuated by a purely pragmatic spirit."[43]

Pragmatism also actuated Bismarck, who switched from a belief in free trade to a policy of protectionism in 1879. "For the abstract teachings of science in this connection" he said, "I care not a straw. I base my opinion on experience, the experience of our own time."[44] Thus, after nearly a quarter of a century of low tariffs, Germany reverted to the protectionist notions preached by Friedrich List in 1841. List had become a firm opponent of *laissez-faire*, arguing that there was a divergence between the individual's short term interests, and the longer term interests of the state.[45] He noted that "free trade" England had enjoyed protective tariffs when passing from agrarian status to an agricultural *and* industrial economy. She preached free trade because it was in her interests – it was safe to do so. List had in fact derived his protectionist ideas from the US, where he spent some admiring years, and developed what later became known as the "infant industry" argument for tariff protection at an early stage of industrialisation. He was in favour of protection for industry, not agriculture, and only as a temporary measure. Economic laws were not universal, and depended on the stage a country had reached. Japan was, after 1945, to be a classic example of the virtues of protection for infant industries. List's book coincided with the completion of the German Zollverein – the customs union of the German states. But this was followed by the British repeal of the Corn Laws in 1846 and the protectionist pressures in Germany receded. "To speak the truth," observed the economic historians Gide and Rist, "tariff duties are never of the nature of an application of economic doctrines. They are the results of a compromise between powerful interests which often enough have nothing in common with the general interest, but are determined by purely political, financial or electoral considerations."[46] The political, financial and electoral considerations weighing on

LEEDS METROPOLITAN UNIVERSITY LIBRARY

Bismarck's mind in 1879 were not only the "infant industry' argument but the need to raise Budgetary revenues to finance imperial expenditure, including social expenditure to ward off socialism.

For Adam Smith, there could be no doubt that "the great object of the political economy of every country, is to increase the riches and power of that country."[47] For him, plain reason dictated that the real wealth and revenue of a country consisted in the value of the annual produce of its land and labour.[48] The England (and Scotland) of 1776 had capital waiting to be employed either by its owners or by lending for a share of the profits.[49] Capital had been accumulated, protected by law and allowed by liberty to exert itself in the manner that was most advantageous.[50] "We see every day the most splendid fortunes that have been acquired in the course of a single life by trade and manufactures, frequently from a very small capital, sometimes from no capital", Smith declared. He was writing on the eve of the Industrial Revolution – a revolution that "capitalists" were waiting to exploit.

Capitalism had been implanted in England long before the Industrial and subsequent scientific and technological revolutions gave it the opportunity to be harnessed to tangible economic growth. Joint stock companies date from the end of the 16th century – there is in existence a complete work entitled "Joint Stock Companies to 1720".[51] According to one historian, Britain's "merchant capitalist" phase was so successful that the industrial revolution was essentially financed from the profits of foreign trade.[52] Joint stock companies began by financing foreign trade and colonisation (or "exploitation"), mining and water supply, as well as banking and insurance. The South Sea Bubble fraud in 1720 was a blow to the reputation of joint stock companies for spreading risk, if not for assembling capital, but they came back into their own to finance canals, railways, docks and public utilities in the period 1760 to 1860. The joint stock companies were there, but the early manufacturers used partnerships, and finance from merchants. The Scots led the way in the formation of joint stock companies for manufacturing, and in links with banks. In 1854 a Royal Commission saw no need for a change in the law of partnership, on the grounds – familiar in many such investigations since – that there was no shortage of finance for industrial enterprises. Nevertheless, some joint stock companies with limited liability were allowed to register from 1855, and limited liability was made open to all in the Companies Act of 1862, paving the way for amalgamations (or mergers) when competition from the US hotted up towards the end of the 19th century. Banks, and the financing facilities of the merchant banks in the City of London, had been well established *before* the Industrial Revolution. But banking can reasonably be said to have followed and supported the early phase of industrialisation rather than to have led it.[53] Banking and the capital markets had more to do with overseas trade and domestic public works than with the start of industrial capitalism.

What capitalism required was safety for capitalists, and a limit to the punishment for taking risks in investment or in the pursuit of gain. The limited liability laws constituted a giant leap into the safety net for the noble breed of Victorian risk-takers. There can be little doubt that limited liability gave a considerable boost to investment: it enabled entrepreneurs to tap a wider market for savings, as typical capitalist projects got bigger and required more capital. The widow could invest £100 without standing to lose £500. C.R. Fay described limited liability as "the legal frame of all commercial enterprise . . . the Magna Carta of Capitalism. The capitalist, sleeping or active, no longer suffers the rupture of his private bench, and still less of his private head, as might have been his lot in the days of Henry VIII."[54] Among other things, limited liability allowed, in Lord Goschen's words, "the marriage of English capital with foreign demand", a reference to the way English entrepreneurs subsequently financed railways and other investments in North and South America and many other parts of the world.[55] Limited liability followed the Bankruptcy Act of 1861, which also helped to systematise capitalism. Until 1705 the law on default had been ruthless. From 1705 it was possible for a bankrupt trader, having paid as much as he possessed in the pound to his creditors, to be discharged and start his financial career all over again. After 1861 *everybody* enjoyed the freedom to go bankrupt.

"If the working man (who enjoys no such limitation in *his* risks) is to compete with him [the capitalist] on equal terms, it must be from within a group, defensive or constructive, which is itself capitalism-proof," said Fay.[56]

The struggle to make the working man (and woman and child), capitalism-proof went on for the second half of the 19th century and the first half of the 20th. For everybody from Bismarck to the British Liberals, progressive social reforms proved expedient, and preferable to revolution. The long recession of 1873 to 1896 brought hardship which strengthened the need for reform – Europe was between the boom caused by the first industrial revolution and the second, which was facilitated by the internal combustion engine and electrical engineering. The recession also revived protectionism in many countries, but not the UK.

From the days of the Communist Manifesto and the International in the 1840s, the revolution of 1848 and the Paris Commune of

1871, through to the meeting of the Second International in Brussels on the eve of war in 1914, one of the burning issues was whether the workers of the world would indeed unite against the capitalists; in most countries a combination of internal reform and nationalism triumphed, with the workers lining up behind their own respective capitalist nation states in the "war to end wars" of 1914–18 – which was itself the outcome of national economic rivalries.

The 1914–18 war brought Communism to Russia, and its successor that was never meant to happen, the 1939–45 war, extended the grip of what Keynes had called Marx's "obsolete" doctrine to Eastern Europe. Capitalism, under what might be called the Keynesian Standard, with considerable initial help from General Marshall, enjoyed its 1950–73 "golden era", throughout which time there were serious Communist Parties in France and Italy (more serious at some times than at others) and a not very serious Communist Party in Britain. Hitler and Mussolini might have disappeared, but Franco's dictatorship continued for part of this period to keep the Spanish and their economy in repressed isolation. And, writing at the very end of the "golden age", the historian James Joll observed: "The search for a middle way between Soviet Communism and American capitalism has continued to be the main preoccupation of the Left in Western Europe – and indeed in Eastern Europe too, whenever there has seemed a chance to take 'different roads to socialism', as in Poland in 1956 or Czechoslovakia in the spring of 1968."[57] But, as Joll pointed out: "Even those who took part in movements of protest or revolt, in Poland and Hungary in 1956, in Czechoslovakia in 1968, attacked the methods used to run the planned socialist economy rather than the socialist economic system as such, and hoped to humanise communism rather than abolish it altogether."[58] "Euro-communists" thought, wrote, argued and debated about a different road to socialism, but never had the political opportunity to take it. "Market socialism", insofar as it was tried in eastern Europe, was 95 per cent socialism and 5 per cent market.

Lenin had asserted in 1916 that the European market for goods and finance was saturated and that the capitalist economies had therefore developed an imperialist struggle to capture overseas markets.[59] His report of the death of the European market proved to be premature, although there is little doubt that the capitalist system made profligate use of raw materials, and especially oil from overseas to sustain its expansion. Throughout the post-1945 period, Lenin's legacy, Soviet Russia, was itself engaged in an imperialist struggle with capitalism, to capture overseas markets and hearts. Perhaps the most dangerous moment for the survival of both systems was the Cuban crisis.

It was American concern – some might say paranoia – about the spread of communism that disrupted the golden age, and took the world economy off the Keynesian standard – the Keynesian standard being for our purposes the twin peaks of economic policy: the combination of Keynesian economic policies within a nation, and co-operation (however reluctant and self-serving at times) *between* national economies.

For, although there are disputes among economists about the appropriate policy reaction to the problems of the post-golden-age period, there is general agreement that the inflation caused by the Vietnam War was the main factor bringing the golden age to an end. The golden age itself had been US-led – all the way from the Bretton Woods agreement in 1944 on the post-war economic order, through General Marshall's Plan for the reconstruction of Europe, to the way that capitalism in Europe, Japan, and elsewhere was actively encouraged to learn from the US lead in productivity – and then proceeded to catch up on it. Moreover the way capitalism took its characteristic modern form – the dominance of the world market by multi-national corporations – was also an American-led trend which others copied.

It is a paradox that in its efforts to make the world safe for capitalism, the US did so much to improve the competition against itself. It helped both Europe and Japan onto their feet; it then operated a fixed exchange rate system, under a dollar standard, which had the effect of leaving other countries reasonably free to adjust their exchange rates to alleviate problems caused by differing inflation rates, or productivity and balance of payments trends, but the US itself could not adjust. From being a major exporter of capital, on the back of a strong post-war current account balance of payments surplus, the US gradually lost its competitive edge, and ended up printing dollars to finance further overseas investment as its current account turned to deficit in the early 1960s.

There was nothing resembling a serious Communist Party within the US (Senator Joseph McCarthy had stamped on the shadow of one), and the Great Society programme of the Sixties developed as a genuine move by the Democrats, inspired by cynical politics and uncynical altruism, to do something about the poor and the underprivileged. President Johnson's dilemma was that the ordinary dictates of sensible Keynesian economic policies required either the curtailment of expenditure on the rapidly escalating Vietnam War, or cutting back on the Great Society programme, which was addressed to education, health, low income housing and other worthy causes. He did not want Congress to provoke the latter by owning up to the true cost of the former. And he also eschewed the classic Keynesian remedy of higher taxes to slow down an inflationary boom.

Inflating its way through the Vietnam War led the US, by then under the Presidency of the Republican Richard Nixon, to two panic moves: caught in "an economist's timelag" between continuing to encourage deflation in the early 1970s and his desire to be re-elected in 1972, Nixon opted for an unheard of (in peace time) period of wage and price controls, plus a devaluation of the dollar in August 1971. It was these moves, rather than the Watergate burglary, which played the major part in Nixon's re-election; they helped to get the US economy moving, by improving the international price competitiveness of US industry; and the wage and price controls dampened inflation, thereby also shortening the length of the recession which had been originally induced to counter inflation. What eventually captured the public's imagination, when it came to light, was the Watergate episode, when the Democratic campaign headquarters had been burgled in the interest of Nixon's re-election. It was what he did to the international economic order, however, that caused the lasting damage. As the US economist Robert Lechachman wrote: "The ending of fixed exchange rates turned out to be disastrous for capitalism. It meant the ending of two decades of certainty, and the start of a new era of instability, violent currency fluctuations, and long term recession."[60]

There is also a view that the agonies of Watergate, and a Presidential involvement in which so many Americans simply did not wish to believe, made the US turn in on itself. At all events, in trying to stamp out the spectre of communism in Vietnam, the US economy had finally overstretched itself, and the "policy" adopted thenceforth soon became known as "benign neglect". The benignity applied to the domestic economy, and the neglect to the rest of the world. After a quarter of a century of remarkable altruism – at least towards other industrial economies – the US administration had become concerned that too many other economies were now standing on their own two feet.

The floating of the dollar was a drawn-out affair, following the ending of the dollar's convertibility into gold in August 1971 (when Nixon also imposed a 90 day freeze on pay and prices and a 10 per cent temporary import surcharge).[61] There was a formal devaluation of the dollar in December 1971 (under the "Smithsonian" Agreement) of 7.89 per cent, and another 10 per cent devaluation in February 1973.[62] The international financial system was now in chaos, with wild speculative movements of capital, and the principal foreign exchange markets were closed for over a fortnight, reopening on March 19 into a world of floating exchange rates.[63]

The problems of the dollar were directly linked to that other great blow to the capitalist system of the early 1970s – the oil shock of

1973, when oil prices were approximately quadrupled within the three months October-December, from a posted price of just under $3 to $11.65 per barrel.[64] The proximate cause of these rises was the Arab reaction to the October war between Israel on the one hand and Egypt and Syria on the other. The Arab states initially intended to use the "oil weapon" (of price increases and cutbacks in production) until Israel withdrew from the territories occupied in 1967 and the rights of the Palestinians were recognised. High demand for oil among the major capitalist countries helped to provoke the OPEC move. So did US aid to Israel during the October war.

OPEC (the Organisation of the Petroleum Exporting Countries) had been founded in 1961, and although the oil producers had become increasingly agitated about their lowly take, the price was still below $2 per barrel in 1970.[65] Early in 1971 it was raised 20 per cent to $2.15 (with a Gulf tax rate of 55 per cent on exports of crude oil). With oil priced in dollars, OPEC stood to lose on the dollar devaluations of 1971 and 1973 if they did not adjust their prices. On both occasions they did so, by slightly more than the devaluation itself, so that by the time of the Yom Kippur War of October 1973 they had some training in flexing their pricing muscles. Before the dollar devaluations they had been planning increases of only 2 and a half per cent a year (plus 5 cents extra per barrel) until the mid seventies.

There were further oil price increases in 1974. In effect the nominal price was quintupled. The price increases constituted a damaging, double-edged blow to the capitalist industrial countries, and the oil-less developing countries, who were big importers of oil: the effect was deflationary, insofar as the price rises acted as the equivalent of a tax increase, removing purchasing power from consumers; but it was also inflationary, in that oil prices added impetus to the wage/price spiral with which most capital economies were having to cope.

Inflation had accelerated in most industrial countries during the boom of 1972–73, which Maddison notes as "the fastest two-year period of expansion since 1950–51 in the aggregate GDP of the advanced capitalist countries", and whose size was boosted by "the collapse of the Bretton Woods exchange rate system and the subsequent easing of demand management constraints".[66] The UK was the most extreme case, with a rise in real GDP of 8 per cent – about three times its average growth rate.[67]

Higher oil prices imparted a classic "exogenous shock" to inflation, adding to the upward pressure on costs at just the time when demand pressures were intense. In the case of the UK and Italy, wage agreements at the time were geared to the cost of living, provoking another sharp upward twist in the spiral. Oil producing countries were suddenly awash with funds they could not possibly spend all at once; it would take them time to absorb their extra wealth in investment within their own countries. They therefore amassed hundreds of billions of dollars of deposits in the international banking system. The well-developed capitalist financial system had no trouble in lending these funds to the hard-pressed developing countries, which, apart from their many other needs, faced the higher oil prices. Little thought was given to the ability of these countries to repay – indeed the money was thrust upon them. One international banker referred thus to the routine procedure at IMF meetings in the late 1970s: "We raise a few routine questions about their economy, then we ask them what their borrowing programme is, and then we lend them money."

This was an exaggeration. But bankers, who are at the heart of the capitalist process of financing trade and investment, are slaves of fashion, and have a "herd instinct". At the time finance ministers and officials of the major capitalist countries were strongly urging the "recycling" of petro-dollars in order to avert the development of a black hole in the world economy from excess savings. Walter Wriston of Citibank proclaimed that sovereign borrowers could not go bankrupt, and the banks thought they were onto a good thing in taking deposits from OPEC and lending them to the developing nations. It is true that countries do not go bankrupt in the sense of being forced by the Government to stop trading when their liabilities exceed their assets. But Governments can default, had done so in the past, and were to do so again. In the case of Mexico, itself both a developing country and an oil producer, the country was being lent money on the security of its oil. Practitioners after the event acknowledged that in this, and other cases, there must have been a lot of double-counting of security going on. There was no central control of this "market" process – lenders were all looking at the same "assets" – and the chickens came home to roost in the balance sheets of the banks during the 1980s.

Despite this massive "recycling" of funds during the mid 1970s, the capitalist economies suffered their first serious recession of the post-war years in 1974 and 1975, with deceleration in economic growth accompanied by severe inflation – the worst of both worlds. There were severe policy disagreements between countries, with some, such as Britain, arguing that the impact of the extra cost of oil imports would simply have to be financed by borrowing, and others, such as Germany and Japan, cutting back domestic demand dramatically in order to offset the balance of payments effect of higher oil prices. The OECD calculated that in 1973–80, real output per head in the major capitalist countries grew by 2 per cent a year, but real income per head by only 1.5 per cent a year.[68] The difference represented a transfer of resources to OPEC countries.

The OPEC group managed to co-ordinate its cartel for longer than free-market economists expected. It was Western capitalism that was in disarray. During the Watergate affair one remark of Nixon's that appeared on the White House tapes seemed to epitomise the end of the "Pax Americana". Asked, during the turbulent times on the foreign exchanges, what he thought should be done about the Italian lira, Nixon replied "I don't give a (expletive deleted) about the lira." Another interesting aspect of the oil shock was that it provided a temporary breathing space for the USSR, which is a major oil producer, and delayed the day when the West would wake up to discover that the "evil empire" was based on a sick economy.

Examining the impact of the events of the early 1970s on the implications for a return to the golden age, a distinguished panel of economists concluded in 1977 that: "A key conclusion we draw from this assessment of factors underlying recent experience, is that the most important feature was an unusual bunching of unfortunate events unlikely to be repeated on the same scale, the impact of which was compounded by some avoidable errors in economic policy . . . this upheaval is not necessarily a sign of permanent change to an inevitably more unstable and inflationary world."[69]

Then came the next oil shock of 1979, making the increase in nominal oil prices during the decade no less than tenfold. The capitalist economies underwent another recession in 1980–81, and, with inflation a more persistent problem than it had been during the "golden age", faith in Keynesian policies waned.

It was the Japanese who coined the term "oil-shock". It was most certainly a shock to capitalism. At great speed the higher price of oil affected its manufacturing and distribution systems, wreaking havoc with the balance of payments of the average oil-importing country. Demand had been growing at a rate which meant that capitalism was precariously dependent on supplies from a few countries – notably Saudi Arabia and Iran – which did not need the money. In the end the price of oil ensured that demand fell. The countries which made the most impressive adjustments over the long term, their governments encouraging conservatism and efficiency in the use of energy, were Germany and Japan.

The slowdown during the 1970s, and the recurrence of recession in the early 1980s, prompted economists to ask not so much whether the mid 1970s recession was the result of special factors that were unlikely to recur, as whether the "golden age" itself was not the result of non-recurring factors. Had not the "golden age" seen boosts to productivity from such "once for all" influences as "recovery from war in Europe and Japan, the reopening of the economies to international trade and the large movement of labour out of agriculture or other less productive sectors of the economy".[70] There had certainly been a "catch-up factor", as the rest of the capitalist world learned about and emulated American technology. Then there was the question whether resource constraints (such as those that prompted OPEC price increases) might now be a permanent part of the scene – as well as broader environmental issues.

Andrew Britton has pointed out: "It is not possible to argue that innovation had lost its impetus, that mankind had run out of good new ideas in the 1970s, when the information technology industry was in its infancy. Technological advance seems to be an inherently explosive process, one which tends to increase at an increasing rate."[71] Equally, it was perfectly plausible that reactions to environmental concerns, and constraints on natural resources such as oil, might throw up new spurs to technological change.

It is possible for the technological and innovatory potential to be as strong as ever, but for defects in the functioning of capitalism to impose constraints on the exploitation of such opportunities. Some economists have pointed to the slowdown in capitalist "accumulation" (or investment) and a fall in the rate of profit during the 1970s and early 1980s.[72] This could well have been due to the slowdown in demand which was induced by governments in response to the inflationary pressures of the 1970s. Britton has suggested that "there was less willing co-operation between workers and management, a change which showed itself both in wage militancy and as increasing resistance to innovation. . . it is very plausible that changes in industrial relations are at least as important to the growth of productivity as are changes in technology or the availability of resources."[73]

What stands out is that managing an economy in the 1970s and early 1980s became more difficult: OPEC, trades union militancy (not so much in the US), large movements of capital and exchange rates in the wake of the breakdown of the Bretton Woods system – all these contributed to inflationary pressures, and to a climate in which fighting inflation became more important than boosting demand and employment. The Keynesian economic consensus was severely shaken, and policy makers lost confidence in themselves. Conditions were perfect for the left to argue that the capitalist system was once more in crisis, and for the right to maintain that the Keynesian standard had failed. These were the breeding grounds for a revival of classical economics, *laissez-faire*, and the "counter-revolution" to Keynesianism, known as Monetarism.

3

The Move to the Right

The Keynesians had lost confidence, and an alliance of New Right and monetarists seized their chance. Despite six years of cautious economic policies, the average inflation rate among the "high inflation" capitalist countries was still 9.2 per cent in 1978–79, compared with a peak of 15 per cent in 1974–75 – after the first oil shock.[1] On the other hand the "low inflation" countries were back to a rate of 3.9 per cent in 1978–79, compared with a peak of 12.3 per cent in 1974–75, and not far above "golden age" experience. The latter group included Japan, Germany, Switzerland and Austria. The former group included the US, the UK, France and Italy. (Within the average the US was 8.3 per cent and UK 10.3 per cent.)

Keynesians everywhere were in retreat: the old "touch on the brake" no longer seemed to do the trick. All manner of factors were blamed for the intransigence of inflation, including the sheer success of previous Keynesian policies and social security provision, which were generally considered to have altered the industrial climate too much in favour of wage bargainers or trades unions; and when wages pushed up prices, these were easily passed on by the oligopolistic multinationals of Galbraith's "New Industrial State", it being obvious that the real late 20th century world was light years away from the atomistic "perfect competition" in which the classical economists used to glory.

For years economic policy had operated on the assumed "trade off" between inflation and growth. Keynes's policies had been thought out in the inter-war period when the last problem on people's minds was inflation, or *rising* prices; the Great Depression was associated with falling prices. Indeed, so concerned were the post-war economic strategists with the desire to avoid deflation and achieve full employment and economic growth that it was generally considered that modest inflation, of 2 or 3 per cent a year, was no bad thing if it brought sustained expansion.

Economic management was not made any easier by the impact the oil shock had on old heavy industries such as steel, which were large consumers of energy, as newer, less energy-intensive technologies came to the fore. Old unions and communities felt threatened; policy-makers lost faith in planning, and this, too, gave scope for a revival of the philosophy of individualism, and belief in the decentralisation of decision-making. The Japanese, however, who were hit especially hard by the energy crisis (as heavy importers of oil), saw the need for a strategic, administratively-directed response to the energy crisis.

Countries such as Germany and Japan still seemed to manage inflation better while also having to cope with higher oil prices. Some commentators resorted to "cultural" explanations, such as that the folk memory of the ravages of inflation was still so strong in Germany that the whole society was geared up to the fight. In the case of Japan itself, the tendency in the West was to assume that the Japanese economy moved in mysterious ways, and that it was in any case a more cohesive and centrally directed society.

The Keynesian view was that, given what both Galbraith and the monetarist Professor Milton Friedman called the "political asymmetry" of Keynesianism (expansionary measures are politically easier than contractionary ones) conventional measures had to be supplemented by incomes policies of some sort, to control wages directly. These had been employed in both the US and UK during the 1970s, but were now politically unfashionable, and the case for them was not assisted in the UK by the breakdown of the Labour Government's working relationship with the trades unions over incomes policy in the 1978–79 "Winter of Discontent".

The monetarists, led by Friedman, argued that there was no trade off between inflation and growth: look what had happened – by being so lax, governments had arrived at a situation where they could not introduce expansionary measures because inflation was too high. At the peak of every economic cycle it got higher. If you wanted growth you had to eliminate inflation. And, by the way, inflation was at all times and everywhere a monetary phenomenon. Forget trades unions. It was governments, or rather their central banks, and they alone, who caused inflation by printing too much money – or, rather, given that cash in the modern economy is only a small part of the monetary mechanism, by allowing the banks to lend too much.[2]

Friedman had claimed to establish close relationships between the movement of the money supply and subsequent movements in prices, although the time lags were "long and variable". The work on which his claims were based was subsequently subject to severe critical attack by the British econometrician David Hendry. Keynesian economists questioned the causation – was it money supply to prices, or was it inflation to money supply? They also doubted the ability of central banks to control the money supply, although they acknowledged that it was always possible to create a good old-fashioned slump by raising interests rates, especially if this rendered the exchange rate too high. Friedman had written copiously in learned journals, but it was in public appearances, journalism and a popular book *Free to Choose* that he made most impact.

Friedman's populist tone had a seductive plausibility. "No government is willing to accept responsibility for producing inflation . . . Government officials always find some excuse – greedy business-men, grasping trade unions, spendthrift consumers, Arab sheiks, bad weather, or anything else that seems even remotely plausible."[3] This immediately lets the usual suspects off the hook, wins the audience or reader to Friedman's side, and prepares the way for an attack on everybody's favourite target: Government. The aforementioned "cannot produce continuing inflation for one very simple reason: none of the alleged culprits possesses a printing press on which it can turn out those pieces of paper we carry in our pockets; none can legally authorise a bookkeeper to make entries on ledgers that are the equivalent of those pieces of paper."[4]

Friedman actually argues that because there are instances of inflation in countries where there are no trades unions, or only weak ones, it therefore follows that trades unions do not cause inflation.[5] Again, in justification of his view that inflation cannot be imported from abroad, he states: "If it were, how could the rates of inflation be so different in different countries? Japan and the United Kingdom experienced inflation at the rate of 30 per cent or more a year in the early 1970s, when inflation in the United States was around 10 per cent and in Germany under 5 per cent."[6] Friedman was cavalier with his facts. The only possible years he could have been thinking of were 1974 and 1975, when in fact there was an internationally induced inflation shock from the OPEC oil price increases. Inflation in both years was certainly "around 10 per cent" in the US. But German inflation was above 5 per cent in both years (7 per cent and 6 per cent respectively) and neither Japan nor the UK experienced inflation "at the rate of 30 per cent or more". In Japan's case the figures for the two years were 21.2 per cent and 11.3 per cent, and in the UK 16.9 per cent and 23.7 per cent.[7]

In all these cases the rate of inflation had been affected by the internationally induced oil price increases. In the instance of Japan, the acceleration was especially marked, because that country was more dependent than most on imported oil, and as a result suffered heavy price increases; given the severe impact of more expensive imported oil on its balance of payments, Japan saw, in addition, a sharp devaluation of the Yen, which also contributed to higher prices. The UK, meanwhile, experienced internationally-induced higher oil prices, large wage increases as the result of trade union wage claims, and a further twist of the spiral from the fact that at this stage UK wage increases were indexed to the rate of inflation.

The UK experience in those years defied *both* the Friedmanite claim that trades unions had nothing to do with inflation *and* his dismissal of the possibility that inflation could be imported from abroad.

Turning to the United States, Friedman maintained that one of the causes of inflation there was a disinclination on the part of the Government to finance higher spending by taxation or borrowing – it preferred to get the Treasury to foot its bills by selling bonds to the Federal Reserve, which were paid for "either with freshly printed Federal Reserve Notes or by entering a deposit on its books to the credit of the US Treasury. The Treasury can then pay its bills with either the cash or a check drawn on its account at the Fed. When the additional high-powered money is deposited in commercial banks by its initial recipients, it serves as reserves for them and as the basis for a much larger addition to the quantity of money."[8] Or, the Federal Reserve could buy outstanding government bonds with "newly created high-powered money."[9] That enabled the banks "to make a large volume of private loans, which can also be represented as adding to employment". Both fiscal policy and monetary policy were biased towards full employment, and there was a reluctance on the part of the government to raise taxes, because that could be represented as adding to *un*employment.

Friedman's explanation of the mechanics of monetary creation is as lucid as one would expect from such a distinguished monetary economist. But the bias in favour of full employment had been there since 1945, and for most of the time inflation had been much lower. Friedman's popular explanation here also pins rather a lot on the Government, and omits the process by which banks themselves, irrespective of government spending, can create money on one side of the balance sheet simply by extra lending on the other – all entirely within the private sector. His emphasis is constantly on attacking governments and government spending, and in this "monetarism" links up neatly with the revival of the New Right, and with various other evangelicals who came together on both sides of the Atlantic: the alliance may have differed in its means, and its degrees of emphasis, but it was united in wanting less government and lower taxes.

Friedman chose to ignore the reasonable hypothesis that wage bargainers might have been getting tougher, and therefore having an impact on the inflationary process. This may be partly because there was less evidence of this in the US than in the UK. And he attacked the Federal Reserve for having "given its heart not to controlling the quantity of money but to controlling interest rates, something that it does not have the power to do. The result has been failure on both fronts: wide swings in both money and interest rates."[10]

(During the recession of 1980–82 the Federal Reserve was in fact going to demonstrate powerful control over interest rates.) It was Government, via central banks, that created inflation by printing money, or rather printing money in excess of that necessary to finance the annual increase in output. Therefore the cure to inflation lay in issuing strict instructions to the central bank about controlling the growth of the money supply.

Governments, during the economic difficulties of the 1970s, got the blame not just for causing inflation, but also for impeding economic performance in other ways. Too much was being spent on the public sector, and not enough room was given to the private sector to manoeuvre, according to this view. Keynes had argued that "economic forces" needed to be brought under control in order to preserve capitalism. Monetarists and the right wing generally now argued that governments should "get off the backs" of the people, and allow these market forces greater scope to provide better economic performance and more wealth. This meant that the size of the public sector and tax bills should be lowered; regulations and restrictions should be eliminated; and, in Britain in particular, the trades unions should be brought down to size. In his Nobel Lecture Friedman himself blamed trades unions for preventing the market from working properly, by pricing non-unionists out of work, preventing the rapid adjustment of the economy to new technology and forcing governments to subsidise housing, health and social security benefits.[11]

One American writer summarised the general approach of the right and the monetarists in the early 1980s as: "The conservative answer to the problems of slow growth and accelerating inflation – as to many other problems – is to use the incentives of higher profits to coax corporations into better behaviour. Any limits on private enterprise, whether by unions, government programmes or environmental regulations, are simply social debris that must be cleared away to clear the broad path to prosperity."[12]

It so happened that the *laissez-faire* approach and monetarism tended to go together: in the 1970s and early 1980s it was common for the monetarists to emphasise also the importance of market forces and deregulation – although it later turned out that some monetarists rued the deregulation of the financial markets as a move which made it difficult to control the money supply. A variety of economic and political gurus made their contribution to President Reagan's policies. One writer better known in the US than Europe was George Gilder, whose equivalent of Friedman's "Free to Choose" was "Wealth and Poverty". Friedman preached the wonders of capitalist consumption – "When you vote daily in the supermarket, you get precisely what you voted for, and so does everybody else." Gilder averred the virtues of being a capitalist, and conducting business and investment, an activity which will prosper if "supply" is freed from government regulation and high taxes.

"Reaganomics' derived from a hotchpotch of President Reagan's own home-spun truths, monetarism, "supply-side" economics, which advocated lower taxes to set business free, and the resurgent right wing. Sidney Blumenthal has pointed out how important former American Marxists, reborn as "neo-conservatives", were in promulgating right wing ideas.[13] As Blumenthal notes, from back in the mid 1960s, when a book called "The Liberal Establishment" argued that "The chief point about the Liberal Establishment is that it is in control", the right wing in the US was trying to rebuild its influence through every means from think tanks such as the American Enterprise Institute to greater prominence in the press.[14] "To counteract this Liberal Establishment, which conservatives believed encompassed both political parties, they deliberately created the Counter-Establishment. By constructing their own establishment, piece by piece, they hoped to supplant the liberals. Their version of Brookings [the liberal US think tank] would be bigger and better . . . The editorial pages of the *Wall Street Journal* would set the agenda with more prescience than *The New York Times*."[15]

William Simon, Treasury Secretary under the Ford Administration, made it his business to develop a "counter-intelligentsia" to attack the traditional East Coast liberal fortress.[16] One of their achievements was to gain widespread credibility for the view that it was government itself that thwarted changes that were good for the economy, not the system of checks and balances which was built into the US constitution itself. Irving Kristol, a neo-conservative, promulgated the "law of unintended consequences" in connection with liberal social policies: "whatever the intention, an opposite effect is achieved".[17] This approach was used by the right to attack "welfare" policies in the run-up to Reagan's arrival in office in 1981. The onslaught on other items of public spending was rendered all the more necessary if the right was to achieve "supply side" tax cuts, *and* the higher defence spending that it felt the military threat from the USSR then warranted. Big business also became more supportive of

the right, forming a "Business Roundtable" to influence public
policy. Chief executive officers of major corporations had become
disillusioned with the post-Second World War consensus. "Federal
regulatory agencies, they believed, hampered productivity,"
Blumenthal writes.[18] "Government expenditures, under the rubric
of Keynesian economics, produced inflation; and taxes inhibited
investment." The economic rise of the sunbelt in the US brought with
it a new breed of right wing, "self help" entrepreneur which lacked
any sense of East Coast "Noblesse oblige". Economic egoism was
once more the order of the day; "private success is the fulfilment of
social responsibility"; "free enterprise, individualism, survival of the
fittest – these were their dogmas."[19] Ronald Reagan's business
supporters were sun-belt entrepreneurs, and "the millionaires
backed him with millions".[20]

Some of those sun-belt industries paid obeisance to private
enterprise but made money directly or indirectly from government
contracts, especially defence. The traditional marxist interpretation
of capitalism as being propped up by an "arms economy" pales
somewhat, as we shall see later, by comparison with the degree to
which communism was propped up by the arms industry. The
"moral case" for "Star Wars" was argued by a right wing think tank
– the Institute for Educational Affairs – founded in 1978 by William
Simon, the former Treasury Secretary, and Irving Kristol, the neo-
Conservative propagandist.

The mixed nature of the factors behind what became the best
known of Reagan's economic policies, the emphasis on tax cuts,
irrespective of the fact that the promised "budget balance" never
materialised, is illustrated by the fact that the "supply-siders"
themselves wanted tax cuts for everybody, whereas another group –
the American Council on Capital Formation – wanted them for
corporations and the rich, the "big savers", who might be expected
to save and invest even more. The argument of "supply-siders", such
as the economist Arthur Laffer, was not the traditional Keynesian
one that tax cuts would increase demand, but that they would act
as "incentives" to make people work harder, and free up the
economy to produce and invest more. This way they would also raise
revenues – although the idea that there existed a "Laffer Curve"
which made tax cuts "self financing" appears to have been produced
by Laffer's disciples. A book attempting to justify supply-side
economics was produced under the aegis of the AEI by a Wall Street
Journal staff member, incorporating the theory of the economist
Robert Mundell that "if the world economy has inflation and
unemployment at the same time, the proper policy mix is tight
money and fiscal ease".[21] Monetary policy was to be directed at

inflation; tax cuts would boost the incentives to work and to raise productivity.

The idea of a "Laffer Curve" in which tax cuts were self-financing was vigorously promoted in the *Wall Street Journal* by Jude Wanniski, who wrote a book *The Way the World Works* propagating supply-side economics and a general move to the right. It did not convince the economics profession, but contributed to the general direction of influential opinion, and was supported by the prominent Republican Representative, Jack Kemp. As Blumenthal comments: "Supply-side economics provided the theoretical underpinnings for old-fashioned optimism" – even if the majority of the economics profession could see no intellectual foundations beneath it. All the New Right required in the US en route to Reagan's election was the taxpayer's revolt over property taxes in California in 1978 – Proposition 13 – and they had captured the public imagination.

The Reagan administration's commitments to large tax cuts, especially for those higher up the scale, were not easy to reconcile with greater defence spending *and* a balanced Budget. But the strength of Reagan's feelings against the "evil empire" was manifest; and they were reinforced by a strong right wing group that wished to dispel the "Vietnam Syndrome". According to the hard right, the Russians still posed a military threat which could only be diminished by a vast build up of arms – and in Reagan's case, by Star Wars technology as well.

For traditional American liberals, the "economic" justification for Reaganomics was wafer thin. "The reality of Reaganomics consists of rearming the United States and (for all but those at the top) reducing US standards of living. It is a militarily dangerous and socially cruel strategy – and ultimately an unsuccessful one. The growth areas it creates, military hardware and, presumably, luxury goods and services for the newly enriched elite, are far from sufficient to replace the former strengths of the US economy", one critic wrote.[22]

Not only did the Reagan tax cuts help the rich – taxes as a percentage of income fell from 48.6 per cent to 38.9 per cent between 1980 and 1984 for those with incomes above $250,000 a year: the way in which certain tax exemptions were removed meant that the proportion of income paid in tax by the lowest income groups actually increased.[23] Then there were cuts in expenditure on food stamps, school lunches, welfare, medicaid and subsidised housing. Galbraith made the point that there was something strange about a doctrine that held that the rich would work harder if they had more money, and the poor if they had less.

Although they rarely made the front pages, right wing philosophers such as Robert Nozick provided a justification for the consciences of the perpetrators of Reaganomics and their beneficiaries. They could rest assured not only that monetarism and supply-side economics were going to turn the economy round, but that, quite apart from that, a redistribution of income and wealth to the rich was morally justified. The Harvard philosopher John Rawls had argued, on Kantian lines, that a just society was one people would choose if they did not know, when making that choice, where they themselves would stand in the society. For Rawls, it is a necessary condition for the good society not only that there should be equality of liberty and opportunity, but also that the distribution of income and wealth should take into account the interests of the poor. This was not far removed from the centre of gravity of post Second World War thinking, although, contrary to a widely held view, there was not a consistent move towards redistribution of income and wealth through the decades: what had tended to happen before the arrival in power of President Reagan in the US and Mrs Thatcher in the UK was that redistribution took place in wartime, and the net effect of peacetime policies for taxation and social policy was to hold the line, and prevent the spread of income and wealth from becoming *more* unequal.

In effect, what raised the standard of living for most people in capitalist countries after the Second World War was economic growth; and varying qualities of safety net protected the weak and the poor. It was a significant moment in the UK, for instance, when the Labour politician and intellectual Anthony Crosland argued that the only way future Labour Governments could achieve redistribution was through growth.[24]

Robert Nozick was even more extreme than Friedman in his views about the unhealthy trend towards welfare and the left. There had been a tendency on the part of post Second World War governments to intervene in economic affairs, with the safety net held higher in Europe than in the US. Nozick argued against the very concept of a "fair distribution" of income or property: "no end state principle or distributional patterned principle of justice can be continuously realised without continuous interference with people's lives."[25] According to Nozick, natural rights make property owners immune from taxation aimed at helping even the poorest members of society. For Nozick the distribution of income is by choice, the result of individual transactions. Nozick attempts to provide the justification, in philosophical language, for what the convicted insider-dealer Ivan Boesky explained in more down to earth terms with words to the effect that "You can be greedy and feel good about it."

The low growth and high inflation that followed the oil shocks of the 1970s had a bad impact on President Carter's popularity in the November 1980 Presidential election. As Robert Lekachman has written: "In November 1980, the actual choice presented to wage earners was between retention of a president and an administration that had cost them income and job opportunities, and a candidate whose appeal was couched in inspiringly affirmative language."[26] Reagan was promising more jobs, more pay, less tax and less inflation: "The astute 1980 Republican campaign and the party's carefully programmed national candidates deployed the lure of renewed growth as an effective cloak for policies certain to aggravate existing inequities in the distribution of income and wealth."[27]

A similar move to the right had taken place in the UK during the 1970s, starting with the setting up of a right wing anti-collectivist group by Mrs Margaret Thatcher and former Cabinet Minister Sir Keith Joseph in 1974. They founded a think tank called the Centre for Policy Studies, which propagated the work of Friedman and the great survivor of the Austrian school of neo-classical economists, Friedrich von Hayek. Hayek's anti-left credentials were impeccable – he was even anti-Keynes well before it became fashionable to be so, and warned of "The Road to Serfdom" in 1944. Hayek had himself served time in the free-market/monetarist Chicago School during the 1950s. Both Hayek and Friedman seized the chance on both sides of the Atlantic to capitalise on the travails of the Keynesian standard during the 1970s.

Margaret Thatcher was in fact an acolyte of Sir Keith Joseph's who only put herself forward for the leadership of the Conservatives when Joseph himself declined to stand in 1974. The CPS and the longer standing Institute for Economic Affairs propagated the faith of markets and monetarism, as did leading economic commentators, but it was probably the general public's disillusionment with the disruptive power of British trades unions – and their link with the Labour Party – which brought Thatcher to power. There was also a public sympathy with the view that taxes and public spending were too high. And, as in the US, the economic management of the country had in any case been a struggle in the wake of the oil shocks; coming to grips with this, and with persistent high inflation, had involved a period of slow growth.

The Thatcher Government arrived in office in May 1979, and the Reagan administration was inaugurated in January 1981. By this time US observers ought to have had a chance to see just how disastrous monetarism had been for the British economy, with the worst recession in post-war years. Unlike the Reagan administration, the Thatcher Government balanced initial cuts in income tax with increases in indirect taxation. Unfortunately, the way they did this, via a near doubling in Value Added Tax, went straight into the consumer price index, and made the job of controlling inflation even tougher.

The British Government found it could not control the money supply, but that the high interest rates which it encouraged in the attempt drove the pound up to a level – $2.45 at one point – which was extremely damaging to the price competitiveness of British industry. Profitability, and pricing policy, are supposed to be at the heart of the capitalism in which Mrs Thatcher so ardently believed. But her enthusiasm for the "free play of market forces" was such that the "market" was allowed to take the pound to a level which posed a serious threat to the important sector of British industry which depended on foreign trade. It turned out that ideological "free market" attitudes towards the exchange rate could seriously undermine the economy's ability to compete in the markets of the real world. Obeisance towards *financial* market forces hampered the effectiveness of the *real* market economy.

In the US, as Lekachman has pointed out, "The failure of Reagan economic policy was readily predictable. Supply-side policies clash directly with monetarism. The success of the former requires easy credit, low interest rates, and a resulting boom in investment."[28] In both countries controlling the money supply proved more difficult than Friedman had predicted – but the central banks turned out to have rather more control over interest rates than the leading monetarist had claimed. In the US, inflation, boosted once again by an oil shock in 1979–80, was brought down by a severe recession engineered by the Federal Reserve. Instead of the great revival of entrepreneurship and business investment urged by the New Right, output collapsed in the early years of both Reaganomics and Thatcherism. In the UK there was a drop of 3 per cent in real gross domestic product between 1979 and 1981; in the US real GDP fell 2.5 per cent in 1982 – half as much again as during 1974–75, after the first inflationary oil shock.[29] Interest rates of close to 20 per cent in the US in 1981 posed a threat not only to domestic US business, but to the entire world monetary system; and the threat of default by Mexico on its debts in October 1982 was an important factor contributing to the timing of the easing of monetary policy by the Federal Reserve – although by then US inflation had been brought under control.

The mechanism by which inflation in the early 1980s was brought down in the US and UK was the old device by which output and employment are hit until the economy cools down. Control of the money supply hardly came into the picture. Of course, when the impact of the Reagan tax reductions and higher defence spending was combined with an easing of monetary policy after the autumn of

1982, there was a marked recovery in the US. In the UK, on the other hand, where the Thatcher Government was more serious than the Reagan administration about cutting the public sector deficit, there was much less of a stimulus to the economy in the immediate years after the 1980–81 recession.

There were subsequent suggestions that supply-side economics had all been a ploy to make the budgetary situation so disastrous that phenomenal cuts in government spending would be forced on the US Congress. Such suggestions have been vehemently denied by both David Stockman, Reagan's Budget director in the early years, and by Paul Craig Roberts, a supply-side advocate who also served in the administration. Stockman wrote: "Years later, in 1985, my old rabbi, Pat Moynihan, would say that we had pushed through the tax cuts to deliberately create this giant deficit. In truth, not six of the six hundred players in the game of fiscal governance in the spring and summer of 1981 would have willed this outcome. Yet caught up in the powerful forces unleashed by the dangerous experiment of a few supply-siders who had gotten the President's good ear, they let it happen just the same."[30] Craig Roberts also points out that "Laffer-curve" forecasts which predicted that the Reagan tax cuts would pay for themselves did not exist, and that the full impact of the tax cuts on lost revenue was forecast by the Reagan administration itself in 1981.[31] OECD figures show that the Federal deficit rose from 2.6 per cent to 5.4 per cent of GDP between 1981 and 1985 under the influence of lower taxes and higher expenditure, with defence rising from 5.3 per cent of GDP to 6.4 per cent between 1981 and 1985.[32]

It takes quite a lot of movement for one category of expenditure to have such an effect on the relative proportions of GDP. David Stockman, the Budget Director of the time, recalls that "they (the Senate Budget Committee) had given the Pentagon a 12 per cent real increase in both 1981 and 1982, and one of 8 per cent in 1983. For 1984–85, Domenici's Committee was drawing the line at 5 per cent."[33] With Stockman trying to fight Defence Secretary's Caspar Weinberger's "last resort" demands for real increases of 7.9 per cent, 7.5 per cent and 6.4 per cent over the years 1984 to 1986, on 23 March 1983, President Reagan delivered a speech in which he unveiled his Strategic Defence Initiative – the concept of a "space-based" anti-missile defence system.[34] Stockman comments: "Whatever its merits, 'Star Wars' was rather dramatically beside the immediate point. We were about to take the 1984–88 defence budget to Capitol Hill, and now the President had, in a fairly spectacular way, taken the debate over Congress's head – all the way to outer space."[35]

Stockman adds that "Domenici was livid. The entire Senate

Budget Committee was livid". The Senate Committee had "accommodated the White House so as to give the President time to rally the nation behind a larger defence budget figure" – now they were faced with this amazing Presidential vision on top. At a subsequent Cabinet meeting, Weinberger then argued against the tax increases Stockman and others were proposing in order to reduce the Budget deficit. "The audacity of it was staggering," said Stockman. "Weinberger was doggedly pushing up defence outlays from $133 billion in 1980 to $377 billion by 1988 – a one-quarter trillion dollar budget increase in just eight years. And now he was throwing stones at the people who were trying to raise the taxes to pay for it."[36]

" 'I can't wait to get my pen out', the President said, grinning enthusiastically," Stockman writes. "And so began the era of the hard-line veto strategy."

Stockman is referring to vetoes on cutting the Budget deficit. Throughout the world there was concern about the size of the US Government's Federal deficit, and about its financial dependence on inflows from overseas, or a rundown of overseas assets, to finance its balance of payments deficit. Such fears contributed to many analyses of the "decline of America as a superpower".

Yet what the combination of Weinberger, the defence lobby and Reagan in particular were in the process of achieving was a veto on the Soviet economic system as well. There was much debate about the size of the Soviet economy and the proportion accounted for by defence, with the CIA and the arms lobby considered by liberals to be exaggerating the figures out of their own obvious vested interest. What was to emerge later was that, if anything, the CIA had been underestimating the degree to which the Soviet Union was an "arms economy". But the most interesting development of all was that the Reagan Star Wars speech, threatening yet another escalation in US defence spending, was devastating news to a Kremlin that was already concerned about the failure of its economy to deliver consumer goods, indeed the basic necessities of life, to Soviet citizens. In fact the concept of "Star Wars" was the last straw.

Just as the UK had allowed its exchange rate to rise much too high for the good of the domestic supply-side, so did the US administration during the early 1980s. The doctrine dubbed "global monetarism", under which exchange rates were left to the vagaries of the market, and countries could only expect to prosper by putting their own houses in order, was assiduously preached at international economic forums, such as OECD meetings in Paris, by Beryl Sprinkel, a hard-line monetarist who also happened to become first a senior US Treasury official and, later, chairman of the President's Council of Economic Advisers. The "strong" dollar, which was adding to the industrial problems Reaganomics was meant to cure, was said by US officials such as Sprinkel, to be the result of a vote of confidence by the world's investment community in the US, where the return on investment was now so good.

In fact, business fixed investment in manufacturing did not grow at all between 1979 and 1985 in the US, compared with an average rate of growth of 5.5 per cent (volume) between 1973 and 1979 – the "difficult" years, when the Keynesian Standard had collapsed, and the New Right was gathering to do something about business stagnation.[37] During the same period there was a collapse of business fixed investment in manufacturing in the UK, which did not regain 1979 levels until the end of the 1980s. Certainly, the easing of monetary policy, the rise in consumer indebtedness made possible by financial deregulation, and the fiscal deficit induced a sharp recovery from recession in the US – GDP rose 3.6 per cent in 1983 and 6.8 per cent in 1984, with senior officials joking in private that "at least the strong dollar is acting as a drag on the recovery". And, certainly, the foreign trade sector of the US economy is only about half that of the UK, as a proportion of GDP. Nevertheless, the lack of international competitiveness of US manufacturing industry brought a reduction of nearly 12 per cent in the volume of US exports between 1981 and 1983, and a phenomenal increase of 23.9 per cent in the volume of US imports in 1984.

The US administration was thus in the curious position of being criticised internally and abroad for the irresponsibility of its "twin deficits" (budgetary and overseas trade) while providing quite a stimulus to demand in other countries via its trade deficit. As one senior European central banker commented at the time (after joining in the general chorus of criticism of the US), "But, when all is said and done, where would all our economies be without the stimulus of the US deficit?" In fact, during the first half of the 1980s, economic growth in Europe was remarkably subdued. West Germany, as the linchpin of the fixed exchange rate area known as the European Monetary System, was conducting an old fashioned trade-off between inflation and growth, with the emphasis on keeping inflation down. German arguments that growth would come if inflation was kept down became known as the "self-levitation" principle of economic management around this time.

Thus, by the time *perestroika, glasnost* and *uskorenie* were unveiled by Mr Gorbachev in April 1985, there was growing concern within the US about loss of international competitiveness, de-industrialization and the rising tide of protectionist pressure within Congress. This led to the dramatic US administration initiative to abandon the free market approach to exchange rates, and to effect a devaluation of the dollar, under the Plaza Hotel Agreement of September 1985. Meanwhile in the UK, where fiscal policy was being conducted much more savagely than in the US, unemployment was still rising and there was not much sign of what was later, albeit fleetingly, proclaimed as the "Thatcher economic miracle". One reason why the Thatcher Government had embarked on its famous policy of privatisation of state assets was as a diversion from the grim domestic economic scene. Ministers had no idea at the time what a national and international winner they were backing.

"Counter-revolution" policies to arrest the alleged relative decline of the leading Anglo-Saxon economies had certainly enriched the higher income brackets, but had hurt the lower income groups, and aggravated the deterioration in the leading Anglo-Saxon economies' international trading performance. These trading problems, of which Japan was seen to be the principal beneficiary, contributed to concerns such as those most notably expressed by Paul Kennedy, about "The Problem of Number One in Relative Decline". Then came the admission of defeat by the Russian and East European economies, which put the "decline" of the US, and the problems of Western capitalism, into perspective.

4

The Collapse of Communism

It is difficult to overestimate the significance of the admission of defeat by the USSR with regard to its economic system. The admission came nearly 150 years after Marx and Engels had warned about the "spectre of communism" haunting Europe. "Spectre" it proved indeed – a phantom solution that nevertheless claimed tens of millions of victims in the course of the pursuit of this most unholy grail. Most societies have undergone some form of collective sacrifice in the transition to the status of a modern capitalist or market economy. Soviet Russia had imposed the most dramatic and sustained sacrifice on its people – and still failed to deliver the kind of reasonably successful, modern consumer society for which most countries in the world evidently strive. What is more, the failure of communism as an economic system had occurred not only in the USSR; it also took place in countries such as East Germany and Czechoslovakia, where the underlying potential for economic success was generally considered to be much better – not least because of the achievements of those economies before the Second World War.

The failure of communism as an economic system is made all the more ironic by the arrogance of the original conception, which was no less than to export the "revolution" to the entire world – a world dominated, when Marx wrote, by capitalism, and when Lenin wrote by capitalism and "economic imperialism". One of the characteristics of the post Second World War period was the rapid withdrawal of the original "imperialist", Great Britain, from empire; another was that markets and trade did indeed expand with capitalist development – as Marx had stated they needed to if capitalism was not to collapse – and with that expansion came an impressive rise in the standard of living of at least a fifth of the world. It would obviously have been more satisfying if a much greater proportion of the world had enjoyed a bigger advance; but nobody could accuse communism of having done any better.

One should not underestimate the scale of the problem the Russians set themselves. It was part of the conceit of communism

that, quite apart from the manifold inherent difficulties in transforming a vast land-mass of disparate and predominantly agrarian
peoples, and quite apart from the choice of what Keynes dubbed "an
obsolete economic textbook", for a long time the system also
required itself to be largely cut off from outside help. Once the
industrial revolution had begun in Britain and spread elsewhere, two
important aspects of economic development were the process of
"catching up" on the technological advances of others, and assistance, in the form of a capital inflow from abroad, to reduce the strain
on domestic savings and consumption.[1] In its efforts at economic
reform, Tsarist Russia had relied heavily on an inflow of foreign
capital; and so, to a lesser extent, had the Japan that was to become
the economic envy of the Western world.

The Tsars had embarked on their attempt at modernisation of the
19th century Russian economy in the wake of their defeat in the
Crimean War, and their fear of foreign domination, as well as in the
face of potentially revolutionary rumblings at home. In the run up to
the "Great Rehearsal" of 1905 and the October Revolution of 1917,
Russian revolutionaries had debated whether a successful revolution
could be mounted before or after the move from feudalism to
capitalism. There was also a great debate among the Tsar's advisers
at the turn of the century about whether to emulate the West, as
favoured by Count Witte (finance minister 1892–1903) who actively
encouraged foreign borrowing, and others who believed in a unique
Russian solution.

Banking got going slowly in Russia in the 1870s and 1880s,
requiring Government financial support and direction. It expanded
rapidly between 1890 and 1914, with Moscow banks tending to
make short term loans to textile and other light industries (on the
model of English clearing banks). St Petersburg banks were more
entrepreneurial, and closely involved in the development of heavy
industry, on a longer term basis, on the model of German investment
banks. The fashionable theme a century later, under perestroika, and
after the historic meeting of President Gorbachev with the Group of
Seven leading capitalist nations, was to be the encouragement of
foreign direct investment in Russia, although potential Western
investors pointed to enormous difficulties. There had also been
difficulties and unhappy experiences a century earlier, so that foreign
investors preferred to use the banks as intermediaries. By 1913 about
half of Russian government debt and half of share capital was held
abroad, and, by 1916, 45 per cent of the capital of the ten largest
commercial banks was in foreign hands.[2] "The joint-stock banks
attached considerable importance to the development of a capital

market . . ." Feinstein states "the principal mechanism used by the banks for this purpose was to make available extensive credits to private investors to enable them to purchase industrial securities which the banks had issued or helped to place. Against this background the St Petersburg Bourse flourished in the years 1908–14, although even then it was secondary to the market in Russian securities in Paris and Brussels".

The Bolsheviks inherited an economy that had been ravaged by the First World War, in which there were only small islands of industrialisation, and four fifths of the population still lived off the land. Industrial production – which had risen rapidly between the turn of the century and 1913 – fell by a quarter between 1914 and 1917, and agricultural output by a tenth. Inflation afflicted Russia, as well as other European economies. The economic crisis helped the revolutionaries to power, but made life difficult for them once they were in. Foreign capital was neither the chosen instrument, nor a feasible one, in an atmosphere where existing overseas debts were being repudiated, property expropriated, the old ruling class persecuted, and civil war raging. And the autarchic regime cut itself off from the classic "catching-up" process of exposure to superior external technology.

The situation was dramatic enough for a partial restitution of private enterprise under Lenin's New Economic Policy, but after Lenin's death (1924) Stalin dropped the NEP and embarked in 1928 on the series of five year plans designed to achieve "Socialism in One Country". The big economic debate between 1924 and 1928 was about "from what source could investment funds be drawn for expanding industry and reconstructing it on a higher technical level, thereby increasing the productivity of labour?"[3] This process required metal and machinery; with foreign loans ruled out, higher export earnings were needed. The main export of this predominantly peasant country had been grain, but in the early 1920s "the marketable surplus of grain was actually smaller than it had been in pre-revolutionary days – smaller by as much as a half."[4] After the land reform of 1917, the peasants had ended up consuming more of the produce they had gained from the landlords and large farmers ("kulaks"). The end of the NEP prevented the peasants from making profits out of food production, which dropped further.

Redressing this mistake, and encouraging large-landowners, would have been bowing to capitalism. Hence the alternative was adopted: the collectivisation of peasant farms. Thus one of the principal problems facing the Soviet Union *between* the wars was that the loss of its traditional grain surplus severely hampered its ability to adopt the classic means of industrialisation – export of raw materials in return for imports of capital goods that would lay the basis for future consumer goods. Without overseas credits, and without substantial export earnings, the two five year plans of 1928 to end 1937 threw all the emphasis onto massive industrialisation in the capital goods sector – iron, steel, coal. It was to be "jam tomorrow". The USSR thus eschewed the familiar "textiles first" approach of other industrialising countries, and output of consumer goods grew at less than half that of heavy investment goods – which were then, of course, diverted into the massive Soviet War effort.[5]

Under the two five year plans, investment more than doubled as a proportion of GDP (to 26 per cent in 1937), exports fell to a mere 1 per cent, and per capita private consumption – providing the "investible surplus" – *fell*.[6] The familiar human costs of the accompanying Great Terror dwarfed anything experienced under the 19th century capitalism which had so offended Karl Marx. If post-war capitalism came to be seen as succeeding against communism and socialism by the simple process of the gradual embourgeoisement of the working class, inter-war communism in the USSR managed to go backwards by removing the bourgeoisie. According to the 1939 Soviet Census the number of collective farm workers rose from 3 per cent to 47 per cent of the labour force between 1929 and 1939, and the working class from 18 per cent to 46 per cent, while the bourgeoisie fell from 16 per cent in 1916 to 5 per cent in 1928 and 0 per cent in 1938. The number of peasant farm workers fell from 47 per cent to 3 per cent. Altogether, half the workforce still worked on the land in 1939, compared with 5 per cent in the UK.[7]

Throughout this period, the output of ideological and economic justifications was endless, but whatever the theories or the rationalisations, the underlying reality was desperately fundamental: to maintain political power for himself, Stalin was prepared to persist with central planning against the odds, and to destroy the peasantry. If it had not been for the Second World War, the system might possibly have collapsed sooner. As it happened, central planning was particularly suited to wartime; the war effort renewed its lease.

The scale of the human losses suffered by the Soviets during the 1939–45 war was awesome. But the military machine triumphed. And the economy possessed enough crucial raw materials, including a fifth of the world's supplies of iron ore and four times more oil production than was available to Germany. (Oil shortages proved fatal to Germany's eastward thrust.) In per capita terms the output of the Soviet economy was probably less than half that of Germany's before the war, but command economies come into their own in wartime, and "her economic system, with its experience of planning over a decade and a half, was much more suited to rapid improvisation and adjustment and to implementing plans and allocations of resources efficiently than the German economy proved to be."[8] One notable feature was the eastward evacuation of much of Soviet industry.[9]

The USSR received about a fifth of the total wartime aid given by the USA to the Allies, under the "Lend-Lease" arrangements. But the war effort involved bigger cutbacks in consumer goods than in either France or the UK, and greater devastation.[10] Although it joined the United Nations the USSR rejected offers of post-war Marshall Aid as "interference . . . in the affairs of those countries with the greatest need for outside help."[11] The USSR had been represented at the Bretton Woods conference of 1944 which led to the creation of the World Bank and IMF, but did not sign the Agreement.[12]

The 1938 Third Five Year Plan had run into the war. The Fourth Five Year Plan was presented in March 1946. Stalin unveiled long term targets for raising the output of basic industries, requiring, in his words, "perhaps three new Five Year Plans, if not more". Post-war reconstruction required that, once again, heavy industry would take priority over the consumer in the next five years.

The USSR began the post-war period with an average standard of living that was significantly lower than in capitalist countries. The Communists had been in power for 30 years by 1947, but it was still possible to make excuses for the practical application of the obsolete economic textbook to what had been essentially a large, underdeveloped economy. One apologist wrote: "Twice within a quarter of a century, twice since the inauguration of the Soviet regime, the people of that country had seen their land ravaged by wars far more deadly than anything that has visited our own island within modern times. Twice, weakened and overwrought by the years of famine and carnage, they had painfully to bend already aching backs to rebuild their shattered economic system, in many respects from its foundations . . . Many have marvelled that men and women could possess the endurance to do such things. Revolution, however, is a strange fire . . ."[13]

During the long Cold War period which followed, both the USSR and the West were fearful of attack from the other side, but it was the USSR which laid the greater emphasis on the so-called "military-industrial complex" – at the expense of the development of a consumer goods sector which was in any case hampered by its imprisonment in a defunct economic ideology. Whereas the emphasis in Western Europe after the war was on a return to a market economy and the provision of consumer goods as fast as possible, the USSR was still pursuing the development of capital goods rather than consumer goods – with the hope that some alleviation could be achieved by providing capital goods to the other COMECON members in Eastern Europe in return for textiles and other consumer goods.

The Soviets were obsessed with the threat from the West, which was used to discipline and threaten their own population. Their paranoia was not mitigated by United States' initial monopoly of the atom bomb. Stalinist cunning mixed with Bolshevik psychology. The population was constantly reminded that the West had encouraged Hitler before 1939 to turn against Russia.[14] However, having seen the way Stalin moved in Eastern Europe, and the development of communist parties in France and Italy, the US could also be forgiven for not being too sure of Soviet intentions either. For Russia in the post-war years it was possible to bargain with capitalism, not co-operate with it.

While being absurdly sympathetic to the repression and lack of democracy and free speech in immediate post-war Russia, G.D.H. Cole was nevertheless prophetic in arguing: "The Soviet Union's general attitude in external policy will be one of pushing, as far as it dares, for its own solution of every problem that comes up, and of yielding only when, and as far as, insistence on its own solution endangers the very survival of the international machinery for the prevention of war. It is, however, of the essence of the Soviet Union's position in world affairs not to allow this machinery to be destroyed; and, accordingly its representatives will, in the last resort, accept within very wide limits any concession that they regard as necessary for its preservation. They will always, however, give way at the last moment, after exacting every concession which they can induce other countries to make."[15]

The Reagan administration in the 1980s was certainly mindful of the analysis of Cole and others that "The Soviet Union respects strength, as it despises weakness and uncertainty of conduct." It could not face the further build-up of US military expenditure and the threat of "Star Wars". It also knew, and despised, its own economic weakness. Maurice Dobb, the communist Cambridge economist, had written in 1963 of the Soviet economy that "since the end of post-war reconstruction industrial production has expanded at an average rate of 10 per cent annually: an expansion which has laid the basis for the present long-term aim (in the 20 year long-term plan) of overtaking 'the strongest and richest country, the USA, in production per head of the population'."[16] Dobb referred to the possibility that the size of military expenditure might be a source of stagnation in the US and UK, which he conceded did not sit too easily with the more familiar Marxist argument that it was the level of military expenditure which was one of the factors helping to keep mature capitalist economies at "boom level".[17]

But when the 20 year period was up, and glasnost, perestroika and uskorenie were declared, it was not a case of the Soviet Union's having overtaken the US, but of calculating by just which multiple the US economy was ahead of the Soviet, and by just how much more, as a proportion of GDP, was military expenditure in the USSR than in the US. It had been known for many years that, because its economy was smaller than that of the UK, the USSR had to spend a greater share on defence in order to keep up in the arms race – or race ahead, as the American right would have it. But the degree to which the communist paradise was itself an arms economy had not been fully realised – despite all the charges that the CIA and the US defence industry ("the military-industrial complex') had a vested interest in exaggerating its size.

Keynes wrote in his "General Theory" that the authoritarian state system seemed to solve the problem of unemployment "at the expense of efficiency and freedom".[18] The history of communism as a political and economic system subsequently testified, in no uncertain terms, to its lack of freedom. The question was: would its efficiency ever improve, or was communism inefficient almost by definition?

It so happened that Gorbachev rose to power at around the time – the mid-1980s – by which both the boasts of previous Soviet leaders such as Khruschev, and the prophecies of Marxist economists such as Dobb, ought to have been pointing to results. To expect to be able to judge the comparative position of the Soviet Union and the West by the 1980s was perhaps unreasonable. The USSR had industrialised so late, and was a very backward country in so many respects, that the appropriate criteria to adopt in judging its progress were thought by some economists to be those of "development economics". There was much fashionable literature about the need for backward countries to go through a period of rapid industrialisation, for which central planning might be appropriate. There was also a widespread feeling of resignation that rapid development, in the early phases, might require an uncomfortable degree of authoritarianism. If the darling of the extreme left was Russia, the darling of the extreme right was Pinochet's Chile, where obstacles to the control of the money supply could be incarcerated or executed. Objectionable though authoritarianism of both right and left might be, the argument went, all countries had to go through a rough period in the process of industrialisation.

Such regimes are all morally repugnant, but the unfortunate

additional problem in Russia's case was that lack of freedom was not contributing towards greater efficiency, even if such a "trade off" is considered tolerable. Relatively rapid rates of growth in the period up to 1950 in the USSR had been characteristic of the early processes of industrialisation. But whereas per capita output grew faster in the USSR between 1913 and 1950 than in the OECD area, it grew more slowly than in the OECD area during the latter's golden age (1950–73), although faster than in the previous period.[19] But, after 1973, the Soviet economy actually grew more slowly than the "oil shocked" capitalist countries. Even making allowance for the backwardness of Russia when it began to industrialise, and for the theory that rapid industrialisation might justify central planning in its early phases, the point about communism was that, in Marxist theory, it should deliver the goods in the later phases of development. This it was patently not doing.

Writing in 1977, Alec Nove noted: "The Soviet-type model is, almost by definition, able to focus upon those questions which, of their nature, are capable of being handled by the centre. These are not just the broad macro-economic categories, but also the development plans of basic industries and sectors."[20] The emphasis on heavy industry – electrification, iron, steel – and on oil and mineral extraction had assisted the Soviet Union's remarkable war effort.

The big economic problems came with satisfying the consumer in peace-time (countries such as the UK had, of course, also had to adopt a "command economy" during war-time). Twenty years before perestroika, in 1965, Mr A.N. Kosygin (Prime Minister 1964–80) was telling the CPSU Central Committee: "In order to expand the economic independence of individual enterprises it is proposed to reduce the number of indices which are assigned from above . . . as seen from experience, the index of over-all volume of output (the planning targets) does not stimulate the enterprise to produce goods which are really needed by the national economy and the public, and in many cases tends to limit any improvement in the assortment of goods produced and their quality. Not infrequently our enterprises are producing low quality goods which the consumer does not want and which therefore remain unsold."[21]

One of the principal economic indices for many years in the OECD countries had been that for consumer spending, or the narrower version, retail sales. Here was the Soviet Prime Minister, in 1965, suggesting this as a novel concept for a criterion of economic success: "Instead of using an over-all volume of production index, it is proposed that the plans for enterprises should incorporate assignments for the volume of goods *actually sold* (my italics). Enterprises will then have to pay greater attention to the *quality* of the goods they produce in order to be able to fulfil their assignment for marketed produce." As Kosygin added, under the existing system, an enterprise was considered to have fulfilled its "plan", and therefore to have been successful, merely by achieving a pre-ordained production target, irrespective of any interest in the goods shown by consumers.[22]

Again, "not enough attention has been paid recently in national economic plans to measures directed at increasing production efficiency . . ."[23] Workers needed incentives; remuneration needed to be geared to "the growth of production, improved quality, increased profits and greater profitability of production."[24] In fact the history of Communist Party discussion on the economy from the 1960s onwards is littered with the need to adapt the system, and to introduce some of the kind of incentives and methods associated with the unmentionable "capitalist" system. But nothing much happened. As Alec Nove wryly observed in 1972: "When I was in the Soviet Union in 1967 and remarked upon the slow progress in implementing even the modest reform measures of 1965, I was several times told by my Soviet colleagues: 'change must be gradual, but we are on the way. Come back in two years and you will hardly recognise the system.' I came back in 1969 and it was all very familiar. These same economists were much more cautious in forecasting change, and less confident about the adoption of major reform measures."[25]

Nove pointed out that the leaders of the Soviet economics profession had been acknowledging for years that "the 'traditional system' is inefficient, that it has outlived its usefulness, that it stands in the way of the effective utilisation and rational expansion of productive forces." The central planning system could continue to enforce priorities, and operated adequately in some sectors of heavy industry, but "the familiar chronic diseases are still causing trouble: over-taut planning, lack of balance between production and supply plans, between the investment plan and the output of building materials and equipment, resistance to innovation, and to technical progress at the lower echelons, the distortion of local initiative by the need to stimulate plan fulfilment, and so on."[26]

Nove's solution, in the early 1970s, involved: first, a clear realisation that the *system* was responsible for continued relative backwardness in the competition with the West ("at present the leaders seem to think that its admitted inadequacies can be corrected by minor procedural and organisational changes'); secondly, a firm leader or group of leaders had not only to be committed to reform, but to have the power and the will to enforce their views on the party and state machine. "No such leaders seem to exist today, and certainly Brezhnev has neither the power nor the will to do the job,"[27] he declared.

In Nove's view then, change towards greater reliance on the market was bound to come, although not in the immediate future. Opinion was divided as to whether this could be done without "prior changes in the political structure, affecting particularly the power of the Communist Party."[28] The "old way" had been outgrown, but "many of us have underestimated the conservatism of the 'establishment' and the strength of inertia."[29]

Inertia received no discouragement from the combination of the breakdown of the Bretton Woods system and the 1973–74 oil crisis which hit the capitalist West. As Maddison points out "The deceleration in Soviet growth since 1973 has been even more marked than in OECD countries but the causes have been different."[30] The USSR was fairly insulated from the world economy. "Although its growth in export volume was halved, its foreign earnings (at least until the early 1980s) were cushioned by the rise in oil and gold prices."[31]

It was a common theme of interviews I myself had with politicians, officials and research institutes in Moscow in 1990 that the two oil crises which had so disrupted the OECD economies in the mid and late 1970s had served to postpone reform in the Soviet Union. But two important developments during the 1980s were: *first*, the fact that the increase in the oil and gold prices was not sustained, and *second*, and generally considered in Moscow to have been far the more important influence: President Reagan's escalation of defence spending, and his ambitions for "Star Wars", finally convinced the Soviet machine that the pretence was over.

By 1985, the Soviet Union ought, according to the Khruschev boasts of the 1950s, to have caught up with and overtaken the West. And it was a good 20 years since Kosygin had talked about the need for reforms. But there was increasing dissatisfaction within the USSR about the generally low standard of living for the 90 per cent of the people who were not immediate beneficiaries of the two tier class system which favoured Party members against the rest. Lateness in embarking on industrialisation was not a sufficient excuse in the face of the manifest success of Japan, which had also been behind the West in the industrialisation process. The problems lay with a system that first, was heavily biased in directing resources towards the military (and the space programme); and second, was as inefficient as its critics always said it would be in the provision of consumer goods. The consumer goods sector was small in relation to the total, and patently failing to deliver what western economists call "consumer satisfaction" (there had been a modest consumer boom in the 1960s and 1970s, which revolutionised life for many Soviets. But this served to manifest the collapse of the system in the 1980s). Moreover, despite the Kremlin's massive investment in secrecy and repression, the general message of the Soviet Union's relative backwardness was being received one way or another by the mass of the population. One of the most outstanding failures of all was in Soviet agriculture, which remained grossly inefficient, requiring one of the world's best endowed regions to import some $20 bn of food a year. The revolution in methods of processing, transporting and storing food – a prominent feature of modern market economies – had largely passed the USSR by.

The "defensiveness" of the Soviet Union could be seen in the way memories of the Second World War were still close to the surface even in 1990 and 1991. The war came up quickly in conversations with the Soviets. The military seemed omni-present. In addition to their ostensibly defensive spending, the USSR had increased its commitments abroad (Vietnam, Cuba, Afghanistan). The OECD quoted US estimates that Soviet military spending rose from about 13 per cent of GDP in the early 1970s to 16 per cent in the mid 1980s (against 5.6 per cent to 6.6 per cent in the US "and a stable 1 per cent in Japan").[32]

The fashionable jibe of the Marxist left against Western capitalism had been that it was an "arms economy". The accusation seems to apply more accurately to the Soviet Union itself. A rule of thumb quoted by Western experts in pre-Glasnost days was that the Soviet economy was only half the size of the US economy, but to equalise the defence effort, spent twice as much on arms as a proportion of gross domestic product. Subsequently, at a meeting in Washington of CIA and Russian experts early in 1990, the Russians suggested that the West had overestimated the size of the Soviet economy and underestimated the proportion accounted for by the defence sector. By 1992 Washington calculated that defence may have accounted for as much as 50 per cent of Soviet industrial production.[33]

During the 1980s, not only did the real price of oil come down: the real cost of extracting oil, and of exploiting natural resources generally, increased. Rising defence expenditure, and greater difficulty in cultivating natural resources, are cited by Maddison as two of the reasons for the slowdown in Soviet economic growth during the first half of the 1980s.[34] But he puts "an *increase* in micro-economic inefficiency" at the top of the list. (The italics for *increase* are mine.) The fundamental productivity performance of the communist system was poor by common consent. But the thought that it was becoming even worse was the last straw.

The political will to make communism work at some level of efficiency, and to preserve the system, can hardly be overestimated. The political will to keep Eastern Europe subjugated distorted the entire economic network – Eastern Europe's dependence on Russian oil after the oil shocks was deliberately used by Moscow to emphasise the alleged virtues of COMECON.

In the end, the big question for the USSR was: how could it change the economy without changing the political system? For the Soviet bosses, political will was always more important than economic logic. Mild cases of this delusion are not unknown in the West, but the attempted triumph of will over matter (or materialism) was taken to absurd degrees in the USSR. In fighting change, of course, the elite were not unlike the capitalists of Marx's time who stood out against reform. They had a lot to lose. Many power groups had a stake in the old Soviet inefficiency: the Party, the bosses of heavy and military industry, the bureaucrats, the armed forces, the barons of state and collective farming, the non-dissident intelligentsia, even large sections of the industrial working class – all protected from reality by all manner of subsidies. "So many people had made life comfortable for themselves, and could be supported because Russia is so rich it can afford to be wasteful", one Western observer commented. The truth was that, when it came, *perestroika* could not work without fatally undermining the Party.

5

Capitalism, Communism and Planning

Russian social democrats revolted against capitalism in 1917 when it had hardly been tried, on the basis of "an obsolete economic textbook" which was itself written during the worst, early, faltering phase of unreformed capitalism. Indeed, the *laissez-faire* capitalism which offended Marx and millions of others was in some ways an enforced system, almost designed to invite revolution or at least reform. Ironically, Marx himself had expected revolution to occur in a more advanced industrial economy than that represented by Russia in 1917.

Every student has his favourite example of why capitalism survived. In *The Millennium Postponed* Edward Hyams cited the Model T Ford as the paradigm of the product that capitalism made available to all; Joseph Schumpeter, in *Capitalism, Socialism and Democracy*, referred to the way that Queen Elizabeth I had thousands of servants working to produce the sort of silk stockings that in the modern capitalist world were available to all.

Policy-makers in the capitalist world struggle perpetually with trying to strike a balance between an acceptable rate of inflation and a socially tolerable level of unemployment, it being generally assumed that this is the prime concern of macro-economic policy. "The choices which policy-makers have to take in respect of budget tax changes and the setting of interest rates are always of broadly the same kind. Should the pressure of demand be raised, risking more inflation? Or should demand be cut back, adding to unemployment?"[1] For most of the post-war era it has been taken for granted that the combination of the existing capital stock (buttressed by technological progress and new investment, which enables output per person to grow by some 2 to 3 per cent or more a year) and the capitalist system itself could supply and deliver the goods. The trick was to run the system with as little inflation and unemployment as possible; on balance the left was more concerned about unemployment and the right about inflation.

It is true that macro-economic "stabilisation" policies were often accompanied by measures designed to boost efficiency at the micro level – "industrial policy" was the vogue phrase in the 1960s and 1970s; "supply-side improvements" were what policy-makers aimed at in the 1980s; but the general ability of the system to deliver was seldom questioned. What *was* in doubt from time to time was the ability of one country's capitalist model to do as well as another – the "grass is greener" syndrome.

By contrast, although it may have persistently feared the Soviet Union's military might, the capitalist world had few serious doubts that the wider communist economy only operated at what Keynes had called "a low level of efficiency". Yet by the 1980s even *that* efficiency appeared to be declining, and at the heart of the problem was the command economy itself. "The fact that the economy was now operating at a higher level, with a more sophisticated output mix, trying to cater for more exigent consumers had made it more difficult to run the increasingly complex command system efficiently",[2] says Maddison. One man using a spade inefficiently in the 1920s was not too damaging. One man failing to use a bulldozer properly in the 1980s meant waste many times greater.

Even Hayek, one of the foremost opponents of communism and socialism, had not been against planning as such. The questions were, and are: when is planning appropriate, and when is it not? And at what level should planning be done?

"Everyone desires, of course, that we should handle our common problems as rationally as possible and that, in so doing, we should use as much foresight as we can command," Hayek wrote. "In this sense, everybody who is not a complete fatalist is a planner, every political act is (or ought to be) an act of planning, and there can be differences only between good and bad, between wise and far-sighted and foolish and shortsighted planning. An economist, whose whole task is to study how men actually do and how they might plan their affairs is the last person who could object to planning in this general sense."[3] For Hayek, it is "not a dispute about whether planning is to be done or not. It is a dispute as to whether planning is to be done centrally, by one authority for the whole economic system, or is to be divided among many individuals."[4]

Or both: the history of "mixed economies" in the capitalist world since their own experience of various degrees of central planning during the Second World War is that of attempting to strike the right balance between *some* degree of central planning (what else are Governments for?) and a wide variety of (often competing) plans in the private sector. Governments make their plans for roads, railways, airports, electricity grids and all the public sector services –

based on reasonably reliable demographic trends and projections; large corporations and medium and small sized businesses like to have as much information as possible about the environment they are likely to be operating in, often plan well into the future, knowing an investment may take 10 years to pay off, and conduct extensive surveys known generally as "market research". Individuals and families make plans for buying or renting houses or flats, their major purchases of consumer goods, and, indeed, for their retirement. "Financial planning" has been a growth business in recent years.

"Indicative planning" of the sort that was fashionable in France for many years, and to a certain extent characterises the Japanese approach, involves both Government planning of the infrastructure and a general attempt to influence the way in which the economy develops, either by direct intervention in industries that are part of the public sector, or through indirect, "arms-length" attempts to influence the manner, or the speed, at which various elements in the private sector develop. (After observation of France and Japan, the British Government made some attempts at indicative planning during the 1960s.) Planning and "intervention" can involve a view of the future – encouraging, protecting and subsidising new "sunrise" industries, or propping-up, or cushioning the rate of decline, of older, declining industries.

Governments in most "capitalist" societies have targets for the rate of economic growth, and some idea of the balance they should like to see between investment and consumption, and about the distribution of income, even if they are vague about how to achieve this. "We must encourage profits and investment" is a classic cry.

France embarked on "indicative planning" at the time of the Marshall Plan, with "le plan Monnet" which co-ordinated public and private sector investment decisions made with the help of Marshall Aid, and with the approval of the donors. Since the donors were the United States, this was never going to be a centrally planned system. The idea was to correct the vision of the "myopic market" so that public and private sectors could co-ordinate their plans, particularly with regard to long term infrastructural investment. The building of consensus in these matters was considered important, and great emphasis was placed on contractual relationships between central government and the regions, and central government and publicly owned enterprises.[5] Planners aimed at reducing the uncertainty facing private sector firms contemplating expansion, and were less concerned about total control of "the commanding heights" of the economy "than about the mundane problem of actual or prospective bottlenecks."[6]

One comparison of French and Soviet style planning emphasised:

"Nevertheless . . . there is one fundamental difference: in Soviet-type economies, the aim of central decision-making is not to influence spontaneous development, but to replace all decentralised decision-making."[7] Thus "At any given moment, the fate of the populace depends in the most direct and immediate way – even down to supplies in the shops for the Christmas and New Year holidays – on the decisions taken by the central authorities."[8]

The problem with the succession of efforts at "reform" in the Soviet Union and Eastern Europe was that they never amounted to more than tinkering with a system that was fundamentally flawed. This even applied to the much-vaunted "perestroika" itself, which was by definition an attempt at "restructuring" the existing flawed system, but was widely misinterpreted in the West as promising something more.

There are many flaws in the various forms of Western "market economy" or capitalist economy. Indeed, it is a contention of this book that, while communism has manifestly failed as an economic system, capitalism as we know it has not necessarily succeeded. Perhaps the most fundamental point about communism was that it was a monopoly – both politically and economically. Until the remarkable events of the late 1980s and early 1990s, there was little else on offer in the communist regimes. In the UK during the early 1980s Mrs Margaret Thatcher used to deflect criticism of her economic policies by witheringly declaiming: "What is the alternative?" In fact the whole point about democratic market economies is that they do offer political and economic alternatives – as Mrs Thatcher eventually found out to her cost.

Democracies that are dissatisfied with their country's economic performance can remove the government at the next election. The one-party state made this option rather difficult. There was no basic political incentive to greater economic performance. Meanwhile it was a commonplace that success and advancement within the Party hierarchy depended, for economic apparatchiks, on the fulfilment of crude production targets, not on the satisfaction of the consumer.

As Janos Kornai and others have emphasised, the communist economy was essentially a seller's market: it ignored many of the fundamental assumptions taken for granted in all forms of capitalism, such as that supply should be a function of demand, that the price mechanism is a helpful allocative and signalling device, and that cost consciousness has its uses. The search for new profitable opportunities, which is linked with the continuing efforts at innovation in capitalist economies, was simply not part of the communist culture. There was no incentive either to improve the product or to maintain the plant.

However inefficient capitalist economies may seem to those who live and work in them, they possess – some more than others – a fundamental dynamism which was notable by its absence from planned economies. Whole sectors of industry were producing things in which no-one was interested, while the things consumers wanted were in short supply.[9]

In Western economies the word "incentive" tended to be rather abused in the 1980s; both the Reagan and Thatcher administrations produced dubious arguments that the not particularly arduous tax rates on individuals and corporations were crippling "incentives". Such assertions tended to neglect the fact that the whole structure of a market economy is geared to incentives to make profits. By contrast, in the communist bloc, as the Economic Commission for Europe pointed out as late as 1989–90: "The central plan is the main instrument of policy and basically decides what individual enterprises should produce. Prices are determined bureaucratically and are used very little as an instrument of planning: producer prices have little influence on resource allocation, and the level and pattern of investment is allocated according to the priorities of the plan rather than the perception of enterprises as to profitable opportunities . . . The incentive structure of this system is such that micro-inefficiency is widespread and responsible for the endemic shortage which characterises the centrally planned economies. More fundamentally, enterprises will not be active in adopting new techniques and raising efficiency simply because there is no strong incentive to do so. The incentive structure, which reflects the restrictive, non-allocative role of prices, also means that new enterprises cannot be set up in response to profitable opportunities and the failures of established concerns. Entry and exit of firms is controlled by the plan . . . the widespread failures on the supply side have provided enterprises with strong incentives to meet their own needs for intermediate goods; this, in turn, has led to a lack of specialisation, overstocking (hoarding) of materials etc., and a lowering of efficiency throughout the productive system."[10]

In the vicious circle of the inefficient communist economy, concern about shortages led not only to hoarding, and a kind of "do it yourself" approach to supplies, but also to the widespread use of barter – thereby fulfilling one of the original aims of the October Revolutionists: the abolition of money. It was, of course, because barter was so inefficient that money was invented in the first place. Inferior technology, and the wasteful use of capital and materials in this un-cost-conscious world, meant that it took four and a half times as much steel to produce a unit of output in the USSR as in the US.[11]

Western entrepreneurs often give the impression that, because of the intensity of international competition, they find themselves having "to run fast in order to stand still." The communist bloc gave the impression of going backwards while trying to stand still. Thus the ECE talked of "a general deterioration in performance which stretches back over two decades or more".

Part of the problem was that a centrally-controlled economy could not cope with the decentralized information-based technology of the 1970s and 1980s. There were no "silicone steppes". The relative stagnation of communist technology was demonstrated to the world during the Gulf War of early 1991, when even the much-vaunted Soviet military technology turned out to be grossly inferior to Western military hardware. Trade statistics show that the inefficiency and obsolescence of the communist economies also began to affect their performance as exporters of cheap goods to Western Europe – with the newly industrialising countries of south-east Asia displacing them. The deteriorating situation had been alleviated to some extent in the 1970s by borrowing to finance imports from capitalist countries; but this policy ran into the high interest rates and debt crisis of the 1980s. As we have seen, the USSR economy itself was granted a lease of life by the foreign currency earnings arising from higher oil prices, but that only lasted until the mid-1980s.[12]

Although for decades the official policy had been to switch the focus from Stalin's early emphasis on heavy industry towards light industry and consumer goods, the entire communist system seemed to get bogged down in what one observer called "the solipsistic growth of the capital goods sector". The basic industrialisation effort had been considered by many to be a relative success, and this was of course geared to heavy industry. But the record became stuck in the groove. In Czechoslovakia in the early 1970s: "More and more steel was needed for production in the engineering industries; new steelworks thus had to be built, which led to the launching of large-scale construction projects, which, in their turn, demanded more heavy machinery. And so on . . . All sectors were working for each other . . . There was always a certain demand, covered by certain resources, but the final result for the populace was minimal."[13] By contrast, the opposite extreme was reached in Britain under Mrs Thatcher: the Government's contempt for manufacturing industry reached such a degree that it was seriously argued the economy's future lay entirely with "services".

One of the ironies of communist economic performance was that, in respect of the two criteria most often quoted in capitalist economies – inflation and employment – it came out remarkably well on paper. Indeed, full employment and negligible inflation were taken for granted. This may give pause for thought by those Western politicians who often argue that, once inflation is under control, all sorts of magical things will follow spontaneously. They may; or they may not. In the USSR, until recently, train fares had not been altered since 1948, and housing rents since 1928.[14] One of the problems of course was that such price controls had grossly distorted the workings of the economy, leading to vast divergences between costs and revenues, and sending the wrong signals about demand and pressure on resources.

"Full employment" was all very well, but the question was: fully employed doing what? Some, we know, either worked for the secret police or spent a large amount of time informing on their behalf. But, quite apart from that, the main point is that, under the communist system, people may have been fully employed, but not in a very productive way – and certainly not productively enough to satisfy their aspirations as consumers. The dissatisfaction may have been greater in Eastern Europe than in the USSR, where many were said to like the haphazard discipline of their work, which often made it easy to moonlight. Others were demoralised by this state of affairs.

It is the pressure to satisfy people *qua* consumers, rather than *qua* producers, that is at the heart of the difference between the communist and capitalist economic systems. This is not to say that consumers in communist countries were not satisfied up to a point, or provided with a very basic standard of living. Nor is it to say that capitalist producers, given half a chance, will not try to take short cuts and "do down" the consumer. Indeed, the history of capitalism is littered with examples of how producers exploited both their workforces and their customers, granted the opportunity. But that tendency provoked a strong reaction over the years, leading to the familiar position where a combination of law, government intervention, consumer organisations and the press all serve, in the characteristic market economy, as watchdogs on behalf of what is known by economists as "consumer sovereignty". But the watchdogs (of capitalism) can be sleepy and ineffectual, as the life and times of the late Robert Maxwell, and the BCCI banking scandal, amply demonstrate.

Hungary was always considered one of the better and more market-orientated communist economies, and in Janos Kornai, it produced one of the most astute students of communism and capitalism. Kornai made a crucial distinction between what he called "pressure" economies and "suction" economies. In "pressure" economies producers are pressing products on the market; in "suction" economies the market is desperate to suck anything it can get from what is laughingly called the "productive system". The concepts are equivalent to "buyers' market" and "sellers' market", but Kornai's analogy provides a vivid description of the contrast between, say, the average display of electronic goods in a Western store, with advertisements screaming at customers to come in and buy, and the queues that would form under the communist system for the most basic consumer products.[15] As Kornai points out: "In the case of *suction* production may detach itself to a considerable extent from the consumer's aspirations . . . In the case of *pressure* the buyer makes the selection. This stimulates the improvement of quality and the economy of inputs. Selection leads to differentiation and concentration. In the case of suction the favourable stimulating effects of selection fail to come about."[16] Of course, it is the natural desire of any primitive capitalist to make a buyer's market into a *seller*'s market, and the duty of a democratic government to preserve competition when appropriate.

Economic advancement is related closely to the development of new technologies and new products, either in a purely innovatory way, or by imitation or "catch-up." Kornai considered the gravest consequence of a continuous state of suction to be the almost complete lack of *revolutionary product development*: looking back over the most revolutionary products of the century – everything from the radio tube to nylon and the silicon transistor – "it should be noticed that with the exception of a *few* initiatives no socialist country figures among those introducing the product in question for the first time", he observed.[17]

The fact that some outstanding results had been achieved in the socialist countries in the whole range of the natural sciences, as well as technical sciences relating to war production, demonstrated that the problem was *not* rooted in the lack of talent or in the weakness of scientific and technical culture. "The problem is the lack of institutions and organisations which despite all obstacles can effect the *introduction* of revolutionary new technical innovations, accepting all the risk concomitant with this work, including that of failure, the struggle against conservatism and deep rooted habit," Kornai declared.

There was little incentive under communism either to take risks with new products and improvements, or – if that were possible – to emulate developments abroad. Kornai asked why the director of a communist enterprise should take risks when – in a state of chronic suction – he was able *without* such effort to sell the products of his firm easily? With the buyers lining up for the firm's old product, why take upon oneself all the trouble involved in the introduction of a new product?[18] By contrast, in the competitive market economies, there is a continual search for new products, or new ways of producing familiar products more cheaply, as firms struggle either to increase their market share, or to fight off marauders intent on grabbing part of that share for themselves.

Yet Western entrepreneurs and industrialists have more in common with central planners than they imagine. The history of modern capitalism, including that of the American "robber barons" and the major oil companies, is one of a continual attempt to sew up markets and sources of supply, either through the achievement of total dominance, or via the half-way house of some sort of cartel arrangement. Western capitalists have proved themselves eminently capable of failing to see any contradiction between their own paeans of praise for the wonders of private enterprise, and the desire to amass as many government contracts as possible for themselves. The monopolistic position of the communist enterprise with its chronic "sellers' market" is, paradoxically, the capitalist's dream.

The Western model of the ideal market economy is one in which everything possible is done to encourage a "buyers' market" by maintaining competition among producers and, with regard to the state and the public sector, "rendering unto Caesar the things that are Caesar's." In recent years the privatisation in the UK and elsewhere of what were previously thought of as "natural mono-polies" in the public sector – such as the public utilities – has confused the issue somewhat. Even so, there is a broad division within the OECD area of 60 per cent private sector/40 per cent public sector with regard to the composition of the national product; and, allowing for that part of public spending which comprises "transfer payments" – the rechannelling of tax receipts towards the sick, the old and the unemployed – the public sector accounts for about 20 per cent of final expenditure. There are differences within the average, with the Scandinavian and Continental European countries tending to be bigger spenders than the US and Japan.[19]

"Rendering unto Caesar the things that are Caesar's" means, in this context, acknowledging that the public sector has an important role to play in the provision of defence, education, health and welfare services, and the basic infrastructure of the economy. Indeed, the public sector plays an important role in underpinning the market sector of the economy, just as the market sector, through the taxes levied on it, makes an important contribution to the provision of public services. The relationship between manufacturing and services (both public and private) is that of a matrix: the two are closely linked, and each serves and derives benefit from the other. But it is exports of *manufactures* that typically provide the bulk of the foreign exchange required by market economies to satisfy their demand for imports.

Whatever they may argue in doctrinal speeches, politicians and officials in capitalist economies are seldom pure in their practical devotion to the dictates of the marketplace. Thus, they are perfectly capable of – indeed, inclined towards – denouncing protectionist and employment-subsidising measures on the part of other countries while happily indulging in them themselves. From the grassroots upwards, in all "market" economies, there are strong political influences militating against the application of pure competitive forces.

The problem with communist economies, however, was that they took anti-competitive measures to extreme lengths. The structure of the communist "sellers' market" was heavily monopolistic, with vertical and horizontal integration of producers carried to much greater degrees than in the capitalist economies. The principal motive force of the centrally planned system, and the criterion by which it was judged, was output for output's sake, almost regardless, from the enterprise's point of view, of whether the consumer was satisfied.

The widespread perception among students of the communist system is that for a long time it did indeed operate at what Keynes had called "a low level of efficiency", but that later even its own poor efficiency standards began to be eroded. To paraphrase Marx's famous phrase about the prophesied demise of capitalism, communism became a victim of "its own internal contradictions".

The growth figures of the early communist decades, with their emphasis on heavy industry, investment and armaments, were achieved by the process known as "extensive growth". That is to say, resources, of land, raw materials and labour, were exploited to the full. This involved everything from virtual slave labour in Siberia to the extensive use of female labour, up to the point where some 85 per cent of the population were "economically active" in the labour force in the early 1970s – a much higher proportion than in OECD countries.[20] In post-war years, especially in the light of the 20 million losses during the war, the emphasis had switched, in theory, to "intensive growth", with gains coming more from higher productivity. But an IMF study points out that the gap between the OECD and the USSR widened over the fifteen years 1975–90; although successive oil shocks, and the policy responses to high inflation, contributed to a slowdown in the growth of the productivity of Western economies during this period, productivity, already relatively low, actually declined in the USSR.[21]

The labour force had been stretched to its limits, and the extensive use of cheap raw materials and energy – insulated from world prices – had brought the country to the state where mining costs were shooting up and, in Abel Aganbegyan's words, it was now "cheaper to save one tonne of fuel than to extract it".[22] Despite the theoretical emphasis on *intensive* growth, economic development had in fact continued to rely on *extensive* use of labour and raw materials right up to 1975. As Aganbegyan concedes: "If you take a typical post-war five-year period, then usually in these five years the basic application of funds and capital investment increased one and a half times, the extraction of fuel and raw materials by 25–30 per cent, and a further 10–11 million people were recruited into the national economy . . . This was characteristic of the whole period, let us say, from 1956 to 1975."[23]

What was wrong with the communist system was that, other than for the setting of a few basic priorities, the central planning mechanism was inadequate to the task of achieving anything resembling capitalist economic efficiency. Aganbegyan notes that in the 1980s the USSR was producing four and a half times more tractors than the US, despite a lower volume of cultivation. "It is obvious that quantity of tractors is not necessary, but they are produced and thrust upon the collective farms and state farms which purchase them as a rule not out of their own resources, but through loans or grants from the state." Meanwhile, in theory the tractor makers were achieving wonderful production targets, satisfying planners and enterprise managers alike. The reward system was geared to production alone. The system had negative efficiency built into it. Unwanted goods were in plentiful supply; wanted goods were in chronic shortage. Again, as Aganbegyan commented: "Shortages are the outcome of an inappropriate economic system and not of any lack of resources or other means."[24] He acknowledged that the productivity of the communist system was two to three times less than that of the average market economy.[25] And IMF calculations suggested the USSR used one and a half times as much energy per unit of output as Canada, an OECD economy comparable in its land mass and extremes of temperature.[26]

Against the average of OECD countries, energy use per unit of output was two and a half times higher in the USSR.[27] The energy pricing system "does not as a rule reflect any notion of scarcity, economic rent, consumer preferences, or the time value of money. It therefore provides little basis for efficiently matching supply with demand, for allocating investment over time or across sectors, or making efficient decisions about the use of input factors."[28]

Matching supply with demand is what economics is essentially about. The tragedy of the central planning system was that it relegated the principal mechanism for doing this – the price mechanism – to such a low level of priority. Although there are many things other than price which determine the demand for goods in a capitalist economy – design, quality, reliability, etc. – prices are an important signal by which the economy adapts to alterations in taste and demand. The average market economy is in a continual process of adaptation to changing circumstances; this was hardly true of communist economies where key prices were held at the same level in some cases for over sixty years.

Of course, economists might baulk at this, but the relative lack of movement in prices was not unpopular with the average Russian. Indeed, the older members of the population remembered Stalin fondly for his annual *reduction* in the price of Vodka. Some Western observers believe there were great political and psychological benefits from the fixed pricing system, not least the five kopek fare on the Moscow subway system. Such benefits suggested that time and change could be halted – but they were part of a system which meant that when modern communications brought conclusive proof of the higher standard of living in the West, halting time and change held its disadvantages. Nevertheless, capitalism has a lot to learn about making city-dwellers and commuters happy with the transport systems run in their name.

The USSR impressed the West (and itself) with the Sputnik and the first man (and woman) into space. But: "Within the industrial sector, most of the technologies were built before the Second World War, or are based on outdated technology from that period. It has been estimated that close to half of industrial production assets are not worth much beyond salvage value."[29] It was true that the resources of scientific talent were there – it was just that the monopolistic, sellers-marker system did not see fit to use it properly. There were bottlenecks preventing the introduction into the production process of the concepts and designs developed in research institutes.[30] The centrally planned system was insulated from the rest of the world, so that for years there was little evidence of a "demonstration effect" from the West having an impact on the USSR itself. Then came the problem that, when the USSR wanted, under Gorbachev, to attract Western business and technology in a big way, the security demanded by Western investors, and such basic concepts as the ability to repatriate profits, became serious obstacles to the possibility of "catching up" in this way.

The question referred to earlier about the level at which planning takes place is crucial to the difference between capitalism and communism. By contrast with the communist experiment of planning "from the top", there were various proposals over the years, often associated with people who styled themselves

"Trotskyists", for planning "from the bottom" under various systems of "workers' control". The nearest practical application was in Yugoslavia, with feeble results. By contrast, what market economies seem to have evolved (consciously or unconsciously) is an economic version of the political principle known as "subsidiarity". Subsidiarity, whose definition appears to have originated with the organisation which Marx regarded as the opium-den of the people – namely the Vatican – is the doctrine, adopted by the European Community, which states that political decisions should be taken at the lowest practical level. This sees a role for the higher powers, the middling powers, and the lower powers, and seeks an appropriate balance between decision-taking at the EC level, the national level, the regional level and the local level.

The *reductio ad absurdum* of the extremist, anti-subsidiarity view was the British Government's decision under Mrs Thatcher to abolish the Greater London Council, which had responsibility for nearly 7 million people – more than the population of many nation states. But just as Government functions are divided in most countries in this way, so a form of *de facto* economic planning takes place in market economies, with contributions from government and the private sector. Governments publish plans for their own spending for up to five years ahead, and these have important implications for the private sector – as do economic forecasts and market research operations carried out by businessmen. Often such forecasts and research efforts turn out to be wrong, but they are the best guide available, they are continually scrutinised and amended, and the individual plans of thousands of firms and individuals can be adjusted accordingly. The important point is that the planning exercises of corporations give them a framework, and they adapt to experience and changed circumstances. Economic planning under the subsidiarity principles of the market economy is a continual process of adaptation.

The combination of continual, but flexible, planning, and adherence to price signals, enabled the market economies to adjust to the implications of the oil price increase of the 1970s in a way that the centrally planned communist system did not. Whether the adjustment was sufficient is another matter: comparison of petrol (or gasoline) prices in Western Europe and the US suggests that the "market" economy of the US has still not adjusted to the long term implications of oil shortages.

As concern grows about population growth, energy shortages, the "Greenhouse Effect", and other environmental issues, what one might call "adaptive planning" is likely to play an ever more important role in economic policy among market economies.

"Leaving it to the market" is not necessarily the answer; indeed, the survival of market economies may, paradoxically, have to be carefully planned.

One of the ironies of communist planning, however, was that environmental concerns were largely ignored. Governmental pressure under the market, or mixed economy system, can force even entrepreneurial cowboys into taking measures which take account of wider social concerns, and not just immediate financial profit. Thus the IMF study maintains that "In Western countries, it has been recognised for some time that the environment and the economy are interrelated, mutually supportive systems."[31] Environmentalists who have had to overcome phenomenal resistance on the part of big business and government can allow themselves a wry smile over such smooth bureaucratic prose. There is also some ambiguity about the phrase "for some time"; many observers would argue that the inter-relationship has been recognised only very recently, and that it is still a long uphill struggle for environmentalists. Multinational corporations, subjected to "regulation and control" over pollution in their home countries, are notoriously less fastidious about ignoring environmental concerns in the third world. And at the Houston summit of 1990, which was supposed to be addressing environmental issues, President Bush said he was not going to risk unemployment (and presumably votes) in the US by adhering too closely to the proposals of officials for reductions in atmospheric pollution. He repeated his opposition to taking serious steps against pollution in the run-up to the Rio de Janeiro "Earth Summit" of 1992.

Under the communist system, however, crude production targets prevailed over environmental considerations. As the IMF study found: "The use of quantitative targets has generated a culture of production maximisation which discourages considerations of quality or of the environmental impacts of production ... the introduction of pollution control equipment 'disrupts' production, lowers output and, hence, decreases the rewards assigned to enterprise staff ... Supply, rather than demand, has driven the economy and produced a distorted industrial sector which is resource-intensive and environmentally damaging." It is calculated that pollution levels were roughly double those experienced in OECD economies.[32] Similarly, when the West Germans began their assessment of the task they had assumed in taking over the former East German economy, they were horrified to discover the high degree of atmospheric and ground pollution.

The British economic commentator Samuel Brittan once observed that it was no accident that West Germany was the most successful West European economy and East Germany the most successful communist economy. Indeed, there were even suggestions by the World Bank and others towards the end of the 1970s that East Germany was in the process of overtaking some of the Western industrial countries. But it was not just the levels of pollution that shocked the West Germans when they took a close look at the economy of East Germany. Productivity levels were a mere 30 per cent of West Germany's; most industries were uncompetitive by international standards, and the general impression – which I can bear out from my own observations – was of an economic junk-heap. That was the most successful communist economy . . .

Even for the Germans, the inefficient communist system was too much. Like the economy of the USSR, the East German economy was centrally controlled, with excessive degrees of monopoly, and of vertical and horizontal concentration of industry. There was not enough specialisation or exercise of comparative advantage within firms or industries; to protect themselves from the inefficiencies of the rest of the system, enterprises became excessively autarchic or self-sufficient themselves, and the bartering system was rife. As in the USSR, one of the many reasons cited for low productivity was absenteeism caused by the need to rush out and queue when certain rare consumer items were rumoured to have made an appearance in the shops.

In the USSR, in 1990, only 150 out of a list of 1,200 basic consumer items were regularly available in the shops. According to official Soviet statistics, the number of cars per thousand inhabitants in 1988 was 55 in the USSR compared with 403 in the leading EC nations.[33] "And furthermore," commented one resident, "it takes you all morning to get petrol."

At the beginning of the 1990s the USSR and Eastern Europe were suffering from the collapse of the centrally-planned, or "administrative" system, without the assumed longer term benefits of a move to a market economy. Indeed, the initial moves – higher prices in certain sectors, and imaginative entrepreneurship by the "spiv" or mafia elements of society – were making things worse, and shortages were being aggravated by panic hoarding. President Gorbachev had been so popular in the West, having evidently brought an end to the arms race and granted freedom to Eastern Europe (while simultaneously displaying more charm and charisma than the average Western leader) that his lack of achievement with the economy had been less widely noted outside the USSR itself.

Perestroika, it turned out, had been yet another failed attempt at repairing a fundamentally flawed system. But this should have come as no surprise to those who had studied such texts as, for example, the widely promoted *The Challenge: Economics of Perestroika*, by

Abel Aganbegyan, published in the West in 1988. Although the author, who was closely associated with the whole perestroika venture, claimed that "during *perestroika* market relations in the USSR will be deepened and broadened"[34] and that the main underlying cause of shortages lay with "the lack of any real feedback between consumer and producer"[35] he was still trapped in the old framework of thinking. "The ongoing perestroika in the USSR is aimed precisely at disclosing the advantages of socialism," he wrote. "Lenin said that socialism must ensure a higher level of productivity than capitalism ... Perestroika must carry Soviet society to a qualitatively new state, when thanks to the advantages of socialism we will surpass the capitalist countries in productivity and other indicators of cost-effectiveness, in quality of production and the level of technology."[36] Much of the book consisted of such vapid boasting and assertion. As for "markets": "Since there is no unemployment and the economic base of society accords with socialist ownership, there is no labour market. A market for capital is not envisaged as part of perestroika. There are no plans for a Soviet stock exchange, shares, bills of exchange or profit from commercial credit."

That was in 1988 but the position changed dramatically in the next few years, leading to the banning of the Communist Party itself, the breakaway from the Union by Boris Yeltsin and the Russian Federation, and Mr Gorbachev's desperate plea to join the bastion of capitalism, the World Bank and International Monetary Fund.

The joint study of the Soviet economy by the IMF and other "market economy" institutions had followed Gorbachev's pleas for help from the Group of Seven "summit" countries in 1990, but preceded the application to join the IMF by Russia and other members of what became, in autumn 1991, the Commonwealth of Independent States (C.I.S.). The basis of the CIS was so shaky that the British Foreign Office preferred to call it the FSU (Former Soviet Union).

We have already referred to the depressing picture of the Soviet economy painted by the IMF study. One sad reflection is to think of the forests of Marxist literature which were published during the past decades about possible improvements and refinements to the basic system. They hardly merit a reference as the catalogue of basic faults is listed by the IMF and OECD.

The consumer suffered not only as a result of the system itself, but also because of the priority given to armaments and investment throughout the post-war communist period. Estimates of the proportion of gross domestic product accounted for directly or indirectly by defence vary from 7 per cent to 18 per cent and even higher[37] Even under perestroika from 1985, investment was given priority over consumption – in order to provide consumption for the future, a tale that had been heard many times before since 1917. Consumer spending accounted for a lower proportion of GDP than in OECD countries,[38] and because of the priority given to crude production targets, services, including distribution (with all that means for the food sector) were well down the scale.[39] It is possible to speculate that if the USSR had not spent so massively on defence, the civilian economy might have done a better job. But it is perhaps more likely that, without the supposed threat from the West that justified the defence industry, the system would have collapsed sooner.

As perestroika was shown up for the non-reform that it was, President Gorbachev signalled in his "Presidential guidelines" in 1990 (the year before the break-up of the Union arose as a serious prospect) that the USSR was finally confronting a possible transformation into a "market economy" – the "spectre of capitalism".

In subsequent chapters we shall look at the differences between types of market economy among the major OECD countries, and suggest that some models are more attractive than others. The IMF and OECD see a market economy as being based on three pillars: first, resources are allocated on the basic of "market" signals; second, there is freedom for competition between producers of goods and services; third, there has to be a supporting framework, comprising contributions from both the public and the private sectors of the economy. The debate about what is the best form of capitalism centres mainly on the third.

The market signals include recognition of prices as the principal market signal, and profits as a guide to the most economically useful activities for investment, combined with autonomy for individual enterprises to respond to those markets signals. Freedom of competition implies both freedom of entry – to counteract monopolistic tendencies – and the perhaps less appealing freedom to exit. The latter is less appealing for obvious reasons; it may be effected with great skill and the minimum of damage; it may also involve difficult decisions with regard to the workforce. But it usually means failure of some sort. The whole point of competition is that there must be losers as well as winners. The limited liability laws proved one of capitalism's greatest breakthroughs in this respect, by restricting the potential losses of investors and spreading the risk. Unlucky creditors may not be consoled by the knowledge that an entire theorem in economics has been devoted to demonstrating that limited liability does not alter the totality of entrepreneurial risk, but merely redistributes it among capitalists – from owners to creditors.[40]

Prices were very emphatically *not* the principal market signal under communism. The views of the central planners at the top, rather than spotters of opportunities for profit lower down, were the main allocative device for investment. Indeed, the British economist and friend of Keynes, Joan Robinson, once noted: "The most important difference in the economy that socialism introduced was in the control of investment. Instead of being divided by historical accident between government, local authorities, a number of profit-seeking large scale enterprises and innumerable little businesses making a livelihood for a family, with no generally accepted view of what it was supposed to be for, an overall plan of investment to build up the strength of the nation was now the main preoccupation of the central government."[41] We have now seen how strong the communist nations felt in reality.

As for the autonomy of enterprises to respond to market signals this was ruled out by definition and practice. One is reminded of the observation by Aldous Huxley, who, writing in 1938, stated: "Capitalism tends to produce a multiplicity of petty dictators, each in command of his own little business kingdom. State Socialism tends to produce a single, centralised, totalitarian dictatorship, wielding absolute authority over all its subjects through a hierarchy of bureaucratic agents."[42]

The model market economy is in fact far removed from the idealised diagrams in all those economic textbooks of perfect, atomistic competition. Although obeisance is constantly paid to the importance of small businesses, the typical market economy is characterised by a predominance of oligopolistic large businesses, themselves increasingly competing in a multinational way, with bases all over the world. Schumpeter, a great champion of capitalism, wrote in 1943: "If all the accusations ever levelled against big business were entirely justified – which is far from being the case – it would still be a fact that the actual efficiency of the capitalist engine of production in the era of the largest-scale units has been much greater than in the preceding era of small or medium sized ones. This is a matter of statistical record ... the technological and organisational possibilities open to firms of the type which is compatible with approximately perfect competition could never have produced similar results."[43]

Since Schumpeter's time, the liberalisation of trade in the post-war years (at least until the 1970s) and the internationalisation of big business have acted to put something of a brake on the monopolistic tendencies of capitalism. But these tendencies have to be constantly watched. Schumpeter himself was so pessimistic that he thought capitalism might evolve into socialism not, à la Marx, because of its internal contradictions, but because of its successes. By accident or design, the oligopolistic nature of international capitalism has proved successful at least for the majority of that 15 per cent of the world's population which lives in the OECD market economies. Whether this is a satisfactory score is another matter.

Prices, profits, competition and freedom of action – these are the great slogans of the market economy. But, as the IMF study points out: "A market system will not function properly without a wide range of supporting infrastructure and services, such as transportation and communications, but also including the free flow of information, a supportive financial system, readily available technical assistance and a coherent legal framework. Such a market system can only function if a majority of investment and ownership is in the private sector."[44]

There is a prodigious amount of history behind the way the capitalist countries managed to evolve the market-based economies whose supporting structures are summarised in that one sentence. The *laissez-faire* period of the 19th century was, as already noted, a system that required heavy government intervention to make it function. The mixed economies evolved in the OECD area represent the result of a seething mass of pluralist forces, with governments and consumers trying to adjudicate between a profusion of conflicting offers, and the public and private sectors in would-be harmonious, but often decidedly uneasy balance.

By contrast the communists spent decades believing that willpower (the plan) counted more than actual facts. For Moscow, an economist was someone who worked out ways of carrying out a command (rather as in the old days an AA man would offer the British motorist the best route from London to Avignon). To submit to "the chaos of the market" was to be a wimp. Communists were not wimps. Soviet communists did not respect economics (or the environment) because they overestimated man. The Russian Revolution had been a triumph of human will, not of historical inevitability. And, even in 1992, with the democratically elected Boris Yeltsin trying to rule through a mixture of chaotic democracy and decree, it was by no means certain that Russia and the former republics were as set as Eastern Europe on the goal of Western capitalism.

6

The Spectre of Capitalism

Most visitors to Russia and Eastern Europe find themselves not so much wondering why the economic system collapsed, as marvelling that it managed to keep going for so long. The shops and general street scenes in Moscow and Leningrad in 1990 reminded one of immediate post-war, austerity-ridden Britain. Sir John Harvey-Jones, the former chairman of ICI, has compared visiting factories in Poland and Hungary to taking a trip in a time machine. "Investment occurred in periodical, vast, centrally directed dollops, usually without any economic focus. Thereafter the manufacturers' task was merely to maintain the planned output. There were no benchmarks for change of any sort – be it quality, cost or quantity. There were draconian punishments for failure and little reward for success, even at meeting the fossilised plans of the central bureaucrats. To keep things running at all took near superhuman drive and determination."[1]

Although Eastern Europe is brimming with visiting "suitcase economists", it is an open question whether their theories and experience have equipped them for problems of this scale. "Classical economic theory . . . makes no mention of one vital ingredient – the time that it takes to build an economic base," Sir John observed. The new generation of Western economists tends to have a touching faith in the power and wisdom of market forces. But the economic historian Charles Feinstein and others looked at the previous development of market economies in other countries, and pinpointed five key aspects of the process: 1) The transition to a market economy took many decades. 2) The role of the state was less decisive than the responsiveness of the private sector, but "nevertheless, where the intervention of the state was conducted on a pragmatic basis, it invariably made an indispensable contribution, giving support to the private sector in many different ways". 3) The private banking sector played a vital role, not only providing loans itself but giving managerial and entrepreneurial expertise and supporting the development of a capital market. But this was a long process. 4) Foreign assistance was involved: technologies and institutions had to be "borrowed" from abroad; foreign capital was needed; rapid export growth helped. 5) Political unity and cultural homogeneity assisted those countries pursuing economic modernisation and democracy.[2]

There is no precedent for a transition from planned to market economy. Britain, and subsequently other countries (such as France, Germany, Sweden, and the United States) experienced a long period of evolution into modern market economies. Indeed, as noted earlier, the Industrial Revolution was "market led", and during the 19th and 20th centuries the governments of Britain and other countries responded to the many excesses of capitalism by introducing legislation piecemeal to institute some sort of social balance.

But there are a number of countries where market economies were introduced or, as in the case of post-war Germany, re-introduced. In the second half of the 19th century both Russia and Japan had reversed their policies of remaining isolated from the rest of the world, including isolation from its technological breakthroughs. Change had been a threat to the old feudal order; but fear of foreign domination led them to industrialise and modernise. The Russian efforts were thwarted by the 1917 Revolution; the Japanese (temporarily) by the Second World War.

The best examples we have of the attempt to introduce market economies, as opposed to the original way in which they evolved in the UK and US, is the experience of post Second World War Europe and Japan, and the more recent surge in the economies of South East Asia. In all cases the process was a long one – taking decades rather than a few years – and state intervention played a very important part. It is ironic that the state's role should emerge as having been important at a time when some of the former communist economies are being lured by the meretricious attractions of wholesale privatisation and the extreme free market; but even the IMF emphasises the limits of the attractions of privatisation, and the need for a state industrial policy to guide the formation of an emerging market economy. "Eliminating the role of the state from central planning and the day-to-day operation of industrial enterprises," the Joint Study notes, "does not detract from the responsibilities of the state to develop a strong and supporting industrial policy which will stimulate competition."[3] Again: "there is no evidence that . . . trying to obtain the benefits of private ownership by giving shares to a wide cross-section of the public (is) likely to do much to increase the efficiency of enterprises."

Paradoxically, the sheer backwardness of the former communist countries offers them one theoretical advantage. "In my view,"

Feinstein argues, "the single most important theme to emerge from the study of modern economic growth in historical perspective is that of backwardness ... Put simply, it is easier for followers to move rapidly towards an already established frontier of best-practice performances than it is for pioneers to shift that frontier forward by various forms of innovation."[4]

Britain was the world's economic leader for much of the 19th century, and the US for much of the 20th. Europe and Japan were helped by the adoption of American technology after the Second World War in narrowing the productivity gap between them and the US. Indeed, by common consent we have now reached the point where Japan has overtaken the US as technological leader in many spheres, having well and truly "caught up".

But it was not until the late 1970s and 1980s that Japan assumed this position of industrial dominance. Widely admired as it is now, and possessing the political sense of purpose and cultural homogeneity that economic historians dream about, Japan still worked hard for over three decades after the war before being taken seriously. As recently as the late 1960s and early 1970s its automobiles and other consumer products were considered to be manifestly inferior to Western goods.

There is also an obvious catch to the "backwardness" concept. Can the potential to catch up be utilised? Four-fifths of the world remains in various states of extreme backwardness and abject poverty, and many of the so-called developing countries suffered a *decline* in their standard of living during the 1980s. The fact of the matter is that embryonic market economies need to attain certain minimum standards before they can take advantage of the potential technological breakthroughs available to those who wish to "catch up".

If burgeoning market economies can achieve minimum standards of economic development (embracing education, social cohesion, administrative competence, and political stability) then "once over this threshold the late-starters can proceed to close the gap by borrowing from the leaders."[5] But arrival at this threshold requires the development of all the fundamental aspects of a market economy that we have mentioned: "Much that is required – including properly functioning financial and labour markets, efficient industrial management and competitive enterprises, reintegration into world markets and convertible currencies – can only be achieved on a timescale measured in decades."[6]

Market signals – price liberalisation, the profit motive, a system of property rights, a financial system, the right to go bankrupt – can be introduced as fast as possible. But such basic concepts and institutions were in place at an early stage of British capitalism. They subsequently have to harmonise with society's way of doing things, and with the outside world's preparedness to co-operate.

There is also a more fundamental question: Is it possible for every country, or even for the majority of developing countries, to catch up? The Marxist model may have collapsed, but some of the traditional criticisms of capitalism have yet to be refuted. There is hardly an example of a capitalist or market economy which does not depend, directly or indirectly, on some degree of cheap labour – at home and (especially) abroad. Traditionally it has been highly convenient for market economies that so many countries offering them cheap commodities are "left behind" and stay behind. (A flood of migration might alter the balance of the equation, as we shall examine later.) There is a perennial debate about whether some aspects of capitalist behaviour towards developing countries are tantamount to exploitation or economic benefit; but, like the proverbial man asked to tell the difference between an elephant and a pillar-box, people tend to recognise exploitation when they see it – *a fortiori* when they suffer it. In the case of Eastern Europe, the first response of almost any economist or businessman in the West to the possible economic opportunities is to say: "Ah, cheap labour . . ."

The biggest conundrum of all may be whether it is possible for the developing world and the former Soviet bloc to achieve the living standards of the Western market economies in the world as we know it. Pessimists look at the population explosion, the finite limits to natural resources, and the ozone layer, and pronounce: impossible. Optimists look at what technology has achieved over the past 200 years, and say: everything is possible. In 1992 we simply do not know the answer. What seems highly unlikely, however, is that capitalism and market forces are going to provide it unaided. In the absence of divine intervention, intervention by governments, and co-operation between governments, would seem necessary.

We have seen that capitalists believe in competition – but only up to a point, preferably a point under their own control. The market economies that were established or re-established after the Second World War were able to flourish in the golden age of capitalism, when trade barriers were being dismantled and the enlightened inheritance of Keynes, Roosevelt and George Marshall saw a period of economic growth the like of which the world has never experienced before. The early reactions of the capitalist West to the implications of the collapse of communism were not entirely propitious in 1990–91; indeed, the simplest requests for lower trade barriers, for example for the agricultural produce of Eastern Europe, fell, for a time, on deaf ears.

The revival of the market economy in West Germany, France, Italy and Japan after the Second World War was accompanied by a strong degree of state intervention. In France, "indicative planning" was regarded as such a success that other countries, such as the UK, flirted with imitations. In Italy a strong state sector was preserved for many years, with dominating state holding companies even in the consumer goods sector; in Japan the Ministry of International Trade and Industry (MITI) was so successful in "indicative planning" that it attracted such bitter criticisms from abroad as: "The Japanese have demonstrated that their definition of the ethic of free trade is not ours. They have also shown that a concerted, covertly organised industrial plan will defeat any number of lone competitors constrained to obey the rules of the marketplace."[7]

Thus Feinstein urges about the strategy for the former communist bloc: "the failure of centralised bureaucratic planning under the old system should not be taken as a justification for the total exclusion of some form of flexible, indicative planning under a new system."[8]

Western Europe and Japan after the war managed to combine the re-establishment of market systems with the democratic process. This was not true of many other areas of the world, including the Far Eastern market economies that are frequently cited as paradigms of successful capitalism: namely Hong Kong, South Korea and Taiwan. The classic textbook recipe for the development of an advanced industrial economy was high investment and savings; this necessitated the sacrifice of current for future consumption, which authoritarian regimes were rather good at enforcing. In the USSR and Eastern Europe the desire for democracy and capitalism have coincided, at least for a time. But even as liberal an economic historian as Feinstein concludes: "The political dilemma is . . . acute. The proposition that economic progress in these countries requires political liberalisation is incontrovertible, but the lesson drawn from the case studies was that it was extremely difficult to reconcile democracy with economic growth when the process was initiated from a very backward position."[9] In the attempt to achieve a modern market economy, governments can either win popular support, or suppress opposition.[10]

The problem in the USSR and Eastern Europe is that these populations have been sacrificing current for future consumption for as long as they can remember. To them the attraction of Western capitalism, as advertised on television, is that capitalism is seen to deliver the goods *now*. The idea of yet more sacrifice is not appealing. Yet the spectre of capitalism demands it in the short term: indeed, 1991 saw a *decline* in the average gross domestic product of the former Soviet Bloc of 15 per cent, as the old command system seized up, and the union and republics debated much, but acted little, on the mechanics of introducing a market economy. In Eastern Europe GDP fell by 16 per cent in Czechoslovakia, 10 per cent in Poland and 8 per cent in Hungary. By Western standards this constituted true economic Depression.[11] In the short term the spectre of capitalism offered the worst of both worlds.

It also brought some of the worst excesses of capitalism out of the woodwork at a very early stage. The pure capitalist will make a profit out of any available opportunity. The collapse of the command system and the prospect of the market system thrust old fashioned black-marketeering to the fore. Some Western economists and political advisers tended to argue that this was just what the former communist bloc required, and the essence of the market economy was captured by these profiteers. "What they need is for everybody to behave like that," was the comment of one Western financial expert.

But, was it? Trading and profiteering within the dying communist system, or with foreign goods obtained with "hard currency" by one route or another, was not the way to build a market economy. The point of the market economy, as developed over the years in *Western* Europe, was to channel such profiteering energies in the right direction, with the appropriate financial and legal infrastructure to support it. While talking in admiring terms about the "black economy" instincts of certain budding entrepreneurs in Eastern Europe, Western industrialists and bankers were not exactly rushing in to behave like entrepreneurs themselves – apart from scattered examples of minor "joint ventures" in the exiguous service industries. Foreign entrepreneurs required a satisfactory law of contract, a recognisable banking system and the ability to repatriate profits from an economy where there were far fewer constraints on the factors of production, including rights over property.

Inflows of foreign capital, whether public or private, seem to have been a prerequisite for the setting up of the widely admired market economies of the West and of South East Asia. And, in order to lay the basis for the subsequent successful flow of private capital, the flows of Marshall Aid under the European Recovery Programme played a vital role during the early post-war years.

We have noted that Marshall Aid during the period of 1948–51 amounted to almost 6 per cent of one year's US national product.[12] When seen from the viewpoint of the recipients, the generosity of that aid appears even more impressive: thus Alan Milward calculates that it amounted to the equivalent of about 10 per cent of national income for Italy and France, and over 5 per cent for the UK and West Germany. "When allowance is made for the special effect of the

availability of goods and services from the dollar area, and for the
cumulative benefits of the mutual expansion of investment and trade
promoted by Marshall Aid, the overall impact of the programme
must 'have been considerably greater,'' Feinstein observes . . . "It
was, for example, a crucial element in the success of the West
German currency reform, of the economic revival which followed,
and of the reintegration of West Germany into the international
economy."[13]

In Japan, West Germany and France after the Second World War
governments devoted large resources to specific investment projects,
and to tax incentives and subsidies for industry and agriculture. It is
well known that the French and Italian Governments had large
holdings in key sectors such as energy, the banks, and many
industrial concerns; but the West German Government was also
prominent in energy, the car industry, banking and a huge building
programme. It also gave special tax concessions for exporters, loan
subsidies and credit guarantees. The emphasis was certainly on
reviving the market sector; but the public sector was seen as playing a
crucial role in assisting this revival.[14] "Both during the transition and
subsequently the major historical lesson is that relations between the
state and the market must be handled on a pragmatic, not an
ideological basis," Feinstein concludes. "The economic activity of
the state must be conducted so as to complement and assist the
private sector, not to usurp its place."

On the initial reaction of Western politicians and economists to
the spectre of capitalism in Eastern Europe, the former Austrian
finance minister Dr Hannes Androsch, who has long been a student
of the boundaries of socialism and capitalism, commented: "The
Western economic order is characterised as much by the role of the
state as by market forces. Alongside the free play of the latter, there
are unseen regulating influences when the overall controlling effect
of the public sector is present. Public and co-operative property
stand side by side with private property, and the criterion of
performance is supported by the safety net of the welfare state to
ensure freedom from hunger and fear." A market economy is too
bitter a pill without the sweetening of a social coating. "One has to
take into account the social and ecological factors as well as the
economic ones. In sum, there is a policy mix of the invisible hand of
the market and the visible hands of public institutions."[15]

In Britain under Mrs Thatcher the ideological belief in the beauty
of the private sector and market forces, and the folly of government
intervention, led to a position where an industrial policy of almost
any kind became anathema; by default the industrial policy became
one of energetic ministers such as the Secretary of State for Wales,

Peter Walker (1987–90), luring foreign investment into the country, notably from Japan. The wonders of Japanese investment and Japanese management practices were a constant theme when Ministers tried to defend their attitude to industry – although this did not go down too well on the Continent, especially in France, where it was increasingly feared that Japanese motor and electronics investment in the UK was a Trojan Horse.

Whatever they say in ritual denunciations of "big government" and "the public sector" most post-war capitalist governments have indeed sought to complement and assist the private sector. In order to be able to compete in the world market, and prosper amid the gale-force winds of market forces, fledgling "market" economies have to be nurtured and prepared. Thus, referring to the post-war experience of Japan, S.Korea, Taiwan, Hong Kong and Singapore (the last four sometimes known as the "Asian Tigers"), Dr Androsch notes that these have achieved their far proclaimed success by relying "less on market forces and foreign investment than on the public hand, which played an important role in the formulation of industrial strategies and measures for restructuring." The emphasis was first on building a manufacturing base through import substitution, then policy was geared towards export promotion. Tax incentives and the exchange rate were used to this end and foreign knowledge and technology obtained through licence or even piracy. The Koreans used interventionist price and subsidisation policies to achieve high rates of savings and investment.[16] All the time their eyes were on the "world market" and thus import-substitution sectors were picked with a view to their export potential and subsidies were removed if industries failed to compete on world markets.[17]

Preparation for market economy status has throughout the period since the Industrial Revolution often involved strategies which are most certainly not recognised as "market-orientated" by purists such as Mrs Thatcher. Yet the orientation of these practices was very much towards the market. Two crucial differences from the communist countries, however, were first, that the successful "NICs" (or "newly industrialising countries") were outward-looking and trying to participate in the world market – whereas the whole philosophy, indeed religion, of the USSR and its satellites had been inward-looking – a fatal mistake. "Korea Inc could be compared to a large multinational firm whose domain of business operation is the world market", writes Yung Chul Park. Secondly, their strategies were not dominated by a belief in the public sector per se, or by the vain pursuit of the beauties of the communist or socialist ideal: they were aiming at economic success, by *whatever* means.

The communists were also aiming at economic success, but they had backed a lame horse and, until the late 1980s, indulged the fatal gambler's practice of "double or quits".

One proxy for "industrial policy" in market economies such as the United States for many years was the close relationship between government and corporations via what became known as "the military industrial complex". Defence and space contracts necessitated a fair degree of medium and long range planning. Much of what counted in the definitions as "the market sector" was dependent for a proportion of its contracts and profits on public sector procurement (in some cases, a very large proportion). Of course, under the capitalist system such corporations were not *confined* to public sector contracts, and it was always open to them to develop business elsewhere – which was not formally the case in the communist countries. Nevertheless, the implication of the "peace dividend" is that a large sector of prominent capitalist firms in the US, UK and elsewhere can no longer rely so much on government contracts from that source to lead their research and development.

Under a successful modern market economy the invisible hand of Adam Smith needs to be in the same room as Androsch's visible hand of public institutions. The communist bloc certainly believed in the importance of education and training, which are also regarded in the capitalist countries as vital ingredients of policy to improve the performance of the "supply-side" of the economy – "regarded", but not promoted fully, as shown by the concern in the "Anglo-Saxon" economies about educational deficiencies in the early 1990s.

We live in a world of necessary and sufficient conditions, and experience suggests that the approach to optimality is best achieved by a benign combination of public and private sector activity. Ruling out the market, as communism attempted to do, means ruling out the most necessary condition for a successful economy. But an excessive hostility towards the public sector, as was manifested by Mrs Thatcher and President Reagan, can lead to the kind of social neglect which is both worrying to those who profess to have social consciences, and damaging to the economy and society itself. During the latter years of Mrs Thatcher's period in office, for example, the British Government came under unusually strong criticism from industry for its neglect of infrastructure investment, especially roads and the transport system generally, which was regarded as hampering the efficiency of the market sector. Similarly, the dignitaries of the City of London became increasingly concerned that widely publicised transport problems of London itself were in danger of diminishing the City's status as the world's pre-eminent financial centre. (When such concerns about "Thatcherism" came to a head, and were referred to by the then Lord Mayor of London in the annual Lord Mayor's Banquet at the Guildhall, on this occasion she was, for the first time, not accorded a standing ovation.)

Thus among the necessary conditions for a successfully functioning market economy is a harmonious relation between the public and private sectors. These necessary conditions include everything from appropriate "supply-side" policies such as infrastructure, education and training, and encouragement of research, to a supportive financial system and the operation of the "market" signals of price, profit and incentive to develop new products and markets. To look at it another way, hostility towards a market system for allocating resources (and, especially, consumer goods) is a severe obstacle to the successful running of an economy, as communist experience has resoundingly demonstrated. But, just as hostility towards the private sector is a barrier to success, so is hostility towards the public sector. This is not to suggest that the antagonism demonstrated by President Reagan and Mrs Thatcher towards the public sector was as serious a handicap to the overall performance of the economy as communist loathing of the private sector. The attitude of the state in the USSR and Eastern Europe towards the private sector for all those years was a phenomenal, indeed overwhelming, handicap to economic performance. But the bias against the public sector shown by the New Right in the Anglo-Saxon market economies was not only damaging to the poor, but did not noticeably improve the performance of the supply-side either. Indeed, as the US examined its own social condition at the beginning of the 1990s, the catalogue of social ills and urban decay finally showed signs of becoming a major political issue for the first time in 25 years. The Los Angeles riots of spring 1992 were a salutary warning.

The US economy in the 1980s and early 1990s was still the largest and richest in the world, and the collapse of the Soviet economy (to, according to some British Treasury officials, about the size, for those 300 million people, of the British economy with a population of fewer than 60 million) underscored the view that reports about US decline had been exaggerated. But in the course of 1990 and 1991, concern about the extent and success of competition from Japan within the US domestic market became a constant theme. And there was a marked recurrence of the contrast, identified way back in the 1950s by J. K. Galbraith, between "Private Affluence and Public Squalor". In this case, however, concern was not merely manifested for the condition of the public sector – the transport system, the schools, the general inner city environment – but also for the manifest increase in *private poverty* across the land. Such had been the diversion of government effort under President Reagan (and not noticeably reversed by President Bush, despite his original promises of "a kinder and gentler America") that, while the rich had prospered, the poorer echelons of society had in many cases either not seen *any* improvement in their living standards during the 1980s at all, or suffered a manifest deterioration.[18] Concern about the condition of American society even prompted the veteran commentator Alistair Cooke to temper a life-long disinclination towards theories of "decadence" and declare: "I believe the feeling is epidemic across the country that daily life, in every sort and size of community, is getting more squalid, expensive and dangerous, and that the US is going, or has gone over the peak of what the Spenglers and Toynbees would call its 'Maturity'." According to Cooke, the "social dangers, deprivations and frustrations" characteristic of the modern American capitalist society raised "three possibilities: one: The second American Civil War, triggered by separate ethnic and regional uprisings. Two: The arrival of a populist dictator (under, as Burke predicted, the banner of liberty). Three: An emergency return to the benevolent form of socialism created by Franklin Roosevelt in the first New Deal."[19]

The America that had devoted so much effort to the defence expenditure which finally convinced the Soviets they could not compete had certainly done so at the expense of resources that might otherwise have been devoted to its more domestic social ills. But it had also demonstrated that, over and above defence expenditure, tax cuts took preference over social expenditures from the public purse. David Stockman, President Reagan's former budget director, had denied that there was ever any right wing conspiracy to wreck the social budget completely by increasing the deficit. But this belief persisted. There can in any case be little doubt that the priorities of the 1980s, or lack of them, had deepened the social divisions within American society which were leading Cooke and many others to such gloomy prognoses. And such prognoses were coming from people who were familiar with the notion that the US is traditionally a "positive society", good at "problem-solving" and "bouncing back".

The limits to American decline were demonstrated by the superiority of its military machine during the Gulf War of early 1991. But the case for the critics was also vividly demonstrated by the fact that the financial underwriter of the Allies in the Second World War, and of the Marshall Plan afterwards, found itself having to conduct the Gulf War largely, and according to some estimates entirely, with other people's money – including a notably hefty, if reluctant, contribution from Japan. We had reached the era of mercenary capitalism. (It was, incidentally, somewhat ironical that

Japan and Germany, our former adversaries in 1939–45, were criticized for being insufficiently bellicose during the Gulf War.)

Thus there were two serious criticisms of the American capitalist model that was, as it were, on offer to the former communist world in the early 1990s. One was that, within its own terms, it was not necessarily as efficient as its theorists would like – a worry reflected by the growing concern about Japanese competition. Second, its own terms were coming under greater scrutiny: the social problems caused by the right wing bias of US society – where even the Democrats are a kind of "inside right" party, on the lines of the traditional Conservatives in Britain, dubbed "the Wets" by Mrs Thatcher – were tolerated as long as they were considered, however harshly, to be a necessary consequence of a system that basically worked well. The openness of American Society, and its manifest belief in human and democratic rights, combined with the American Dream in which all think they or their children can eventually come good, or even become President, are values that have often overcome opposition to the harshness of the system for "losers" or the less fortunate.

"Europeans like to think of the American model as *laissez-faire*, red in tooth and claw" says Michael Ignatieff, "but it is actually a form of state capitalism in which the great corporations of the military-industrial complex fatten on the largesse of the state, while the poor and disadvantaged get a firm dose of *laissez-faire*."[20] Yet it was an idealised version of the American model which was being most promulgated in the context of Eastern Europe by Western economists in 1990 and 1991. Indeed, at a World Bank seminar in Bangkok at the annual meeting of the World Bank and International Monetary Fund (October, 1991) the US model of capitalism was being lauded as supreme, despite the perceived threat from the Japanese model – and Western Europe's mixed economy was ignored.

The emphasis was all on "freeing up" the former communist economies as fast as possible. As Dr Vaclav Klaus, Minister of Finance of the Czech and Slovak Federal Republic, summarised it, the name of the game was "stabilisation, liberalisation, privatisation and clarification". It all sounded so simple. While the Group of Seven deliberated on how to handle the Soviet Union's requests for financial and technical assistance, Lawrence Summers, Chief Economist for the World Bank, declaimed confidently: "Spread the truth – the laws of economics are like the laws of engineering. One set of laws works everywhere." They are not, of course. The simile is absurd. The laws of engineering are far more reliable, and consistent. Economic laws involve people and their institutions. The behaviour of people and institutions is not entirely predictable – unlike the way the reaction of a suspension bridge to the pressures of an army of vehicles may be gauged by the engineer. What is helpful in seeing how the spectre of capitalism may affect the prospects for the Soviet Union and Eastern Europe is historical perspective, and observation of what has happened elsewhere, rather than hysterical enthusiasm for simple solutions which "stabilise" inflation and the budget, and then allow market forces to deliver the desired prosperity. The omens are not entirely favourable.

"Structural transformations of economic systems are a plunge into the unknown," said Adam Przeworski after a comparison of political and economic reforms in Eastern Europe and Latin America. "They are driven by desperation and hope, not by reliable blueprints. For political reasons, the reform strategy most likely to be undertaken is not the one that minimises social costs. It is the bitter-pill strategy that combines a turn toward markets with transformations of property. And even if such reform programmes enjoy initial support among individuals and organised political forces, this support is likely to erode as time passes and the suffering continues."[21]

The terrible thing about the *sudden* adoption of capitalism is that the two great necessary conditions preached by the "reformers" are in conflict. "Price liberalisation", needed to "make markets work" and introduce such basic concepts as "relative prices" and "opportunity cost" (the avoidance of distortions caused because the full economic costs of various processes were not taken into consideration under the command economy) almost inevitably involves a disturbing acceleration in inflation as people rush to protect themselves from higher prices. According to Grigory Yavlinsky, the economist charged by President Gorbachev in 1991 with the task of drawing up an economic treaty for the disintegrating republic, over half the budget deficits of the USSR were caused by simply printing money. "Stabilisation" is an uphill task in the face of "liberalisation".

The tragedy, also, is that unemployment is bound to get worse. The mere introduction of competition, both internally and against the rest of the world, guarantees that the former eastern bloc employees are less protected. There is less hoarding of labour. And the collapse of the administered system before a fully-fledged capitalist or mixed economy system is in place leads to sharp falls in economic activity, which also aggravate the unemployment problem. The reductions of 10 to 20 per cent in output experienced in Eastern Europe in 1991 (industrial output fell by 35 per cent in Poland between 1989 and 1991) were reminiscent in scale of the figures recorded in the Great Depression which afflicted Western capitalism in the late 1920s and early 1930s.[22]

There is all the difference in the world between recognising the characteristics of a market economy and trying to adapt to one from a command structure. It took literally hundreds of years for the Group of Seven leading industrial economies to evolve into their present diffident pre-eminence. (Even the much envied Japan is far less sure of itself than outsiders might imagine – as we shall see later.) The record of "capitalist" institutions such as the World Bank and International Monetary Fund at assisting in the advancement of underdeveloped economies is at best mixed, as the condition of so many Latin American and African nations amply demonstrates. Yet, in their desperation, the east European economies were driven into the hands of the IMF some years ago; and the final indication of Soviet capitulation was the formal application sent by President Gorbachev to join the IMF at around the time of the London Economic Summit of July 1991. This was followed up by Yeltsin's Russian Federation, and by other "Soviet successor-states".

Comparing the hopes of Eastern Europe with Latin American experience, Adam Przeworski noted: "The bare facts are that Eastern European countries are embracing capitalism and that they are poor. These are the conditions Eastern Europeans share with masses of people all over the world who also dream of prosperity and democracy. Hence, all one can expect is that they too will confront the all too normal problems of the economics, the politics, and the culture of poor capitalism. The East has become the South."

As they talk about "stabilisation" and "sequencing", economists from the World Bank, IMF and University faculties sound wonderfully plausible and sure of themselves. "Stabilisation" involves reducing the balance of payments and fiscal deficits and controlling inflation; "sequencing" is the buzz-word for securing the right order of priorities between achieving "macro-economic stability", competition, a legal and regulatory framework, privatisation, development of the financial sector. The "in thing" in 1991 was to achieve stabilisation first; yet the actual experience of the G7 over centuries was an evolutionary hotchpotch, in which stabilisation as we know it was only understood, let alone achieved, rather late in the day.

Working from "a technical economic blueprint based on theories developed inside the walls of North American universities" the glib technocrats from the West offer those embracing capitalism "choices that are not easy to explain to the general public and decisions that do not always make sense to popular opinion."[23] In Western democracies governments have learned either to carry the

people along with them, through the arduous processes of consultation with trades unions, interest groups and the people's representatives in parliament and the media, or to suffer at the ballot box.
The non-democratic alternative is to stifle opposition and impose
your will that way.

But that is what the countries of Eastern Europe have been trying
to escape from. The interesting thing about the spectre of capitalism
in eastern Europe is that rejection of communism and yearning for
democracy are part of the same process. The impetus for change in
Poland grew out of the Solidarity trades union movement. "Adjustment" and "restructuring" of the economy subsequently hit the very
industries – shipbuilding, steel – which were the backbone of the
reform movement; unemployment soared among the original
supporters of democracy and the move away from communism,
leading inevitably to a backlash.

Poland is an economy that was much influenced by economic
theories developed inside the walls of North American universities
and smoothed and polished in the comfortable surroundings of the
World Bank and IMF. The negotiations between the government
and Solidarity in spring 1989 were taken by the West to result in a
"broad consensus on future political and economic reforms".[24] But
what they and the June 1989 elections showed most convincingly
was a broad anti-communist consensus. The subsequent economic
programme introduced by Poland's first post-war noncommunist
government was widely described as a "big bang" or "shock
treatment" – and thoroughly deserved such metaphors. As with so
many metaphors, not to say clichés, adopted by the economic and
financial establishment, however, the origins and implications of
such phrases were conveniently brushed aside by the enthusiasm of
the "reformers". The people were told that the treatment might be
painful, but that the pain would not last very long.

On 1 January 1990 the Polish government introduced a "stabilisation" package which included: tight fiscal and monetary policies;
punitive wage controls; comprehensive price liberalisation, including the cutting of subsidies and drastic increases in previously
controlled prices; the freeing of foreign trade; the reduction of
import tariffs; a 46 per cent devaluation against the dollar; and
"internal convertibility" under which residents could obtain foreign
exchange for imports of goods, but must equally surrender all
earnings of foreign exchange to the "pool" managed by the central
bank.[25]

Part of the "stabilisation" programme in these cases involves the
so-called "monetary overhang" of people's savings: the reformers
speak unashamedly of "confiscation *de jure* through monetary

reform or *de facto* through inflation."[26] "Excess" money in circulation can be "sterilised" through privatisation, purchase of financial assets, temporary freezing of bank deposits. "Apart from the confiscation route, all the elements of this stabilisation package require the creation of new, market-oriented institutions and the introduction of new laws," says the ECE.

Fears about "monetary overhang" in cases like that of Poland seemed to involve the assumption that there was a hoard of money waiting to be spent once controls were lifted and shortages eliminated. The spending of such money would be inflationary, it was feared. Yet it was also cynically assumed that, as prices were freed, there would be "corrective inflation" to dilute the value of the monetary overhang.[27] Between December 1989 and January 1990 the monthly rate of inflation rose from 17.7 per cent to 79.6 per cent. Immediate Polish experience of the spectre of capitalism was therefore one of roaring inflation and vast losses in the value of savings. An IMF pamphlet in 1991 brushed this aside, noting that, after the immediate impact of "big bang": "Inflation has been substantially reduced from the very high levels experienced around the end of 1989. Shortages, a source of chronic social unrest in the past, have largely been eliminated." It conceded, however, that "the decline in output was larger than expected and unemployment rose. In part, this reflected the limited supply response to liberalisation. Inflation remained higher than foreseen; in substantial measure, this outcome was a direct result of excessive growth in credit and wages in the second half of the year."[28] Output declined by 13 per cent in Poland during 1990 (a 21 per cent fall in the state sector being mitigated by a 17 per cent rise in the smaller private sector), and private consumption by 24 per cent.[29] As the ECE commented: "The steep fall in real wages may partly reflect a too restrictive wage policy in view of the erosion of forced savings by hyperinflation in the fourth quarter of 1989."[30] The shock of price freedom for domestic enterprises, and the need to pay world market prices for goods from the Soviet Union, brought another inflationary surprise to Poland in the second half of 1990 and early 1991. The country suffered an inflation rate of 585 per cent in 1990. Not surprisingly, wage demands rose; forecasts for both wages and prices given to the IMF during loan negotiations early in 1990 proved way out, and part of an IMF credit was temporarily suspended. A bigger and better credit was subsequently negotiated with the IMF early in 1991, founded on more false hopes of the achievement of "macro-economic stabilisation".

By 1991 an impressive array of economists assembled by the EC Commission was beginning to have second thoughts about the early enthusiasm for "stabilisation" of the Polish and other East European economies. The talk was of "L curves" – under which output collapses, and then stays low for years, rather than "J" curves, under which a small fall is soon followed by a dramatic improvement to well above the initial position. The World Bank forecast that 1989 output levels in Eastern Europe would not be regained until 1996, and some were even more pessimistic than that. By April 1992 we were being told: "Pre-transformation levels of per capita GDP in Poland may not be reached before the year 2000."[31]

Introducing the EC survey, the economist Richard Portes, an expert on Poland, acknowledged that huge mistakes had been made in bringing stabilisation to the Polish economy. The central feature of economic liberalisation was "a drastic change in relative prices, which is supposed to bring restructuring. But there will be adjustment costs. These will be lower, the greater is factor mobility. But deep-rooted problems in both capital and labour markets have substantially raised these costs of adjustment."[32] Portes suggested that by concentrating on the behaviour of households and the "monetary overhang" the economists had in effect ignored the basic problems of productive efficiency. "It is much harder to change the behaviour of firms than of households", he said. Not enough emphasis had been put on "the necessary changes in corporate control and the financial environment for state firms and on transforming the banking system."[33]

But here again, history shows that such institutions and methods of corporate ownership and control took decades, indeed centuries, to work out in the advanced capitalist countries. The fact that mistakes were made with "sequencing" does not mean that different "sequences" from the economists' blueprints would have done much better. To conduct macro-economic policies, you need a macro-economy. As Hannes Androsch has pointed out: "Shock therapy carries the threat, as the examples of Poland, Yugoslavia and elsewhere have shown, of the creation of a shock with but little or no therapeutic value. It is necessary, aside from stabilisation, freeing of prices and deflationary measures to control inflation, to increase the range of goods and services offered. Yet improvements can only really be made at the level of the economic unit – the firm, the factory, the enterprise. It is there that the national product is generated."[34]

The North American academics and their lamb-like disciples encouraged a price free-for-all onto a monopolistic industrial structure, thereby guaranteeing hyper-inflation. It was hyper-inflation in post-First World War Germany which led to rampant unemployment, the political and social collapse of the Weimar

Republic, and all the calamities which the architects of post-Second World War Europe were determined should never occur again. The inflation in Poland that arrived with the spectre of capitalism did not compare with the "wheelbarrow" inflation of Weimar. But it was nonetheless severely disruptive of the social consensus necessary if the country was to persevere with the new-found religions of democracy and capitalism.

A classic mistake made by the advisers to the Polish Government was to pay too much attention to the so-called "market rate" for foreign currency when advising on devaluation of the zloty. Portes acknowledged that the "black market" rate for currency before the stabilisation programme was misleading, representing essentially the demand for luxury goods by people in the better-off income brackets.[35] The devaluation was excessive, certainly producing a transformation of the foreign trade balance, but also contributing yet another upward twist to the spiral of hyper- inflation.

The much vaunted process of "privatisation" had hardly got off the ground in the Poland of 1991 and 1992. This is not surprising – it was bound to take considerable time, except in the minds of the draftsmen of instant blueprints. But it did mean that any magic hopes for improved micro-economic performance from privatisation were misplaced. In the general chaos domestic firms cut back investment and foreign investors were sluggish in coming forward – not least because there was great uncertainty about how things would turn out, and a natural – and, as it happens, well founded – caution on the part of foreign capitalists. Economic advisers subsequently conceded they had underestimated the problems caused by controversies over restitution of property to the original owners.

With things looking pretty bleak in the early summer of 1991, President Lech Walesa mournfully observed to a high-powered visiting EC delegation: "We have done all the things the West asked of us – now where is your investment?"

Poland's initial taste of market economics brought serious inflation and unemployment, and corruption in abundance. The democratic test of the spectre of capitalism in Poland came with the general election of Sunday, October 27, 1991. Sixty per cent of the electorate did not vote at all, and the reformers – the Democratic Union – only just won more seats than the Communists. The Times correspondent in Warsaw, Roger Boyes, concluded: "Poland's general election has shattered the consensus in favour of radical market reform . . . there will be repercussions throughout Eastern Europe and, perhaps most significantly, in Russia."

If ever there was a communist country which was prepared for the

arrival of the spectre of capitalism it was Hungary. Indeed, Hungary
had been haunted by the knowledge that communism was an
economic disaster since the 1960s, and much of the significant
"reformist" literature had emanated from Hungary. The only limits
on Hungary's flirtations with capitalism before perestroika in the
USSR were fears about how much the Hungarians could get away
with without bringing down the wrath of Moscow on their heads.
After all, that wrath had already descended once, in the shape of
Soviet tanks in Budapest in 1956.

Whereas in Poland the capitalist spectre devoted too much
attention to the "macro" rather than the "micro" – and with
spectacularly destabilising results for what was supposed to be
macro-economic "stabilisation" – in Hungary the micro-foundations were much better laid. Indeed, the OECD commented
"Hungary has achieved substantial progress in market-oriented
structural reforms. However, it has had more difficulty in reaching
macro-economic stability." Even as Western economists were
conceding that they had, on the whole – and most certainly in Poland
– devoted too much attention to capitalist "macro" policies rather
than the micro-foundations on which the macro-economy is built,
Hungary's progress with the basics of a market economy made an
impressive list.

To begin with, the Hungarians discovered privatisation even
before Mrs Thatcher. Admittedly, their concept of privatisation was
confined to housing for a long time, rather than industry. But the fact
of the matter is that in the mid-1970s the Hungarian Government
had embarked on a process of selling public sector housing to
tenants, at knock down prices which the tenants could afford and
which eased the burdens on the government's (pre-capitalist) budget.
At the beginning of 1990, some 78 per cent of Hungarians lived in
owner occupied housing – one of the highest percentages of home-
ownership in the world.[36] What is more, even before the privatisation process, the proportion of the population in owner occupied
houses or apartments was still remarkably high – at 73 per cent in
1970. This was in complete contrast to the position in, for example,
the USSR, where 72 per cent of the urban housing stock was state
owned.[37]

The visitor to Russia during the perestroika years used to note how
there was much talk of "markets" but little understanding. In
Hungary there was more understanding, but a limit on practice.
Thus, despite the reform conscious nature of the Hungarian
government for several decades, the "socialist" sector still accounted
for 94 per cent of GDP in 1988.[38] As the IMF has noted: "Hungary
was the first centrally planned economy to introduce a broad

market-oriented reform, in 1968. It has been undertaking economic reforms ever since. And yet the first freely elected government in forty years – which took office in May 1990 – inherited a poorly performing, over centralised economy with low external reserves and the highest per capita debt in Eastern Europe."

Many of the fundamental elements of capitalism that we in the West take for granted had already been introduced into (or returned to) Hungary by 1990. The 1980s saw the introduction of a comprehensive tax system, company and bankruptcy law, a more sophisticated banking system, and the development of financial markets. The Budapest Stock Exchange reopened in 1990. Progress was at an early stage – the more "commercial" banking system still seemed to be allocating similar lines of credit to the same old borrowers – and the degree of real competition between enterprises was decidedly limited.[39] Nevertheless, the proportion of goods and services liberalised from price controls more than doubled from just over 40 per cent in 1985 to 89 per cent in 1990.

Despite its more Western orientation, Hungary was still dominated by its trading relationship with other communist countries until the late 1980s. It remained a relatively inefficient economy by Western standards, with little spur to that most important capitalist dynamic – innovation – coming from its main eastern trading partner, the USSR. But rising aspirations for better living standards introduced a familiar capitalist practice – that of living on credit. Indeed, the West allowed Hungary to build up such a huge per capita level of debt, that the formal adoption of capitalism at the end of the 1980s was constrained in its prospects from the start by the crippling burden of servicing this debt. Its active foreign trade policy after the twin blows of the collapse of trade with the USSR and the higher cost of oil imports at world prices was impressive, and the degree to which Hungary has succeeded in raising its exports to OECD countries has been staggering. But all the time it has been running fast to stand still, because of the huge accumulation of debt – some 40 per cent of its export earnings, or over 10 per cent of GDP, being required to pay the interest on accumulated overseas debts – and because the end of subsidised oil and other raw material imports from the USSR alone cost it a further 4 to 5 per cent of GDP.[40]

Thus Hungarians faced an enormous, some would say intolerable, squeeze on their living standards in the early 1990s: there might have been a fairly advanced "capitalist" or "market" framework in place by comparison with the USSR and other Eastern European countries, but the strains on the population were daunting. The beginnings of the "adjustment" to market economics in 1990–91 also coincided with a recession in many OECD countries and the loss of a large segment of the previously captive market of the USSR. This induced a fall of 4 per cent in GDP in 1990, and a further slide of 8 per cent in 1991.[41]

Much price liberalisation had actually anticipated the formal adoption of a market economy or, rather, the adoption of the goal of a market economy: the objective adopted in 1990 by the Hungarian State Property Agency was a reduction in the state's ownership of trade and industry from 90 per cent to 50 per cent within a few years. Within the first year about 5 per cent had been privatised.[42] There was also no "monetary overhang" to worry about. Even so, the price changes that took place in the early 1990s, and the natural desire of wage earners to keep up, produced a wage-price spiral that, while not at Polish levels of hyper-inflation, brought an inflation rate of 28.9 per cent in 1990, which accelerated further in 1991 to 36 per cent.[43]

In order to put the balance of payments into shape to service foreign debts, Hungary has to devalue from time to time, and this further aggravates the inflationary problem. The country started the formal transition to capitalism at the end of the 1980s with a per capita income way below the average of the OECD market economies; its citizens' aspirations and ambitions are high, but they are being asked to make extreme sacrifices in real wages in order both to service the overseas debts and to *reculer pour mieux sauter* by undergoing the "transformation costs" of moving to a market economy. Capitalism brings them, among other things, the mixed blessing of inflation and tough "counter-inflation" policies. Ironically, the spectre of capitalism was asking Hungary to pay its way in the world with a vengeance, while those arch capitalist countries, the US and UK, were both unashamedly running large balance of payments deficits, and expecting other capitalist countries to finance them.

Real wages in Hungary have been on the decline since 1988, bringing increasing resort to second jobs. Food and basic general expenses absorbed 45 per cent of the average household's disposable income in 1989, 55 per cent in 1990 and over 70 per cent in 1991. The OECD commented drily: "There are limits to the capacity of the population to make further adjustments in its consumption pattern."

These were the kind of horrors facing the East European economy which was probably most in favour with the capitalist world. And its problems were mounting despite the fact that foreign investors from the world of better-established market economies have been attracted by Hungary's relatively liberal, open and easy regime for outside investors – who are offered attractive tax concessions and protected property rights. Hungary, with a population only a few million larger than London, had attracted over $1.5 bn of foreign investment by the end of 1990, representing, according to the OECD, "well over 50 per cent of all foreign capital directed to central and eastern Europe".[44] Early in 1991 the IMF considered the government's reform programme – "designed to put in place the most important elements, including the institutional framework, of a contemporary market economy within three years" – sufficiently impressive to offer it balance of payments help totalling $1.6 bn over three years, plus up to $0.5 bn to cover the higher cost of oil imports. This compared with expected annual debt service repayments of close to $4 bn a year in 1991–95.[45]

Both Hungary (population 10 million) and Czechoslovakia (population 15 million) were generating interest out of all proportion to their size or importance in the world economy in the early 1990s. But this was for obvious reasons. One of the first effects of the political liberalisation of Eastern Europe was that Czechoslovakia changed its name to The Czech and Slovak Federal Republic (or CSFR). In most assessments of the impact of capitalism on the CSFR, it was given a head start by comparison with Poland and Hungary, because of its low "starting" inflation rate (1.5 per cent in 1989, against 18.8 per cent in Hungary and 260 per cent in Poland), low foreign debt ($5.8 bn, against 19.5 bn for Hungary and 36.5 bn for Poland), and relatively high per capita income.[46] One interesting comparison of the latter was provided by calculations that, at the beginning of the 1980s, Czechoslovakia's per capita income was 70 per cent of that of Austria, compared with 52 per cent in the case of Hungary and 45 per cent for Poland.[47]

Most such comparisons have proved, since Eastern Europe was opened up, to have grossly overstated the real standard of living in the relevant country. (Calculated at the commercial exchange rate, Hungarian per capita GDP in 1989 was only a seventh of the OECD average.) What is generally accepted is that Czechoslovakia was a prosperous economy before the war (Hitler was attracted, among other things, by its industry), but that it subsequently became the most planned and centralised of all the East European economies; and, after the tragic events of 1968, it was the least tempted to flirt with economic reform. The 1980s were a bad decade for economic performance in the entire communist bloc, but Czechoslovakia did worse than most, and is generally reckoned to have fallen further behind both Western countries and Hungary. According to some economists, the underlying productivity of the CSFR gives it a comparative advantage in key industrial sectors over Hungary and Poland.[48] But the more Western experts have looked at the CSFR, the more antiquated and monopolised large sections of its economy appear to be. Moreover, it was especially dependent on the Soviet market, which all but collapsed in 1991.

The CSFR was less prepared for reform than the other two countries, and also started later, its "big bang" occurring in January 1991, under the radical finance minister Vaclav Klaus, who eventually won a debate against more cautious colleagues, such as Valtr Komarek, who was first Deputy Prime Minister in charge of economic reform in 1990. Klaus, a former pupil of Mrs Thatcher's sometime economic adviser Sir Alan Walters, has almost upstaged Milton Friedman in his devotion to the free market. Klaus took the simple view, from within the walls of those North American universities, that privatisation takes a society from communism to the marketplace, and convertibility of the currency transforms it from a closed economy to an open one, providing the competition that is so desperately needed.

The Hungarians put the emphasis, German-style, on the establishment of a *social market economy*, with a strong safety net for the poor and unemployed. They also give the impression of favouring a gradual, evolutionary approach – so much so that some observers argue that so far the main impetus to reform came with the liberalising measures of the last *communist* regime in Hungary. But the CSFR's "Scenario of Economic Reform" (published 4 September 1990) states baldly: "It is of paramount importance to place emphasis on the market economy as our true goal, *market economy with all its positive and negative aspects*, a goal that we seek to accomplish at the earliest possible date."

This is a remarkable hostage to fortune. President Havel's economic advisers wanted a gradualist approach, with a conscious attempt to minimise unemployment. Komarek warned that the Klaus programme of full liberalisation of prices and exchange convertibility (for CSFR enterprises) from January 1991 was foolhardy: the monopolistic position of many state-owned firms, and the many imbalances and rigidities in the economy, could aggravate inflation and unemployment, as well as causing a rise in foreign borrowing.

Klaus went full steam ahead, with the result not only that social tensions increased within the CSFR, but that tension between the two parts also mounted. Before the Second World War, the Czechs (as opposed to the Slovaks) had had one of the highest standards of living in Europe. Under the communist regime, it was the Slovak part of the economy which became more closely geared to the Soviet system, especially in the build-up of its defence industries, and other heavy industries. The pre-war gap between Slovakia and the Czech economy narrowed under communism, but this left Slovakia more vulnerable to the collapse of the USSR. Much higher prices for basic materials from Russia, and the drastic fall in demand for its goods, combined to hit the Slovak economy in 1990–91. The additional impact of the short-run deterioration in economic prospects caused by the Klaus reforms both aggravated the Slovak economic crisis and gave Slovak nationalists a perfect scapegoat for their separatist demands. "Hence politics began to shift leftwards in Slovakia and resistance to rapid market economic reform became bound up with the desire for greater autonomy."[49] By the summer of 1992 the separatists were in the ascendant.

The Klaus reforms were ambitious, to say the least. The CSFR was the most backward of the trio of Poland, Hungary and Czechoslovakia – the most tainted by communism, with the least experience of market-orientated reforms before. The risks being taken with price liberalisation and inflation were severe – there was glib talk of would-be sophisticated wage indexation agreements to keep the fall in real wages to 12 per cent in 1991 and 10 per cent in 1992.[50] These are the kind of reductions in living standards that are very unlikely to ward off social unrest.

Long term hopes were being pinned on foreign direct investment – such as Volkswagen's takeover of Skoda and judgements by banks – in the end "reliance on market forces to bring about the required restructuring of East European industry entails relying on the financial institutions, especially the banks, to make correct judgements about the long term viability of different firms (or even entire branches)."[51] The worry being expressed in the CSFR in 1991 was that the monopolistic position of big industries would enable the inefficient to survive, while bank credit was being withdrawn from potentially viable firms.[52]

Once again, the impression given by the early stages of the transition from communism to capitalism in the former Czechoslovakia is that macro-economic policies from within the walls of North American universities have been at a premium, but the market economy to which they apply will take a long time to be formed. One Czech economist has suggested: "This overly liberal and macro-economic approach to economic policy may, in the face of a present sluggish state of the evolution of markets, become the rock on which Czechoslovak economic reform founders." As noted, even the best macro-economic policies require a macro-economy to which they can be applied.

The scale of the problems facing Eastern Europe was a theme of the first annual meeting of the Board of Governors of the European

Bank for Reconstruction and Development in Budapest in April 1992. As one official summarised: "The situation is tough. The recipes we thought would work are not working. Privatisation has not spread as fast as we hoped. For macro-economic policies, you need a micro-economic build-up."

The EBRD Governor for Poland complained that the country might be suffering from "reform fatigue," noting that "problems to be solved in the course of transition are by no means straightforward and there are no ready-made prescriptions how to deal with them." In particular, while encouraging the spread of capitalism to their country, foreign creditors were not willing to take any commercial risk: "Virtually all foreign credits are available only against state or major state-owned banks' guarantees ... So, paradoxically, credit assistance intended to support the transition to private-ownership based, free-market economy may be utilised only through increased initial involvements of the state."

In April 1992 the success of privatisation at a superficial level was apparent to anybody who walked the streets of Budapest, or who thumbed through that most capitalist of hotel bedside bibles, the Yellow Pages. Indeed an EBRD study suggested that more than half of the "small assets" of Poland, Hungary and Czechoslovakia had been privatised.[53] "However," declared the EBRD, "the pace of larger privatisation (those enterprises with more than 100 employees) has been disappointing so far and systemic restructuring efforts have barely been started." Hungary was in the lead, so far, but even Hungary had privatised fewer than 10 per cent of its enterprises. Only a handful of medium to large enterprises had been privatised in the former Soviet Union. At the current pace of privatisation in the former Communist countries, more than half the state enterprises would remain in the public sector for over a generation – if they survived, that is: it was being increasingly recognised that much of the communist inheritance of "enterprises" was simply not viable in the medium term.

The general view among bankers and officials connected with the former communist bloc in mid-1992 was that the entrepreneurial spirit had been revived more in Hungary than in Poland or Czechoslovakia. But thus far it was apparent principally among small shopkeepers, taxi drivers and consultants, rather than in the heavy and consumer goods industries which are the backbone of a modern economy. It did strike one however that, given their relatively small populations, it might be a mistake to think in terms of rebuilding an entire complex economy in countries such as Hungary and the CSFR, and a certain degree of specialisation might be called for – Hungarians cited financial services and computer software as potential growth areas: indeed, Hungary boasted one world market leader in "architectural software" for Macintosh computers.

The catastrophic fall in demand and output in the former Soviet bloc did not produce much in the way of a search for new markets. Many observers have noted a tendency for enterprises to sit back and hope somebody will come to their rescue – as if the old command economy would be the *deus ex machina* with new orders. One Hungarian firm, Videoton, has been in the process of reconstruction after seeing a collapse in demand for its defence electronics, and a fall in Soviet demand for its TV sets from 200,000 a year to 20,000 in 1991. Euroinvest, the privatisation consultancy which bought Videoton, said in April 1992 that the firm had had 25,000 employees five years earlier, 12,500 when taken over, but that the workforce was immediately halved to 6,000. A typical Hungarian concern was: would there be a major switch from the use of Hungary's Ikarus buses in the former Soviet Union to makes such as Mercedes? Unemployment had quadrupled from under 2 per cent in 1990 to over 8 per cent at the end of 1991 (GDP having plunged 8 per cent), but was widely expected to double again by the end of 1992. Given the collapse in real wages during 1991 and 1992, the surge in unemployment was hardly a testimonial to the classical economists of North America who see falls in real wages as the textbook answer to unemployment. Indeed, the substantial fall in real wages in Eastern Europe generally "proved economically counterproductive, socially unfair and politically dangerous".[54] Falling real wages actually *reduced* the incentive to reallocate labour to more productive uses, and allowed "inefficient sectors to maintain over-employment and inhibited productivity growth".[55]

Little Hungary had so far received some 60 per cent of the total of foreign direct investment in eastern Europe. Germany, which is also the biggest foreign investor in Poland and the CSFR (as well, of course, as in the former East Germany) was also the biggest investor in Hungary in 1991. With the entry of General Electric, Ford and General Motors into Hungary, the US was now in the lead. But the cries in this most attractive, to Westerners, of former communist economies, were becoming desperate. "Unemployment is high and increasing, we need capital investment, we cannot get out of this hole without help," said Professor Joseph Veress, General Secretary of the Hungarian Economics Association. "Hungary today," said the Prime Minister Jozsef Antall, "is in a recession that is depressing living standards, hampering investments and thus slowing down the modernisation of infrastructure and of productive structures . . . our economy needs a large volume of foreign capital . . ."

But private foreign investment flows into Central and Eastern Europe had amounted to less than ECU 4 billion ($4.8 bn) and to the former USSR less than ECU 400 million ($480 million) between the fall of the Berlin Wall and spring 1992.

While pleading for foreign capital, the Hungarians were proving such hard bargainers that, although they were leading other countries, the privatisation process was still considered painfully slow. "They try to squeeze more out of a stone than you can really squeeze out of a stone," said one Western accountant.[56] Its cautious approach in this matter might prove more sensible than the gadarene rush towards privatisation in the CSFR. There was a naïve view in Prague that everything would come right for the economy when Finance Minister Klaus "sold" the economy to the people early in 1992. All would win prizes – "everyone will get vouchers". While Hungary was moving cautiously towards 49 per cent foreign participation in Matav, the state telephone company, Czecho-slovakia had seen some 8 million people (half the population) subscribe $35 each for vouchers which, later in the year, in the words of *The Wall Street Journal Europe*, "allow them to bid for shares in a massive privatisation blow-out sale". This would certainly produce dramatic figures for share-ownership (far more than in the UK, for instance) but it was hardly relevant to the management of business. Indeed, *The Wall Street Journal Europe* suggested: "It might reduce the scope for drawing foreign capital and expertise."

One of the most bizarre aspects of the collapse of communism has been the way that, in the former Soviet Union itself, the most primitive forms of capitalism and market economy have come to the surface. By spring 1992 Moscow and other Russian cities had spawned a proliferation of street markets, modern versions of medieval bazaars, where citizens would sell their possessions in order to finance the purchase of basic necessities whose prices had been "deregulated". A senior Western banking official who travelled round the republics advising on financial reform found a world of feudal baronies, where local chieftains, formerly party officials, ruled the roost. The pursuit of the free market had reached the point where, as it were, anarchy ruled: at one stage he was told he could certainly travel from A to B by plane – provided he personally bought the fuel. "Yeltsin issues orders," this official said, "but do they reach beyond the walls of his office?"

The EBRD President Jacques Attali asked: "Do we want to build a market economy or an economy dominated by the mafia? It is ill-advised to free market forces in the short term without first having put in place the necessary institutions. Without such institutions, there is a black market, not a market in the proper sense."[57]

On average, industrial production, gross domestic product and real purchasing power fell by 15 per cent in the year to spring 1992 in the former Soviet Union and Eastern Europe. Such a collapse of economic activity is unprecedented in the post-war OECD world, and comparable to the disruption caused by the Great Depression. But severe tariff and non-tariff barriers affected the import of agricultural products and steel, textiles and chemicals from eastern to western Europe. One Easterner observed: "We live always in a shortage economy. The difference lies in where the shortage is – whether it is in the shops or, as now, in our pockets."

In Eastern Europe the extreme free market theorists had managed to achieve what, in different circumstances, they had achieved in the US and UK in the early 1980s – policies nominally designed to assist the supply-side which in practice made the supply-side worse. The difference was that the starting point was a much graver, and altogether different, economic situation, and the penalty for going wrong was also much more serious (although not necessarily for the foreign advisers, who would merely pack their suitcases).

In the former Soviet Union, where the approach to Big Bang therapy was that much more delayed, there was an estimated drop of 17 per cent in output during 1991. But this was more a reflection of the economic structure falling apart in advance of the famous market-orientated reforms and stabilisation policies. The impact of these was largely yet to come. In 1991–92 autarchy and anarchy prevailed over the disintegrating structure of the former Soviet Union, with the old command structure collapsing, and the very worst features of capitalism rearing their ugly head.

Enterprises and regions turned in on themselves, with multiple trade restrictions imposed not only between the fifteen former republics, but also within the Russian Federation. In Leningrad/St Petersburg, for instance, the mayor Anatoly Sobchak, became the representative of factory managers whose main concern was the provision of food for their workers. "Many big factories," Anatole Lieven reported, "are no longer anything that a Western economist could recognise as a factory: they are food procurement units." The factory's transport section, or its construction unit, would repair to the collective farms, where they would work in return for food, which was then sold to other "effectively non-working workers" at subsidised prices.[58]

"Here we have factories which made rockets that went to the moon," said one St Petersburg colonel. "Are they now supposed to get rid of nine-tenths of their staff and compete with the Third World in making cheap pots and pans?"

While the flow of production within the former Soviet Union was disrupted, and the bulk of the official economy became fragmented – a case of every factory manager for himself and his local loyalties – the once hidden black market economy increased and multiplied. But the figures who counted as, or were aiming to be, new millionaires, were not engaged in investment or production. They were classic "spiv" traders. There was the man who took belts full of dollars to South Korea and returned with fashionable training shoes to be sold from his 15th floor apartment base. People who bought cars in Poland could sell them in Moscow for a profit, in 48 hours, that exceeded a university professor's salary for ten years. More ambitious businessmen were trading oil, gas and commodities for "hard currency" with which to import cheap consumer goods. And of course there was a proliferation of activities to attract foreign tourists and businessmen in Russia's "dollar economy", where visitors were happy to spend what to the Russians was a month's, or even a year's, salary on everything from smart consumer goods to the services of a profession that was far older than communism. This was wild west, or perhaps wild east, capitalism, but it was deficient in the kind of productive capacity required to build a decent market economy beneath the froth.

Although inflation had certainly taken its toll with the price liberalisation measures of 1991 and 1992 (and aggravation through shortages and hoarding) the so called "market rate" for the rouble against the dollar had become absurd. Tradeable Russian goods were selling, in roubles, for a twentieth of the world value. Thus the rouble was grossly undervalued on a purchasing power parity basis. Hence the emphasis of both Moscow and some Group of Seven members on the need for a currency stabilisation fund, to give Russia the foreign exchange reserves with which to keep the rouble at a more realistic level. Meanwhile the desire of many of the separate fifteen "successor states" to flex their independent muscles with their own currency did not look as wild as it appeared. Under the system by which the Kazakhstans of this world had no budgetary disciplines but shared a common currency, fiscal and monetary policy were only distantly related, and a kind of competitive inflation process developed. Separate currencies, or separate currency blocs, would "bring the governments of the former Soviet republics face to face with the monetary consequences of their fiscal imprudence," it was hoped by a growing consensus of despairing economists.[59]

As the G7 tentatively acted on former President Nixon's proposal for an historic gesture to help the former Soviet Union in April 1992, it certainly seemed that, in the absence of such assistance, the former communist bloc would have stood very little chance of making the transition with which even the East European countries were having severe difficulties. But *would* Russia and the other states pull off the move to a market economy, as opposed to the unfortunate combination of a disintegrating economy and fringe cowboy capitalism, even *with* large-scale assistance from the West? By August 1992 the divide between the theoreticians and the practitioners seemed to be immense, and the early costs of the experiment with free-market capitalism were taking their toll.[60] The potential for political instability seemed endless, and, quite apart from the widespread concern about the weakness of Russian democracy and the chances of an eventual military takeover, there was the nagging underlying question: do the Russians and the "successor states" really want to embrace the spectre of Western capitalism anyway?

7

The German Model

The economic failure of communism led to glasnost and perestroika. The new mood in Moscow made it possible for the Berlin Wall to come down without reprisals from Soviet tanks. The liberal mood in Czechoslovakia and Hungary allowed emigrants from East Germany a free, if convoluted, route to West Germany in the months leading up to the collapse of the Wall. But the mass movement of hundreds of thousands of East Germans to the prosperous West German Federal Republic threatened to endanger the social stability of West Germany itself. Thus the carrot of seizing the historic chance offered by Gorbachev's regime to reunite Germany was accompanied by the stick of mounting alarm about what might happen if East Germans were not offered the promise of economic incentives to remain where they were. The monthly flow of migrants from east to west became an important economic and political indicator during 1990.

The West German Chancellor Helmut Kohl had the historic vision to seize the opportunity of German reunification when doubts were being voiced by both the British Prime Minister Margaret Thatcher and President Mitterrand of France. More controversial were the terms on which Kohl conducted the economic and monetary union with East Germany in mid-1990, and the promises he made – before being re-elected later that year – that the costs of reunification could be met without higher taxes in the West. In particular, by opting for a one-for-one exchange rate between the D-mark and the Ostmark, the West German Government ensured that large parts of East Germany's industry would be rendered uncompetitive in both the German and international markets. The politics of the terms of reunification were all-important to Kohl. The main reason why the Chancellor opted for the "one for one" exchange rate, and promised higher wages, was to win the vote for his own party in the subsequent election.

If the East German economy had continued as a separate country, some sort of exchange rate could have been determined which allowed for the differing productivity levels in East and West.

According to official estimates made in mid 1991, the actual productivity levels in the former East Germany averaged a mere 28 per cent of West Germany's. Adopting the same currency value for the products of East German industry was bad enough. But the powerful movement in the former communist region to bring wage levels up towards Western Germany's levels compounded the problem. What was more, the West German Government and industrialists soon found that large chunks of the eastern bloc's shipbuilding, chemical and textile firms were extraordinarily backward; and even the electronics sector, which had been highly thought of in the West, was much further behind western standards than had been expected. The "people's paradise" had also neglected the quality of its infrastructure and hospitals, and allowed concern about pollution simply to pass it by.

The Bundesbank President Karl Otto-Pöhl had vehemently opposed the one-to-one exchange rate, which amounted to a multiple up-valuation of the old Ostmark. The Bundesbank's advice was ignored – an ironic example of the limits to its much prized independence – and early in 1991 Pöhl described German economic and monetary union as "a disaster". Having thus been overruled, he subsequently resigned.

For the German Government, making a success of economic and monetary union with the former GDR was not only important in itself: it became a test case for the success of the whole Eastern bloc's adaptation to the spectre of capitalism. Given Germany's crucial relationship historically and geographically with Eastern Europe, to say nothing of the fears of massive migration if things went wrong, it was more important for Germany than for most to facilitate a smooth transition in the east. But the process of monetary union with eastern Germany can be seen as the absorption of a region into an economy, rather than the rebuilding of an entire economy as was being attempted in Poland, Hungary and Czechoslovakia.

As such, it probably qualifies for the title of the most expensive regional rescue-operation in history. Transfers of funds from Western Germany accounted for some 60 per cent of the former East Germany's GDP in 1991. In order to improve the infrastructure, subsidise uncompetitive industries, invest in new ones and finance huge unemployment costs, the West Germans were diverting about DM 140 bn a year to the eastern part of their country alone. This was the equivalent of nearly £50 bn, or $90 bn a year – almost twice the combined OECD countries' aid to developing countries, and four times the assistance contemplated to the much larger former Soviet Union. Some of this transfer represented physical investment by West

German firms, but a large part was accounted for by direct transfers from the West German budget, bringing the budget deficit to over 5 per cent of GDP. The aim was to save what could be saved from the existing capital stock; to make ambitious new capital investments in both the private sector and the public sector infrastructure; and to provide unemployment and other social benefits. As an IMF study noted: "It is clearly essential to the success of economic integration that capital flow east rather than labour flow west, and that income growth and new opportunities are sufficient to meet reasonable aspirations on the part of the residents of East Germany."[1]

The Treuhandanstalt (or Trust Fund) found it necessary to "liquidate" about a quarter of the first 2,000 enterprises it handled for privatisation. The provision of jobs, rather than original property rights, became an important criterion in mid-1991 for the allocation of enterprises to the private sector. Existing enterprises were hit by both the competitive losses associated with the one-to-one exchange rate and the rise in wage levels, and the collapse in business from eastern Europe and the USSR. Of course, the loss in competitiveness aggravated the east German economy's losses of business in a situation where orders generally were falling in the former communist bloc.

A senior official in Bonn commented in May 1991: "In an ideal world we should simply have closed the place down, and started again with a green field site." As it was, to build up the economy of the eastern region in a way which provided employment and prevented mass migration to the western part of the country, the Bonn Government estimated that throughout the 1990s there would have to be an average annual rate of investment of DM 140 bn in the public and private sectors combined.[2] Terrifying forecasts of 50 per cent unemployment rates in parts of East Germany were circulating during 1991. The ultimate irony was that, in the face of this short-term "disaster", in Herr Pöhl's words, the easterners had been adding to the problems of the industries that employed them by using their new found political freedom to spend their money on West German goods.

In the closing months of 1991, the wilder unemployment forecasts were not being fulfilled, because various employment protection policies (i.e. subsidies) remained in being. There were hopes that, having plunged by 70 per cent since 1989, manufacturing output was steadying and even picking up in response to new investment. With new construction in the lead, the Bonn Government was forecasting a 10 per cent rise in East German GNP for 1992.[3] But American observers concluded in the autumn of 1991 that "high costs and low productivity of labour presently make East German production unprofitable in almost all sectors at any given level of output."

The general tendency of most observers was to assume that, with the power of the West German economy behind it, and the political determination – nay necessity – to succeed, the former East Germany was better placed than the other Eastern economies to face up to the spectre of capitalism. West German subsidies would provide the infrastructure; and the basic legal, financial and social framework required for a market economy was all there in the very concept of German monetary union or German Economic, Monetary and Social Union (GEMSU), to give it its full title.

Indeed, what was on offer to Eastern Germany was the equivalent of a very-special Marshall Plan, far bigger in scope than anything conceived of for post-war Europe. What was not on offer was the potential attraction to multinational firms of an educated, but low-cost workforce, as in countries such as Poland, Hungary and Czechoslovakia. This was an educated, but high-cost labour force, and it was hardly surprising that the vast majority of early investors in East Germany were from West Germany – some 90 to 95 per cent according to official estimates in 1991.

The determination of the German Government to make GEMSU work was fully apparent in 1991, although there was a question mark over how long the younger generation might feel the necessary level of commitment – especially since, notwithstanding Herr Köhl's earlier promises, taxes were temporarily raised to help pay the subsidies towards eastern Germany. The other problem which soon made itself felt was the impact of higher interest rates in slowing down both the West German economy and those linked to it via the European exchange rate mechanism as the Bundesbank struggled to keep the inflationary impact of GEMSU under control.

Although widely acknowledged to be a model European economy – probably the most admired model – the West German economy had not grown noticeably fast in the 1980s. Indeed, in international forums such as the OECD and the G7, the West Germans often came under assault from other countries for apparently being perfectly content with export-led growth, and for not going out of their way to stimulate the domestic economy. There were several years when domestic demand hardly grew at all in West Germany. The Americans, in particular, felt the Germans were not doing enough to contribute to the growth of world trade, and even Mrs Thatcher – that arch non-interventionist – had been known to express frustration with German economic policy.

It was at about the time some ill-judged articles began to appear in the British press (1988) suggesting Germany had caught "the British disease" that German growth began to speed up again. The combination of an export boom, and faster growth in domestic demand (fuelled by tax cuts in 1990), produced an investment boom in Germany even before the effects of unification. When the world economy slowed down in 1990, "exports" from West Germany, which had grown by 8 and a half per cent in 1988 and 1989, also grew by 8 and a half per cent – but the third year's figure included "exports" to eastern Germany.[4]

There was thus a West German economic boom in 1990 and early 1991. But tax increases to help finance the costs of reunification, and a marked slowdown in world trade, affected German growth in the course of 1991. And, as wage earners in the Western part hit back against the costs of unification to them, wage demands for increases of up to 10 per cent began to take on a British aspect. Having been overruled on the terms of unification, the Bundesbank flexed its muscles over monetary policy in 1991–92, and introduced several increases in interest rates aimed at cooling the economy. In 1991, with German industry concentrating on the requirements of the East, Germany went into current account balance of payments deficit for the first time in many years. Forecasts of the inflation rate rising to 4 and a half or 5 per cent caused great concern about the possibility of even tighter monetary policies, and the general expectation of official and private forecasts was that the reunification boom would slow down in 1992, which, indeed, it did. But the Bundesbank's truculence had some impact in moderating the wage bargaining climate.

Thus, ideas that German reunification would act as an economic "locomotive" to the rest of Europe had some validity – the rest of Europe benefited from a marked increase in exports to Germany in 1990–91 – but were to prove short-lived. The successful absorption of Eastern Germany into the West German economy was the overriding domestic, political and economic objective of the German government; the principal aim of the Bundesbank was to ensure that this did not endanger its reputation as the inflationary watchdog of Europe. Indeed, in the closing months of 1991, the importance of the Bundesbank as the custodian of economic virtue was dominating another important unification process: the goal of European economic and monetary union.

Before his resignation of July 1991, the President of the Bundesbank, Herr Pöhl, had fought hard against the revival of proposals for European economic and monetary union. There had been such proposals during the 1970s, and they had come to nothing in the face of the harsh realities of economics and politics. In the second half of the 1980s, however, the concept – always an ultimate "goal" of the Founding Fathers of the European Community – had been revived once again by France, with a big push being given to

EMU, as it was known, by the European Commission and its President, Jacques Delors, a French socialist politician, and a former finance minister.

In a sense the Delors Report on monetary union was dreamed up at a time when "Eurocrats" had nothing better to do. The work of the Delors Committee was conducted by European central bankers, who were instructed by the European Council (the EC heads of Government) to produce a "conditional report", in their "private capacity" – as individuals, not central bankers. This was a somewhat surrealistic approach, and of course the central bankers behaved like central bankers, drawing on their considerable resources of advisers, and ending up with a blueprint that owed more to their central banking views than their "private" views. The basic brief was: if there were to be economic and monetary union in Europe, how should we (the politicians) go about it? What the politicians received was a harsh, central banker's view of necessary conditions, with the emphasis almost entirely on counter-inflation policy, the goal being price stability rather than economic growth or low unemployment. After the publication of the Delors Report, a phenomenal amount of the energy of European finance ministry and central bank officials was devoted to detailed technical work, including much dotting the "i's and crossing the "t's".

Both during the preparation of the Delors Report, and in the course of the subsequent work which led to the adoption of the goal of monetary union in Rome in December 1990, and the attachment of a formal target date at Maastricht in December 1991, a number of central bank officials privately expressed their astonishment at the way the politicians were so happily accepting so much of what they had recommended in the "conditional" report. "When the politicians wake up to what all this implies for their own powers, they are bound to backtrack," one senior official observed at an early stage in the process. Yet, in the end, the European Council accepted a tough set of conditions on targets for inflation, interest rates and budget deficits at their Maastricht Summit, and the UK was left isolated in demanding what became known as an "opt-out clause". Even Britain's reluctance was generally seen as having more to do with concerns, on the part of Mrs Thatcher and the right wing, about "sovereignty", and the Conservative government's anxiety to appease its own anti-Europe lobby, than with serious questioning of the hard economics of monetary union.

The Delors "blueprint" for Europe had been conceived before the events of 1989 brought the oppressed citizens of Eastern Europe out into the glare of capitalist sunlight. It was soon to become apparent that this *annus mirabilis* also represented the unfreezing of European history, and the revival of all manner of nationalist, ethnic and religious tensions. The amazing events of 1989 onwards might have seemed enough for the EC to cope with, without the additional burden of implementing the (amended) Delores blueprint. On the contrary: by contrast with the view of the British Foreign Office that the "widening" of the EC – the entry of EFTA (European Free Trade Area) countries such as Sweden and Austria, and coming to terms with the desire of Eastern Europe for "association" with, and ultimately membership of, the EC – should take precedence over the "deepening" process of Delors and After, both Paris and Bonn decided that events in Eastern Europe in fact added weight to the case for EMU.

The whole Delors process had been led by the French because, under the exchange rate mechanism of the European Monetary System they found that their economic policies were in effect subject to the views and actions of the German Bundesbank. The French saw the chance for greater influence for themselves under a European central bank, on whose board they would be represented. But the fall of the Wall, and the German unification process (which, as we have seen, President Mitterrand at first tried to resist) added considerably to French fears of German domination of Europe. (Whether *anything* could prevent German domination of Europe is another matter.) From being primarily motivated by economic consider-ations, the French push for closer European Union also gained momentum from the desire to tie Germany down in Europe and avoid the resurrection of Greater Germany. Somewhat to their surprise, and to the considerable chagrin of the British, Bonn reacted to the events of 1989 and 1990 by seizing upon economic and monetary union, provided this was accompanied by a big push towards political union in Europe, with much greater powers for the European Parliament in Strasbourg. The generation in charge of German policies was as desirous as any country of tying Germany down in Europe – of a European Germany, rather than a German Europe – and of resisting a recrudescence of old, pre-war, nationalist pressures.

The Bundesbank, and other sceptics of EMU, had hoped that the enormous problems associated with Germany's own monetary union, after unification, would give pause for thought. Herr Pöhl had delivered a number of speeches pointing out the moral of the lessons German Monetary Union had for European Monetary Union. These had little impact within Germany, and it was not until around the time of the Maastricht December 1991 European Summit itself that the German public seemed to wake up to the prospect of the loss of the D-mark under a Single Currency, the Ecu. By then the European leaders had committed themselves to adopting a single currency in

1997 or 1999. Meanwhile, although it hoped that EMU would somehow go away, the Bundesbank, under both Pöhl and his successor, Dr Helmut Schlesinger, had endeavoured to ensure that the conditions for EMU would be as strict as – preferably stricter than – the statutes of the Bundesbank itself.

The Bundesbank and others had repeatedly pointed to the difficulties of uniting different countries, with different economies and different productivity levels, under the same currency regime.[5] Under normal arrangements between countries, an economy that loses competitiveness against others, either through higher inflation or poorer productivity (or a mixture of both), is free to devalue its currency. This puts it back, at least for a time, on an equal trading footing, enabling it to export more, and import less (or prevent its imports growing quite so fast).

In the absence of the freedom to vary the exchange rate (a condition which occurs by definition if an economy enters a "single currency" area) poor economic performance is accompanied by loss of business and employment, and ultimately, by emigration.

Within countries, the poor economic performance of particular regions can be compensated by subsidies from the central government. The Mac Dougall Report, 1977, found evidence that up to 40 per cent of regional economic differences can be compensated in this way. (Within the UK, Northern Ireland is an example of a region that is heavily subsidised from the centre). But Mac Dougall and his colleagues estimated that, in order to provide sufficient regional compensation for the likely casualties of a single currency union, the Brussels budget would have to be raised from about 1 and a quarter per cent of EC gross domestic product to between 5 to 7 per cent. Such a change never looked politically likely in Western Europe, even before the question of the financing of help for Eastern Europe arose. Although German monetary union, as we have seen, was a special case, its enormous costs nevertheless provided a graphic illustration of the problems of currency unions. But such questions were little debated, with public attention tending to focus on the obvious attractions of not having to change money as one travelled around Europe if a single currency were indeed to be introduced.

Whether the emphasis was put on a European Germany or a German Europe, it was difficult to contest the view that Germany had emerged as the dominant economy of Western Europe. This was apparent not only in the way German economic policy was exercising an hegemonic influence over the rest of the European economy, but also in the general admiration for German economic and industrial success. The European Community itself had been conceived by the Founding Fathers primarily as a means of creating sufficient union and harmony between Germany and the rest of Europe – especially France – to ensure that there would never be another war in Europe – or, at least, in Western Europe. The end was political, but the means were economic – beginning with the European Coal and Steel Community in the early 1950s, and continuing with the customs-union of the European Economic Community, the setting up of the European Monetary System in the late 1970s, and the Rome/Maastricht goal of economic and monetary union, and a single European currency, by 1997 or 1999.

For much of the post-war period France had been seen as a dirigiste economy, with a high degree of state intervention and "indicative" planning, including state control of some banks and consumer industries. The state sector accounted for only slightly more than the OECD average of around 40 per cent of GDP, but – after a shaky start – from the mid-1950s the confident leadership of the elite of the French educational system seemed to be all-pervasive, with links stretching across the public and private sectors, and a general impression to the outside that this was a successful system which knew where it was going. The advent of President Mitterrand's government in 1981 saw a short-lived burst of independence and "socialism against the trend" of President Reagan's United States and Mrs Thatcher's Britain. When a burst of expansion and a series of social measures and wage concessions to the unions brought chaos in the foreign exchange markets, Mitterrand retreated from "socialism" and France adopted a prolonged period of orthodox economic policies, designed to bring French inflation down to the level of Germany's.

France had for years seemed to be inflicted with an inflation rate which one British official sarcastically described as "9.9 per cent, recurring". After being forced to devalue early on in the "Mitterrand Experiment", France then adopted at least some of the tone of the more "market-oriented" economic policies which were the prevailing fashion in many other quarters.

The French Government's actions did not necessarily speak as loudly as its words in this respect, notably during the brief stint as Prime Minister of Madam Edith Cresson (1990–92). The French in practice continued to manifest protectionist tendencies towards, for example, imports of Japanese motor cars; and whatever the spirit of the freer competition enshrined in the rules of the European Single Market (due to be inaugurated on 1 January 1993) old habits die hard with regard to the subsidising of state-controlled industries.

In macro-economic policy, however, the French desire to emulate German inflation rates was such that relative price stability was bought at the expense of employment; by the end of 1991 the OECD was forecasting an inflation rate of 2.9 per cent for France in 1992[6] compared with 4.0 per cent for Germany. But the price paid was that unemployment was likely to be twice the German rate, at over 10 per cent of the workforce. The boost to economic activity in Germany during 1990 and 1991 because of reunification was often described as "Keynesian" – and certainly the Germans liked to give the impression that the unification boom was also stimulating other European countries: the volume of German imports rose by an unusually high 10 per cent or so in both 1990 and 1991. But the assistance to the French economy from this source was not enough to counteract other factors, including the impact of maintaining a strong franc in the exchange rate mechanism, and in effect being dependent on German monetary policy. As German interest rates rose in the closing months of 1991, and remained high in the early months of 1992, because of the Bundesbank's onslaught on inflation caused by the unification boom, the "Keynesian boost" was defused, and German economic policy became a drag on the whole of the EC.

In its almost slavish devotion to the German lead in economic policy, France was being followed by Britain. Having delayed putting the pound into the exchange rate mechanism of the European Monetary System until October 1990, the British Government was imposing the kind of painful adjustment – low, or in its case, no economic growth, and high unemployment – in the search for a better inflation performance on German lines – that France had undergone during the 1980s. But whereas, under a single currency, it would, by definition, be impossible to alter the exchange rate against other European countries, it was perfectly possible to do so under the rules of the ERM. It was just that, in both the French and the British cases, national pride had become a more important consideration than the familiar trade-off between more basic economic objectives – at least until mid-1992.

At times of economic depression and high unemployment, people naturally feel threatened, and all manner of unsavoury prejudices tend to be unbottled. "Orthodox" macro-economic policies in France were exacerbating racial tensions in 1991–92, with blatantly racialist demagogues such as Le Pen having a field day, and even more decent politicians such as Valery Giscard d'Estaing and Jacques Chirac making speeches with racialist overtones. The strains of unification were also being felt in Germany, with outbursts from the extreme right, and public sector strikes over the costs of unification. In Britain, where it was at last being more widely recognised that there had been no "economic miracle" under Mrs Thatcher, the general state of confidence in the economy was at a decidedly low ebb; industrialists, fighting for survival under one of the worst recessions since the 1930s, were cutting back investment as they approached the 1992 "Single European Market"; and homelessness was a growing social ill after years during which public sector housing construction had been cut back in the pursuit of Mrs Thatcher's ideal of a thriving free market sector. Yet the Major Government in 1990–92 seemed paralysed by the desire to achieve German-style low inflation at all costs – although, perversely, this did not in the end threaten its own 1992 electoral prospects.

At the time of reunification, the Bundesbank itself would have been perfectly content with a revaluation of the D-mark: this would have eased the inflationary pressures of unification, among other things by encouraging German consumers to buy more cheaply from abroad, during a period when so many resources which previously went into the German export surplus were being absorbed by the rebuilding of Eastern Germany. But neither France nor the UK wanted a realignment of the ERM. While complaining about the impact of German monetary policy, the other major European countries were in fact doing much to make it as painful as possible for themselves. Just to ram things home about what it was prepared, and not prepared, to do, the Bundesbank made sure that the rules for "stage two" of the approach to economic and monetary union (due to commence on 1 January 1994) would not involve any dilution of Germany's control over monetary policy.

The Anglo-French pursuit of German-style economic success was subjugating quite a lot to the conquest of inflation – as luck would have it, at a time when the stance of German counter-inflation policy was even more aggressive than usual, because of the impact of unification. Paradoxically, the Bundesbank itself was never as confident of its own counter-inflationary powers as observers from abroad. During the long post-war period when German inflation rates were negligible by the standards of other countries, by far the most important point stressed by Germans themselves was the horror of inflation which was felt in their bones – and which had a benign effect on the wage bargaining climate. All major industrial countries are subject, from time to time, to such inflationary shocks from abroad as those provided by OPEC in the two "oil shocks" of the 1970s and early 1980s. Also, at certain stages of the business cycle, or in circumstances where monopolistic pricing is dominant, rapid increases in profits can be inflationary. But, on the whole, some two thirds of producers' costs in industrial nations are accounted for by wages and salaries, and it is differing rates of wage inflation that explain the major differences in recorded inflation rates.

Until the "unification shock" produced unaccustomed demands for increases in wages and salaries, during 1991–92, the Bundesbank had a relatively easy time conducting monetary and counter-inflation policy, because underlying inflationary pressures were that much less than in most other European countries. This happy state reflected a greater consensus about economic and social policy than certainly existed in, for example, the UK.

The consensus was apparent at both the macro and micro level. Under the German "social market economy" there was a productive compromise between the raw spirit of capitalism and the needs of the wider population for the assurance of a reasonable safety net. There was less confrontation between capital and labour than in the "Anglo-Saxon" model familiar in the US and UK – as well as in Australia and New Zealand. As the German Government puts it: "A central feature of the German social market economy is the co-operation between unions and management because they recognise they are economically dependent on each other . . . free collective bargaining has to take public interest into account."[7]

A great sense of harmony between what the Germans and other Continental countries like to call "the social partners" was apparent to any visitor from Mrs Thatcher's England during the 1980s. Similarly, the general theme of German "corporate governance" was one in which managements had closer, longer term links with banks than in economies such as the US and UK, and the spirit of "hostile takeovers" was notable by its absence. This pragmatic approach to industry and business was buttressed at the macro-economic policy level by an ethos which was less vulnerable to fashion than in the US and UK, with a pronounced emphasis on continuity of policy, rather than lurching from one extreme to another. Many international officials who had previously been critical of Germany's apparently self-serving approach to international meetings on "policy co-ordination" had come to admire the Germans for the results they produced.

By spring 1992, however, things were turning very sour. While there were now some signs of uplift in the former east German economy, the budgetary costs were continuing apace. It was increasingly recognised that the terms on which reunification had been conducted were a heavy burden on western Germany. First the government had said tax increases would not be necessary; later there was a temporary, special income surcharge. There was nothing like the sort of tax increase required to offset the costs, and the Bonn government was warning of dire restrictions on public expenditure in the West for the next few years.

The way frustration really showed through was in the wage claims made to offset the inflationary consequences of unification. Most of the weight of combating inflation was being placed on the Bundesbank's shoulders and the central bank was trying to slow monetary growth, and encourage savings, with its high interest rate policy. The burst of public sector strikes in April 1992 was a sign of a very severe strain, and even reactivated suggestions that Germany had caught the British disease. Such ideas were far-fetched – in similar circumstances the British inflation rate would no doubt have been double or treble the 4–5 per cent rate that was causing all the trouble. But the general outburst of *schadenfreude* at Germany's troubles, coupled with bitter attacks on its general economic policy stance by the US and UK, did not bode well for future international economic co-operation.

Bonn was not only financing the costs of unification: it had also – inevitably, given its geographical position in Europe – undertaken the lion's share of recent financial assistance to the former Soviet Union, including, for instance, much of the cost of removing Russian troops from German soil. There was not much enthusiasm among the German public for further contributions to the EC budget to finance the transition of the poorer countries of Western and Southern Europe towards economic union; and the prospect of the loss of the treasured D-mark (due to be replaced by the Ecu under monetary union) was a further bone of contention.

One of the politicians who had worked hardest for *ostpolitic* and the collapse of communism was Hans-Dietrich Genscher, who resigned from Helmut Kohl's government on 27 April 1992, after eighteen years as Germany's foreign minister. Genscher had quietly spotted President Gorbachev as a man "to do business with" several years before Mrs Thatcher. On the day he resigned he declared: "Germany's foreign policy direction is clearly set, and the commitment of our foreign policy to Europe is unshakable." But the June 1992 referendum in Denmark reflected dissatisfaction with the "centralising" tendencies of Brussels, and in France, too, there were signs of a political reaction against the Maastricht deal; with the EC seemingly impotent in dealing with the civil war in Yugoslavia, the question had to be asked whether the impact of the spectre of capitalism on Europe was not putting intolerable strains on the European vision. The Soviet threat had bound European nations together after 1945. Was the realisation of the Cold War aim of the collapse of communism going to prove an obstacle to closer European union? Notwithstanding any threat to EMU, the many preparations for the 1992 Single Market (due to be officially in-augurated on 1 January 1993) meant that the EC was already a *de facto* economic union. But the German government wished to press on towards a single European currency, its economic strategy being driven by the overwhelming desire for European Political Union. "Only through resolute commitment to the realisation of European unifi-cation can we obviate a relapse into the destructive nationalism of the past," declared Chancellor Helmut Kohl.[8]

8

The Japanese Model

The spectre of capitalism haunts not only the former USSR and Eastern Europe, but the whole world. As long as communism (or socialism) and capitalism were seen as alternatives – however undesirable they might be – most discussion concentrated on the differences between communism and capitalism, without too much emphasis on the different forms of, and approaches to, capitalism. With even Vietnam knocking on the capitalist door in 1992, and capitalism creeping up the coast of mainland China, communism had been relegated to the role of Captain Oates in Scott of the Antarctic. It had gone outside, and was likely to be some time.

But capitalism comes in many forms, with those forms that make the most noise not necessarily producing the most favourable impression. During the decade of the 1980s when communism finally collapsed, the loudest capitalist noises were undoubtedly made by the US and the UK, with President Reagan and Mrs Thatcher the most vociferous proponents of the virtues of the capitalist system and the wisdom of market forces. Since Reagan and Thatcher were the leaders most closely associated with the hawkish "defence" policies that finally unnerved the grey men of the Kremlin, confusion of their form of capitalism with the only "alternative" to communism was perhaps understandable. The scope for confusion was also greatly enriched by the policies of the World Bank and the International Monetary Fund, which preached and applied nostrums dreamed up within the walls of North American universities to countries that were far from the most suitable recipients of such wisdom.

As the biggest, richest and least scathed victor of them all in 1945, the US was the best placed to involve itself in post-war reconstruction efforts, and to influence the course and philosophy of the official multilateral institutions. With the biggest voting power on the World Bank and IMF boards, it was still a dominant voice during the 1980s, when the "free market" ideas of the Reagan administration were preached to the rest of the world, with the willing support of a Britain that still held great influence in World Bank/IMF circles – an influence that reflected its empire and victor status in 1945, rather than the position of its economy in the 1980s.

Thus the dominant capitalist philosophy was the Anglo-Saxon version, which was biased in favour of free markets rather than intervention and controls, individualism rather than the team, and which was of a more confrontational nature – between government and industry, and between employers and trades unions – than Japan or Continental Europe. But even Anglo-Saxon capitalism is not a consistent philosophy: there was more "welfare" in Mrs Thatcher's England – for all her efforts to downgrade the role of the state – than there ever was in the US, even under the most enlightened Democratic administration. Meanwhile in Germany, where "social partnership" and a reasonable degree of "welfare" were built into the system, the prime role of the market was certainly not forgotten. While Mrs Thatcher had regarded "redistribution of income" as a dirty slogan, the German government was happy to proclaim that one of the key features of its economic system was: "Redistribution of income through pension, health and unemployment insurance schemes and many other measures to help the weak and needy." Nevertheless, Bonn added firmly: "To see this income distribution – as some people do – as the real 'social' component of the social market economy system is a fallacy. This system is what it is, not because it redistributes income, but because its efficiency and economic strength give it the freedom to spread prosperity wider."

The Scandinavian economies, such as Sweden, which appeared for a long time to have achieved an idealised form of what we earlier termed "social capitalism", saw a reaction in the early 1990s, when a political party more orientated towards the market, and less "welfare", came into office. But although this was hailed in the US and UK as yet another sign of the death of "socialism", it is more likely to constitute a reversion towards the Continental European mean. Public spending, as a proportion of GDP, had been extremely high in Sweden. All that was being contemplated was a move towards the OECD average – but nothing like a conversion to the raw capitalism favoured by the American Right.

The most telling example of the deficiencies of the school which equates capitalism, or the market economy, with the Anglo-Saxon version embodied in the US and UK is surely Japan. Yet, ironically, Japan's post-war reconstruction began under American occupation. As one writer has observed: "General Douglas MacArthur, with the title of Supreme Commander for the Allied Powers (SCAP), came into his satrap like Lord Curzon taking over as Viceroy of India." The Americans wanted to make Japan into their ideal of a classless society, and, 45 years later, "Japan is much closer to the egalitarian mass society, with fewer extremes of poverty and wealth by far than in America."[1]

Japan is the economy most admired and feared by other capitalist economies around the world, and the relationship between government and industry is much closer than would be dictated by the ideal US/IMF "free market" model. On the other hand state provision for education is low, and both education and the social safety net are heavily dependent on family and other private sector finance. Appreciation of social needs is there; its manifestation, and the way in which these needs are met, take a different form. The famous homogeneity of Japanese society and Japanese culture is sometimes seen in heavy government intervention in industry, sometimes in the "paternalism" of the big corporations and the "life-time employment" system.

Capitalism comes in many guises. The extreme, *"laissez-faire"* version of capitalism was a system that, paradoxically, had to be imposed. Communism was a system that required much *greater* imposition: the enforced abolition of nearly all private property rights was a major policing operation, justly meriting the sobriquet "totalitarian". But capitalism as such was never imposed – until recent events in Eastern Europe, that is. Capitalism was a natural evolution of history, taking on board man's natural desire for private property, his inclination to trade, his scientific discovery and technological application, and the legal and financial institutions and statutes that lubricated the wheels constantly turning in the marketplace. As one writer recently put it: "Ranging from the United States to Japan, from Singapore to Brazil, from Kuwait to Mexico, (capitalist) economies share only one obvious characteristic, namely a substantial cluster of privately owned firms that use markets and contracts as the principal means to acquire their inputs and dispose of their outputs."[2]

The economy that the US and EC most fear, indeed envy, is that of Japan. American and European experts, with the British well represented, have been thick on the ground in Eastern Europe, advocating the swift adoption of Reagan/Thatcher style capitalism. Just what resemblance does the post-war approach of Japan bear to what is being urged on Eastern Europe now? As for the individual capitalist, so for the nation: the natural instinct is to sew up sources of raw materials and outlets for the supplies of one's manufacturers and traders. To the outsider, Japanese capitalism is formidable, even frightening. But for many Japanese the underlying fear is that they live a perilously insecure existence, dangerously dependent on imported raw materials – notably oil – and vulnerable at any time to a breakdown in the world trading order which has provided such valuable outlets for the popular products of their engineering and science-based industries.

Japan's pre-war attempt at building up a "Co-Prosperity Sphere" in East Asia ran into the buffers of the Second World War. After the war she was forced to drop the military aggression which had accompanied her economic expansion plans of the 1930s, and given extensive American help in building a more outward-looking economy, and a society no longer dominated by the imperial old guard and their institutions. The Americans insisted on the unravelling of monopolies, the setting up of democratic institutions, and a pronounced emphasis on education. Defence expenditure was cut to a minimum; up-to-date American technology was made available; Japan became the major industrial supplier, under US direction, for the Korean War: it was subsequently a base for US forces in peacetime, and given a phenomenal financial premium for the privilege – this "special procurement" expenditure paying for nearly a third of her imports of commodities in the first half of the 1950s. "Japan Inc." was helped back on its feet by the United States of America – not by market forces.[3]

Having received such generous assistance, however, Japan then proceeded to become the international giant of the market economy with such a sense of mission and purpose that one of the foremost Western experts on Japan felt able to write: "Some regard her economy as essentially state-directed, while others attribute to vigorous private enterprise the credit for their country's post-war success. It is paradoxical that one can find ample evidence that makes both propositions appear plausible."[4]

The truth appears to be a judicious mixture of public and private endeavour. Some capitalist countries find that, despite the great breakthrough of Keynesian economics, life in the international marketplace can be difficult if you do not adjust your economy fast enough (Keynes's theory was, after all, essentially about a "closed system"). Communist countries in general, and the former USSR in particular, managed, in the COMECON bloc, to combine a closed economy, in which there was little disruption from outside, with intensive state direction, and negligible attention to the signals from the marketplace. The oligopolistic tendencies of the much less "planned" American capitalism led Galbraith to point to a cosiness and degree of producer planning under American capitalism that was a long way from the right wing's idealised model of atomistic competition. The consumer was under the producer's control to a far greater extent than he realised ("The New Industrial State").

The cosy model of capitalism that America had evolved into from the days of the 19th century robber barons was eventually to face severe competition from Japanese capitalism – indeed, concern about what the Japanese were doing to US industry and jobs was to run in tandem in the US press during 1990 and 1991 with the triumphalist tone of the reporting on American capitalism's victory over communism. The liberal trading system in which the US believed, and which it had encouraged through the GATT process, allowed Japan to undermine the complacency of such inward-looking corporations as General Motors. Market research was invented by the Americans; but their Japanese pupils were to apply it far more widely, and wisely.

Japan's post-war industrialisation did not happen sporadically, or by chance. It was planned. But whereas the USSR went monotonously for production targets, irrespective of the subtlety of consumer tastes beyond certain basic needs, Japan built innovation and adaptation into its very concept of planning. The welfare state, non-industrial infrastructure and other options were subordinated to the requirements of rapid industrialisation. Education, banking, the tax system, the Government machine itself – all were geared closely to the requirements of Japanese industry. "Infant industries" were protected from overseas competition, but competition was encouraged between domestic concerns. It was not so much a case of the Government trying to "back winners" in the case of individual firms, as of the Government sponsoring the race *within* individual industries, and subsidising those who were running towards the sunrise. Subsidies for declining industries were limited to transitional arrangements for the redeployment of people and physical resources, rather than for permanent propping up of "lame ducks." And subsidies for such vital aspects of the market system as the rail network were taken for granted. Agriculture, too, as in many other "market economies", has been subsidised in Japan.

In common with the raw entrepreneurial capitalist, Japanese capitalism explores every opportunity, and does what it can get away with. This means that, while running a highly efficient and adaptable manufacturing base, Japan has not hesitated to employ the kind of protectionist devices that are more associated in the textbooks with less efficient economies – and which are in theory, but not in Japanese practice, supposed to be inimical to economic efficiency. Japan, in common with Germany, seeks its own economic interest.

Japan has sometimes been described as a "corporate state". It does not operate the economy, in the way Mussolini did in pre-war Italy, with the unions subjugated and all opposition suppressed by a police state. But the needs of business and industry rank so high in the scale of priorities that some students have maintained that the Government essentially plans what business does, and others that big business in effect runs the Government. What is clear from most studies is that there is close and serious consultation between government, industry and the banks and the financial system generally; that the interests of the nation are certainly taken for granted in such consultations; but that there is competition is indubitable – "even among the oligopolists there was keen rivalry for market shares", as G. C. Allen has put it.[5]

For "market share", even more than crude profits, is what businessmen, outside the confines of the textbooks, are most obsessed with. But the difference between the Japanese approach and that of the American is that Japanese capitalism has a more dynamic concept of markets, and a longer term approach to them. Moreover, the state and business is more closely intertwined in the pursuit of market share.

Week in, week out, businessmen in most countries are conscious of their share of the market. Apart from the case of very small, one product companies, this means that large and medium sized corporations, with operations in many products and many markets, are continually assessing the course of their sales in relation to those of their rivals. And there is no doubt that the typical capitalist corporation looks many years ahead, and is continually responding to market forces, and trying to develop new products and new markets.

The classic approach of businessmen left to themselves is one of "if you can't beat them, join them." If the law, and even a sense of morality, prevent a businessman from coercing his rivals, or their customers, into submission, the next natural move is to settle for some cosy "market sharing" arrangement, under which competition is more apparent than real, and every producer and seller derives some benefit – including that from collectively acting to keep new entrants out of the market. It is against such collusive arrangements that anti-monopoly and pro-competition laws are set up, and the legal textbooks are replete with examples where "market sharing" has been discovered and action has been taken against the offenders.

The problem for the rest of the world with Japanese capitalism is that Japan does not appear to wish to share the market with anybody. It looks around the world at what markets it can penetrate, and does its best to do so. It examines world market trends, identifies likely areas of growth, and encourages the highly competitive corporations that make up "Japan Inc." to get in on the act. In the early post-war period the policy was explained by one Japanese administrator: "Carefully select industries, prevent ruinous competition at the infancy stage, nurse them up to a competitive stature and then expose them to outside competition."[6] Officials and industrialists worked together. In the early post-war days, they went for products which were likely to be in greater demand, in the world as a whole, as incomes grew, and which, whatever the costs at the beginning, promised to benefit from technological progress and lower costs eventually.[7] This policy continues. Over the decades the emphasis shifted from steel and shipbuilding to cars, synthetic fibres and electrical industries, then engineering, petro-chemicals, and electronics. By the late 1970s Japan was already anticipating the huge demand for video recorders, microwave ovens and better cars in the 1980s. In 1991 the government announced that it was subsidising research among leading manufacturers to try to effect a final breakthrough in the elusive search for an electric car whose batteries did not have to take up so much space as now, or be recharged so frequently.

In the early days Japan was in such a hurry that it simply bought or copied the results of other countries' basic research. Later, with "catch-up" – in some cases "overtake" – came much greater resources committed to its own research. While the US and the UK were gradually allowing much of their engineering industry to be described as "smokestack", Japan oversaw a dramatic increase in the proportion of her exports accounted for by engineering goods – from 28 per cent in 1954 to 79 per cent in 1979. This corresponded with a fall in the proportion accounted for by textiles and clothing from 40 per cent to 5 per cent over the same period.[8] When low wage competition afflicted the Japan that had once relied on cheap goods and low wages itself, the country simply shifted production of cheap goods, such as textiles, to other areas of Asia. As G. C. Allen comments: "Japan may be said to have been engaged in exporting part of the low-productivity sector of her 'dual economy.'"[9]

The Japanese approach of directing the country's marketing efforts on a strategic basis, in certain concentrated areas, has been widely regarded as unfair and disruptive. But the fact of the matter is that in important areas it has worked and added to the advantages of Japan's other fundamental economic practices. The fashion for "supply-side" economics began in the West during the 1980s, but Japan had been concentrating on the supply-side for decades. All the basic factors regarded as important for improving a country's industrial performance were taken for granted in Japan, including high standards of education, a culture conducive to capitalism and business, concentration on research (once this could no longer be borrowed from abroad) and development, receptiveness to innovation, high standards of quality, design and marketing, government policies supportive of industry, and, in particular, an emphasis on as stable an environment for business as possible, notably through a lack of the "short term" approach which characterises the financial sectors in the US and UK; and, perhaps above all, the willingness to pull together and react and adapt fast in the face of external shocks – such as the two oil crises of the 1970s. Add to this the successful system of industrial relations, flexible wages, and "single enterprise unions" – which both assisted adaptation at the micro level and meant that wage inflation was seldom a barrier to expansionary policies at the macro level, and the Japanese economy constituted a highly skilled and adaptable workforce, well managed, and not knowingly undersold by government policy.

Added to all these supply side advantages has been, at various periods, the bonus of an undervalued exchange rate. Most people think of Japan as, in the late George Mikes' words, "the land of the rising yen". The natural result of prolonged low inflation and high productivity has been to raise the value of the yen; but there have been long periods – such as the first half of the 1980s – when, in addition to all its other advantages, the Japanese trading offensive has enjoyed the extra advantage of a relatively undervalued currency. As if this were not enough for the success of the Japanese "industrial capitalism" model, the political dominance of the Liberal Democratic Party for so much of the post-war period has meant that the Japanese economy was relatively immune from the disruptive short term changes that stem from inter-party rivalry and frequent changes of government and policy in other capitalist countries.

Behind the growing concern in the US in 1991–1992 about the threat to domestic jobs from Japanese competition lay some comparative statistics which, on the face of things, looked almost like a modern version of Mr Micawber's famous definition of the boundary between happiness and misery in the conduct of one's economic affairs. In 1989 Japan's exports were equivalent to 9.7 per cent of her national income, and her imports amounted to 7.9 per cent. The difference accounted for the infamous trade surplus of $64 bn, which so inflamed world economic opinion. The comparable statistics for the USA were: exports 7.2 per cent and imports equivalent to 9.4 per cent of national income. Adding to the frictions between the two countries was the fact that two-thirds of the Japan surplus could be identified with its bilateral trade with the USA.

Behind the Japanese trading success lie much more impressive percentages for individual manufactures: thus 95 per cent of video cassette recorders produced in Japan in 1990 were exported, and 48 per cent of colour television sets. As much as 45 per cent of cars made in Japan were for export – and so on, with the jackpot being hit not by cash registers (a mere 87 per cent) but watches (91 per cent of which were exported).

Japan, with a population half that of the US (124 million against 250 million) had a GNP per capita of $23,500 in 1989 against $20,900 for the US. It accounts for 19.2 per cent of the total output of the OECD area, against 35.8 per cent for the US.[10] Its choice of the passenger car market as one area of concentrated attack is borne out by the fact that its market share of world production was almost 28 per cent in 1990 against 17 per cent for the US.[11]

On most of the criteria studied by economists when assessing economic performance, Japan seems to do all the right things. Investment ("gross fixed capital formation") is 32.1 per cent of GDP, compared with 20.5 per cent for Germany, 19.6 per cent for the UK and 16.6 per cent for the US.[12] Its applications for patents – an important indicator of an economy's general dynamism – totalled 334 per 100,000 of population in 1988, compared with 261 for Germany, 133 for the UK, and 112 for the US. Its share of the OECD market for exports of manufactures was 14.71 per cent against 12.81 per cent for the US and 7.25 per cent for the UK, but below Germany's 18.18 per cent (1987 figures).[13] However, when it comes to shares of the world export market for "high tech" manufacturing industries, Japan is ahead of Germany (22.6 per cent, compared with 14.95 per cent). High tech was once very much a special preserve of the US, but the latest figures show that even here Japan is marginally ahead of the US (22.6 per cent compared with 21.7 per cent) – the small size of the gap no doubt reflecting the continuing pre-dominance of the US in defence equipment.

The American neurosis about Japan, and the latter's economic and political self confidence, were epitomised in the ill-fated visit by President Bush to Tokyo in January 1992: what was originally conceived of as an historic diplomatic meeting to emphasise the importance of the US/Japanese relationship in the Pacific following the collapse of the Soviet Union became a disorganised begging mission, with the President and leading US car makers pleading with the Japanese to open up their markets. There was manifestly something strange about a trading relationship under which the Japanese had won a market share approaching a third in the US, whereas US auto-makers had about 0.25 per cent of the Japanese market. But, protectionist though the Japanese undoubtedly are towards imports, they are able to cite the fact that European car-makers had been more successful in penetrating their market than the US. The foreign share of the Japanese car market was 4 per cent in 1991, or 200,000 units. Of these, 150,000 were from the EC, and 30,000 from the US. US cars were too big for Japanese roads and consumers, and did not pass the stringent anti-pollution tests. Perhaps the most embarrassing point to emerge however was that

American auto-markers had concentrated on shipping left-hand drive cars to Japan which, in common with Britain, continues to use right-hand drive cars. This was, as it were, to drive straight into the hands of Japanese critics who said the US corporations were not really serious about penetrating the Japanese markets.

On that occasion the Japanese gave the Americans a humiliating lecture on the need to invest in distribution networks and manufacturing sites in foreign markets if one is serious about capturing market shares. Then came President Bush's embarrassing collapse at a state banquet, followed the next day by what one observer described as "a patronising analysis of US problems delivered by the (Japanese) prime minister, Kiichi Miyazawa". In his speech, Mr Miyazawa said: "I might say the US society is a great society. But there are homeless people; there is the problem with Aids and so on, and for various reasons education is not as high as in the past, and US industries are not as competitive as in the past. Since Americans are aware of these problems I am convinced they will overcome them because I believe that the United States is a great country."[14]

The Bush visit ended ignominiously in what appeared to be a "managed trade" agreement under which Japan undertook to purchase certain numbers of US cars and components, and other products, in order to reduce the trade imbalance. This bilateral arrangement contrasted strongly with the theoretical commitment of the US to multilateral trading agreements and the General Agreement on Tariffs and Trade. But it followed a pattern of development whereby, when pushed, Japan undertakes to import more, although her proportion of manufactured goods imports, in relation to total imports remains far the lowest of the major industrial countries – at 50 per cent, against around 80 per cent for the US and UK.[15] Within weeks of the Bush visit, the Japanese prime minister was denying that there had been any "agreement" – saying only that Japanese car manufacturers would make "efforts" to import more.

There was growing threat of trade friction and indeed a drift to protectionism and trade wars as other capitalist economies became aware in the early 1990s of how intense the pressure of competition from Japan now was. As early as 1983 an American author had proposed action against Japanese competition in a sustained diatribe unashamedly entitled *The Japanese Conspiracy – The Plot to Dominate Industry Worldwide – and How to Deal with It*. Among the suggestions made by the author, Marvin J. Wolf, were that the Japanese must be induced to "discontinue the cartelization of industries, which creates a handful of large, effective organisations able to overwhelm foreign competition," and, "most important,

Japan must show that it is willing to play by Western rules by having MITI commit administrative harikari."

The "cartelization" of industries is a reference to the way that Japan, after being instructed by General Mac Arthur to break up the *zaibutsu*, or trading empires in which banks and industrial groups were closely linked, managed to evolve a not dissimilar system again, in G. C. Allen's words, "not by the imitation of, but rather by the skilful adaptation of, Western models to her own needs". The big corporate and banking groups – *keiretsu* – are distinguished by close links between firms, and with banks, and by systems of "cross shareholdings" which render large sections of industry invulnerable to the threat of takeover. It is worth remembering that Japan did not start dismantling controls on capital flows until over 20 years after the war (from 1967). It was fear of foreign takeovers that strengthened the trend for interlocking shareholdings. By 1989 the US administration had in fact begun the so called "Structural Impediments Initiative" talks with Japan, aimed at the kind of things Mr Wolf and others were complaining about. The SII talks covered everything from the cross shareholding system to price formation, the financial system, general trading practices, wholesale and retail distribution, land policy. Throughout the 1980s and early 1990s Japan was under pressure from the US and European countries to do more to expand domestic demand and let in imports. What Washington seemed to be set on was conversion of the manifestly successful Japanese capitalist system to something more approaching the less successful Anglo-Saxon version. If you can't beat them, ask them to join you, was the approach.

Many observers of Japanese capitalism have asked themselves the question: what is it that can be attributed to differences in the *system*, as opposed to the culture – in other words, what could be borrowed or adapted to make other industrial economies less fearful of Japanese competition? In the end the answer seems to boil down to the combination of the investment and pace of innovation which is allowed under a version of capitalism which is less obsessed with short term considerations and the free play of *financial* market forces than the West.

Thus, although the Japanese version of capitalism is very much geared towards the acquisition and expansion of markets, the operation of the financial market has been less disruptive of the real economy than in many other countries. To put it in the fashionable jargon: there is much less *short-termism*; in particular the system is not geared to satisfying the short term requirements of shareholders for dividends, or of other participants in the market to "take over" their rivals against their will. The satisfaction of shareholders in the short term, and the desperate desire to avoid being taken over, is seen in Anglo-Saxon capitalism as promoting the short-term pursuit of profit, as against the long-term goals of the strategic building up of market shares, and general investment for the future. The theory, from the classical economics textbooks, is that markets and profits provide the best test. But in practice, financial markets are very short term in their outlook. To take but one example, the leading British company ICI devoted much of its time in 1991 to fending off a takeover threat from Hanson Industries; ICI, with its ten year programmes of research and development, was seen as vulnerable to a company that could satisfy the markets with its profits and share price – but did so partly by being savage in cutting the research programmes of companies it took over.

During much of the 1980s it was the kind of smart operator who could make money and boost short-term profits that dominated the headlines and became fashionable under Anglo-Saxon capitalism. In the US, men such as Ivan Boesky, Michael Milken and Donald Trump were for a time glamorous figures under a financial culture which glorified money-making and "deals", as opposed to longer term considerations. Keynes had long ago pinpointed "money-making and money loving" as "the essential characteristic of capitalism", but the *degree* to which money-making and financial manipulation were glorified under Anglo-Saxon capitalism may, literally, have been counterproductive. There is an important distinction between making money and earning it.

This is not to say that there were not also financial scandals in Japan – there were plenty in the 1980s and early 1990s, and there is a long tradition of them. But the fundamental basis of Japanese capitalism, when it comes to manufacturing industry and the production and marketing of the goods that consumers want, appears to be more geared, in the long term, towards the real market than the financial one.

A long-time student of Japan, Professor Ronald Dore, has suggested: "Japan's is in effect a different form of capitalism . . . managers see their primary duty not as being to their shareholders but rather to their employees . . . hostile takeovers are practically unknown in Japan. Whenever anybody attempts one, practically the whole business community rallies round to the defence." Dore points out that Japan's financial system is more like the British than the German, in that the stock market bears a close relation to the total capitalisation of industry, but that "in effect there is no market for total corporate control. This means that managers are not continuously concerned with the price of their shares, their market valuation in relationship to their assets, the likelihood of takeovers etc. – allowing them to concentrate on long-term developments in the firm, because they are secure themselves."

Under the Anglo-Saxon model, the possibility of takeover is supposed to be a spur to competition – a threat that keeps managers on their toes. It might be a more appropriate metaphor to say it diverts too much of their attention towards guarding their backs, instead of concentrating on the direction in which the firm should be going.[16]

Given that they are less concerned with short-term profits than their Western counterparts, and that they aggressively pursue sales and market shares, the Japanese have caused concern not only to Anglo-Saxon businessmen and governments, but also among the economists who like to think that capitalism conforms to their theories. (One may note in passing that a number of writers have emphasised that economists were not high on the list of Tokyo's priorities for consultation when the post-war miracle was being planned.)

As the American economist Alan S. Blinder has pointed out, this means that: "First, Japanese firms have a natural competitive advantage over Western rivals who maximise profits. The *kaisha* (Japanese companies) can flourish (by their own standards) even in markets that will not support a competitive rate of return. This edge grows progressively larger in industries on the cutting edge of technology, where learning curves are important. Second, the hypothesis can explain why cost increases may not induce Japanese firms to retrench. Third, it may explain why Japanese firms behaved as if they had a cost of capital advantage when they did not."[17]

Blinder regards "size maximisation" as the objective of the Japanese firm, including under this head the goals of maximising growth, maximising market share, and maximising employee welfare. The latter has been dubbed "Peoplism" by Professor Itami:[18] under "peoplism" capital owners are not the sovereign powers they are under theoretical capitalism; nor is the state. Itami's point is summarised: "Peoplism is identified with employee sovereignty, dispersed sharing of information among a wide spread of employees and organised markets with emphasis on long-term economic gains through long-term relationships."[19]

If it is capitalism at all in Japan, it is a much more refined and honed capitalism than the raw capitalist ideal whose very mention can draw instantaneous applause from any gathering of businessmen or right wing sympathizers in the West. Blinder raises the question from classical economic theory: "Why does the Darwinian process not eliminate firms that fail to maximise profits?" He plausibly suggests that the answer may lie with the following factors: one, as is clear from the repugnance towards contested takeovers, Japanese firms do not live in terror of the takeover predator, in the way that "non-profit maximisers" do in the West; two, growth orientated firms may draw "more and better work" from their employees.

What particularly irritates Americans is that Japan gets "more and better" work from teamwork, not individualism. The Anglo-Saxon appeal to self-interest and the harnessing of greed towards productive uses have little appeal in Japan. "Economic Man" (or "Person") takes more forms than the classical textbooks allow. In Japan the whole team is geared to rapid improvement and renewal of the product, whereas US textbooks associate individual initiative with speedy response to change. This may be a cultural characteristic which is difficult, if not impossible, to transplant. In Anglo-Saxon capitalism, individualism and short-termism appear to be associated. In Japan both the Government and the banks back the team, in a long-term relationship. Moreover Japan seems to have developed an effective combination of economies of scale among the large, competitive corporations that produce and market consumer goods, and a myriad of small suppliers, with low stocks and a rapid response to the changing demands of committed clients, to whom they remain loyal. Loyalties and relationships in business are not necessarily inefficient, but the takeover culture of Anglo-Saxon capitalism tends to erode such concepts.

One must not forget that the relevant Japanese firms tend to offer the security of life time employment, with the incentive of promotion and a large profit-sharing element in the pay system. And, as Ronald Dore points out, "managers are paid salaries which cause them to identify with employees rather than shareholders. This contrasts with Anglo-Saxon 'remuneration packages' which are geared heavily to short term performance." Blinder's third factor is that "technical change proceeds faster in a size maximising environment with employee participation." (A student of the traditional British scene would have added "and employee co-operation".) He is thinking of "large firms in which management enjoys considerable autonomy, especially in technologically progressive industries with steep learning curves" – broadly, the type which produces all the goods with which the Japanese have saturated the high streets, shopping malls and car showrooms of the Western capitalist countries.

The pursuit of growth and market share is graphically illustrated by a comment from Akio Morita, the chairman of Sony, in 1987. "Competing in a market we understand, such as our own, Japanese companies sometimes misbehave with their cut-throat tactics. Companies will go after an increase in share of market by cutting prices to the bone, sometimes to the point where there is no chance of anybody making a profit on the product. The winner for market share becomes the one who can afford to lose money in the market the longest."[20] Another close student of the Japanese scene observed: "Japanese companies are highly geared (that is, they have a high ratio of debt to equity) and, if you applied Harvard Business School criteria of their net worth, they would be close to bankruptcy. But you can rely on MITI or the Bank of Japan to keep a firm going if it is considered competitive in the long run."[21]

The general approach of Japanese capitalism, or "peoplism" is well captured in the title *Growth Through Competition – Competition Through Growth* of a book by Professor Hiroyuki Odagiri. The author says he is "tired of hearing simple-minded arguments that what the Japanese have been doing is totally different from the *laissez-faire* economy of the West." He argues that the Japanese economy and Japanese management "are based just as firmly on competition as those in the West, possibly more so." It is the "possibly more so" which is especially interesting. And the really important question is: what are they competing *in*?

Japanese companies believe in competition, and they believe in planning. The Japanese capitalism that so terrifies the rest of the capitalist world is a system of what one might call "competitive planning". Research and development seem to be referred to far more often in books about the economy and business written by Japanese themselves. There is an English language television programme in South-East Asia, beamed out from Tokyo after the main news, which in the UK would probably be called "finance" or "City", but is in fact entitled "Economy and Science". Japan used to copy others; now they copy themselves. Morita notes: "We (at Sony) have poured billions into our technical laboratories for R and D and others have watched us and taken advantage of our up-front investment by moving into our field after we have pioneered it."[22] He casually states, of the technologies of the 1990s: "Those areas that are expected to receive the greatest emphasis – opto-electronics, digital technology, video technology and laser technology – happen to be our specialities."[23]

The role of "pooled research" between companies is part of the competitive process: "I see the principal role of co-operative research as a signalling device to indicate important areas for long-term research attention, and as a stimulus to proprietary company research." "Fierce rivalry makes it a point of honour for a company to become involved in new, high profile technologies . . ." Again, " . . . Engineers are at the helm of many of the leading Japanese manufacturing companies, and a technical orientation is pervasive.

A strong belief in R and D and in the most modern facilities and equipment is nearly universal."[24]

There was intense "competitive planning" in the bitter battle that went on between JVC and Sony over the appropriate system for VCR machines – a battle which was eventually won by JVC, when Sony's Beta format conceded defeat in 1988 to JVC's system, known as VHS. The principal Japanese electronics firms have recently been competing in the development of a more powerful semi-conductor, and the next generation of supercomputers, whose potential uses are awesome, and towards which the Government has contributed research funds. But the signs are that so far the US is maintaining its leadership in the technology of supercomputers.

Odagiri has observed, about the financial news in the two countries, "all the news in the UK relates to the selling and buying of companies, or to fighting against proposed purchases. All the news in Japan, on the contrary, relates to product development and investment either internally or by joint ventures. Businesses, to the British, are something to be bought and sold like commodities. Businesses, to the Japanese, are something to be developed and expanded internally."

Making money, buying and selling, doing deals – these were the practical manifestation of the right wing ethos of President Reagan and Mrs Thatcher. Odagiri cites an interesting comparison between the way an announcement of an IBM "Restructuring" plan was reported in the *Financial Times* and the *Nihon Keizai Shimbun*. The former concentrated on the reaction of Wall Street and the implications for the share price; the latter on how many jobs would be lost. "Companies, for the British, are first of all objects of investment: for the Japanese, they are places in which people work together."

Odagiri thinks one reason why the competitive aspect of Japanese capitalism may have been overlooked is that Anglo-Saxon observers are dominated by the fairy-tale, neo-classical concept of perfect competition in atomistic markets. They have failed to realise that there can be other forms of competition – odd since so many of them make ritual references to Adam Smith, whose *Wealth of Nations* showed he had a much more strategic view of competition. Indeed, it would be interesting to compare a modern Smith's version of *The Wealth of Japan* with the kind of neo-classical economics that are taught to Eastern Europe and the former Soviet Union.

A common theme of visitors to Eastern Europe in 1991 was that government officials did not understand the concept of markets, and that the kind of black marketeering and deal-making observed in the streets was just the sort of thing that should be encouraged. This came strangely from people who also affected to subscribe to the rule of law. Seldom, at seminars on Russia and Eastern Europe in 1990 and 1991, was anybody on the panel to be heard suggesting that perhaps the Japanese model was more appropriate to those facing the spectre of capitalism than the models constructed within the walls of North American universities. As Odagiri points out: "A market with a limited number of participants can be more competitive than an atomistic market. A market not perfectly competitive today may still be competitive in the long run."[25]

We have seen that the advent of the bankruptcy laws was an important element in the evolution of modern capitalism: competition implies winners and losers, and entrepreneurial figures are given the opportunity to start up again. Quite apart from the consideration that, if Japan Inc. is so successful, it is other *nations* whose firms are more threatened by bankruptcy, in modern capitalism the risks are spread within large, diversified firms. Odagiri maintains that bankruptcy (with its waste and dishonour) is also a less appealing option in Japan because of the different concepts of what has come to be known as "corporate governance". In the absence of controlling shareholders – who can accept a takeover bid or not, as they please – Anglo-Saxon managements are subject to takeover, or "shareholder's revenge". Bankruptcy tends to be the market discipline for smaller firms, and takeover for larger ones – unsuccessful firms, that is: large Anglo-Saxon firms like taking over successful small firms at the right price, whereas Japanese capitalists prefer to expand "from within". But, as Odagiri notes, since, in Japan, managements consider themselves to be accountable to *all* the *stakeholders* "from the shareholders to the employees, the suppliers and the customers", it follows that "the cost of bankruptcy is disproportionately large."[26]

For Odagiri "the growth maximising behaviour of Japanese management strengthens competition because to attain growth the firm has to increase capacity in existing markets or enter into new markets. The two key concepts of growth maximisation and competition thus become complementary."[27] Commenting on Alan Blinder's observation that Japanese firms pursue growth rather than profits, the long-time member of the International Monetary Fund staff, Jacques Polak, asks, with what seems an air of despair for one who has been so closely associated with the propagation of the Anglo-Saxon model around the world: "But how can a firm that does not maximize profit survive in international competition?" The proof of the pudding is in the eating. Blinder (and Odagiri) notes that Japanese companies are not disciplined by the stock-market in the way American companies are. Blinder – again, in common with Odagiri – believes firms that concentrate on maximising size and growth draw better results from their employees, and may have a "virtuous circle" effect on the speed of technical change.

The IMF's Polak concedes the battle: "If large corporate firms in Japan produce more, at lower prices, other firms must produce less at higher prices than if all were guided by profit maximising. But since it is precisely these large firms that dominate Japan's exports, the outlook is grim for Western competitors unless they catch on, start maximising size, and they may discover that in that way they achieve higher profits after all."[28]

An important concept to emerge not only from studies of Japan but also from many a conversation with individual Japanese officials and businessmen is the simple, old-fashioned belief in loyalty and the value of long term relationships between companies, their customers and suppliers, and *within* companies between the organisation, the employees, and the senior executives. As one MITI official puts it: "Such long term relationships give the firm a feel for how many products it can buy for the next five years, which in turn helps the manufacturer to invest, leading to lower costs for both the producer and customer." The official was speaking to a group of a dozen, mainly Anglo-Saxons, and added with a gentle smile: "A long-term relationship is not always wrong."[29]

By contrast, typical of the trend of Anglo-Saxon capitalism in the 1980s was the popularity, during the vogue period of financial deregulation, of "transaction banking" as opposed to "relationship banking". This might provide "finer margins" and short-term profits – but ran the risk of alienation between manufacturer and banker when the business climate soured. Also typical of that period was the frequency with which chief executives would move from one firm to another, often for a well-publicised increase in the "remuneration package", and by definition not displaying much loyalty to individual firms. By contrast, in Japan: "The external market for managers is very limited."[30]

Japanese capitalism is much more interested in shifting the entire emphasis of production from one market to another than in moving executives from firm to firm, or altering ownership in response to the dictates of short-term financial market considerations. Aldo Morita notes: "In the United States and Europe, the steel makers or computer manufacturers or automobile companies periodically say they cannot compete with foreign technology, and their reaction is always to put people out of work . . . Japanese companies attempt to avoid letting any workers go, but try to use them to bring the company back to health."

Thus: "When the electronic analog technology began to give way to digital technology, we did not fire our analog engineers. Our analog engineers eagerly learned a new field. They had to, to survive. Learning new technologies is a way of life for us in Japan, and others will have to do it: it is not possible or desirable to cling to the past."[31]

There is, of course, a difference where "clinging" to traditions has nothing to do with international economic competitiveness. It is not necessary to pull down beautiful villages, à la Ceaucescu, in order to adapt. But it may well be advisable, from the point of view of the national standard of living, to eschew clinging to out-of-date products and practices in the industrial estates outside the villages. A rather unusual, and not easily imitated, method of adapting to change was described by a British businessman who moved to Hong Kong. "In England whole communities erode over a generation in the face of the competitive winds from abroad; in this place they merely move down a couple of floors."

A corollary of the Japanese emphasis on loyalty and long-term relationships is the importance, in that country, of the group, rather than the individual, both in decision-making and in general economic activity. Indeed, one American observer goes so far as to conclude: "At its root, the Japan model (of the economy) promotes the strength and welfare of the group, not the individual. The strength of the country, the welfare of the company – or company group – and the reputation of the family are promoted over individuals." Japan is seen as promoting growth through "dynamic efficiency, not static efficiency", so that although life-time employment, and sub-contracting based on loyalty, not short-term considerations of the market price, may raise costs in the short run, "the pay-off comes in the willingness of individuals and enterprises to change and adapt to new situations since they feel secure in their basic relationship."[32]

Notwithstanding the desire of free market purists in the West to interpret otherwise, such Asian tigers as Singapore and Taiwan have followed the Japanese model rather than the Anglo-Saxon one. But it has its costs, and any visitor to Japan soon sees that high GDP per capita figures on paper do not necessarily translate into US/UK style consumption.

Both industrial production and real consumption rose by over 50 per cent in Japan during the decade of the 1980s, with greater emphasis also being placed on public sector investment, pollution controls and the general quality of life. Nevertheless, in his list of "What Can the World Learn from Japan?" the American economist Lawrence B. Krause felt it necessary to include, in 1991: "Be prepared to work very hard and consume very little. Workers average between 48 and 50 hours per week over the year (including holidays and vacations) in Japan and the Asian NICs. This leaves little time for leisure, and the money should be saved anyway." But Krause felt he had to acknowledge that the lesson of the Japanese model was that "without active government participation, countries trying to catch up will have little hope of succeeding." Moreover, "without both vigorous adaptive firms and active governments supporting them, even affluent countries like the United States are likely to see their living standards eroded."[33]

In the slanging match which followed President Bush's visit to Tokyo in January 1992, the speaker of the lower house of parliament Yoshio Sakurauchi said Americans wanted "high pay without working for it", adding contemptuously that America was "Japan's sub-contractor".[34] He said 30 per cent of the US workforce was illiterate. Apologies and explanations flowed across the Pacific, but within weeks the Prime Minister Kiichi Miyazawa criticised US graduates for lacking "the work ethic" and preferring jobs on Wall Street to engineering. He also attacked the kind of financial innovations that had been born in the US financial system during the 1980s, such as "junk bonds" and "leveraged buyouts" (which often allowed the tail to wag the dog in ownership of US industry). As Miyazawa acknowledged, there had also been a "bubble economy" in Tokyo during the 1980s, when the price of financial assets and real estate rose to dizzy heights. But one interesting contrast between the US and Japan in handling the excesses of the financial boom of the 1980s was that the governor of the Bank of Japan, Mr Mieno, deliberately embarked on a strategy of reducing the level of the market to more sustainable levels, whereas in both New York and London the reaction to the excess of the 1980s was seen as having unfortunate consequences for wealth and spending power, and contributing to the recession of 1990–91.

We have seen that there is something of a "grass is greener" syndrome in examining the economic performance of countries. There is also a long-established economists' view that, as countries "catch-up" and leaders become jaded or top heavy, there may be a natural tendency for industrial economies to "converge" in their performance. There may also be a tendency for the various *forms* of capitalism to converge – if only because one lot may catch the disease of another, or an inferior performer attempt to ape the success of a superior.

Some observers of the Japanese scene were deriving solace in the early 1990s from the view that big problems lay ahead for that industrial powerhouse; and some Japanese themselves, such as Akio Morita, began to criticise aspects of Japanese capitalism. Morita went so far as to argue that "the Japanese style of management is dangerous", and that by putting engineering at the heart of the economy, making efficiency the focus, Japanese leaders had been too narrow in their approach. Morita urged a package of reforms, including shorter working hours, higher pay for workers, fairer relations with suppliers, higher dividends for shareholders, and greater attention to the protection of the environment.[35] In their vast programme of overseas investment, Japanese firms in the 1980s and early 1990s had demonstrated that their management approach could achieve similar levels of productivity abroad to those at home (superficially suggesting, in the UK's case, that the problem all along might have been management rather than the trades unions. On the other hand, they insisted on single union plants, and had the pick of the available workforce in areas of high unemployment).

According to a Western market research chief with great experience of Japan, Morita "does not make the case on the grounds of altruism; his argument is that Japan derives a competitive advantage from its work culture and that it should modify it to world standards to stall any protectionist backlash."[36] It is certainly the case that, paradoxically, the nation that is seen by all the world as both protectionist itself and devastatingly successful in international markets is actually dependent on a reasonably open trading order for its continued export success. That success has been achieved despite a proliferation of "voluntary export restraints" on shipments out of Japan to many countries.

In the case of the US market, Japan's voluntary export restraints, and the growth of the "managed trade" that Anglo-Saxon capitalism ostensibly does not believe in, were associated with the damaging effects on the US trade balance of the rise in the dollar during the first half of the 1980s. This, it will be recalled, was the heyday of the Reagan period, when dollar "strength" was boasted about, allegedly reflecting the high returns available in the successful US economy, whereas that very "strength" was sapping US domestic industry, via the effect on price competitiveness.

The Plaza currency agreement of 1985 inaugurated a period of co-operation between the G7 industrial countries, after "market forces" had been allowed to play havoc with exchange rate relationships during the first half of the decade. There was an unspoken bargain under which both Japan and Germany assisted the US – according to some observers, because it was in their interests to do so, given that their security depended on US protection in both Europe and the Pacific. It has been suggested that, following the collapse of communism and the nuclear threat from the former USSR, Japan and Germany no longer have any interest in such a "security for financial help" bargain.[37] Whatever the accuracy of this judgement, it is certainly true that Japan saw to it that it financed much of the US balance of payments deficit during the 1980s – thereby, to a considerable extent, lending the money for US consumers to buy its exports. Indeed, from 1945 onwards the US had needed Japan as a bulwark against communism in South East Asia, and Japan had in turn required US protection. But even if the security reason for easing America's problems by buying Treasury bills has diminished, the interest of Japan in warding off a general move to protectionism is considerable.[38]

It is worth emphasising again the paradox, in 1991–92, of Anglo-Saxon dominated multilateral institutions preaching their own form of capitalism to the rest of the world, while the Anglo-Saxon economies themselves lived in fear of competition from the Japanese form of capitalism. Japan itself had certainly benefited from a combination of its own protectionism, and the security protection of the US navy. Japan's protectionism was described by one writer as "the willingness to go along only at the pace that suited Japan and to allow foreign competition only as far as it was useful to learn from."[39]

Even in 1992, World Bank economists calculated that Japan had trade barriers covering about a quarter of its imports, whereas the US and EC had restrictions on a sixth of their imports. Much of the latter constituted restraints, sometimes described as "voluntary", on shipments from Japan, and anti-Japanese sentiment was certainly mounting.[40] According to the Japanese Economic Planning Agency, some 30 per cent of exports to the US were under some sort of trade restraint in 1989.[41] Moreover, as was evident almost daily in the news from the United States, Japanese efforts to surmount protectionism in the US, or anticipate further moves, by increasing inward direct investment, were not necessarily dampening anti-Japanese feeling itself. Typical of the feeling that Japan was not playing fair was a remark from a distinguished trade economist, an admirer of Japan and a strong believer in free trade, who said "it is not for nothing that there are 200 items on the Structural Impediments list (of Japanese barriers to trade, in the eyes of Washington). And you try arguing in Japanese in the Tokyo law courts . . .".

But, as in the case of the British Empire and other countries in the past, dominant trading nations begin to have a vested interest in free trade, however protectionist they themselves may have been at a certain stage.

There are several ways in which the trade frictions allegedly caused by Japan's success might be assuaged in the future. One is, as Alan Blinder concluded: "If the Japanese practices that I have characterised as size maximisation really amount to a more sophisticated way to maximise profits, then Western firms may be expected to catch on."[42] Certainly, with the proximity of out-standing examples of nearby Japanese investment within the US and UK, especially in cars, those countries have a chance to study the miracle at close quarters. There were also suggestions in mid-1992 that leading Japanese companies such as Nissan and Matsushita were being forced by recession to make fewer model changes and concentrate more, like western capitalists, on profitability. But they were doing so from a position of such strength that Western observers might be rash to derive too much comfort from such reports.[43]

Another route would be if, as many observers hope, Japan begins to suffer the classic problems of advanced industrial societies, and its performance begins to deteriorate anyway. Some observers claimed to detect problems in store for Japan in the forecasts of a demographic shift leading to an unusually large ageing (and dependent) population; but this is a trend the Japanese spotted themselves as long ago as the 1970s, and began to make provision for – as Adrian Hamilton has written: "The most immediate require-ment was to increase the pressure on pension funds and savings institutions to raise returns in preparation. By the late 1970s, the institutions were growing both more sophisticated and, in line with corporations, more anxious to diversify their funds into foreign holdings, both as a hedge to a slowing down of the Japanese economy and as a quick route to higher returns."[44] (What a pragmatic Japanese solution – to keep dividend payments low domestically in the interest of longer-term growth, but to seek out the dividend income which less growth-orientated market-economies were offering abroad . . .)

Typical of the view that the problems of others will catch up with Japan is the observation of Saskia Sassen, of Columbia University: "Yes, Japan has immense economic might. But its might is based on an economic system that extracts immense social costs. In the long run these costs weaken and tear at the economic fabric. It happened in the United States, and the first tell-tale signs are appearing in Japan." Illness associated with overwork became a common news item about Japan in the US and British newspapers early in 1992, as a long-term sign that there is hope for us all.[45] Similarly, there were worries about the more "consumerist" younger generation, higher levels of debt, and so on. But the average level of private savings in the country dwarfed the debt figures. As one observer put it: "There is no doubt that Japanese have begun to spend more than they did in the past, and that the younger generation no longer regards personal debt from credit cards and banks as shameful. But, despite all the arguments of the disaster theorists, it also looks as if Japan can afford it."[46]

In addition to planning for higher investment returns to provide for an ageing workforce, Japan was also adapting to its threatened demographic problem – namely a labour shortage – by increasing use of part-timers, and a rapid rise in fixed investment, which rose during the 1980s from 16 per cent to nearly a quarter of GNP – "i.e., the capital intensity of GDP rose to offset the lower growth of the labour force."[47]

One change being forced on Japan in the early 1990s by outside pressure is "deregulation". As that other process much touted during the 1980s – "globalisation" – takes its toll, it could be argued that Japan will suffer accordingly, and that, for instance, the era of "cheap finance" for industry, in a restricted market, is over. But Hiroyuki Odagiri notes: "The conspiracy theorists will say that such changes are bound to undermine Japan's strength. We disagree . . . We see no reason why these changes should conflict with growth maximisation and competition. In fact, we take the view, quite contrary to the conspiracy theorists but consistent with mainstream economic thought, that any policy change in the direction of deregulation can be expected to contribute to competition and efficiency in industry. The only irony is that this may not be brought about internally by the voting power of consumers but by external pressure."[48]

9

The Inter-dependence of Market Economies

Competition and the profit motive are characteristic not only of individual capitalist or market economies, but of the relations *between* them. Under competitive capitalism there is a chronic tension between the interests of the residents of individual nations as consumers, and their interests as producers. It may suit the consumer in the US or UK to have no restrictions – "voluntary" or otherwise – on the import of Japanese consumer goods; but producer groups – the representatives of employers and employees – think of their own profits and own jobs, and the politicians, on the whole, are aware that there is a limit to which people can consume imported goods if they do not produce enough themselves in exchange. (Although in one sense producers and consumers are all the same people, in another sense they are not. That is one of the big international economic problems.) The behaviour of US and European car manufacturers towards the Japanese threat is a case in point.

But capitalism, like life, is infinitely complex. We find that Japanese car manufacturers surmount restrictions by direct investment in overseas markets – following a long established practice of British and US firms. We find that domestic car manufacturers, while protesting from the rooftops about unfair competition, adopt the "if you can't beat them, join them" approach, and that they, for example, US auto makers, sell Japanese cars under their own brand names in the US[1] and British car firms have links with Japanese manufacturers, offering shareholdings and employing their technology. When investing directly in overseas markets Japanese firms can claim that they are providing local employment, although seasoned competitive capitalist businessmen in the UK will maintain that these are merely "screwdriver factories", and that companies do not invest abroad out of the goodness of their hearts.

Three important trends in capitalism during recent years can be broadly summarised under the headings: globalisation; regionalisation; and inter-dependence – of both multinational firms and countries – an inter-dependence which might also be labelled "competitive collaboration". Some aspects of these trends have pointed towards protectionism; others have suggested a process of interlocking interests which, if carefully handled by public policy, both national and international, could still achieve benefits on the lines of the years of the golden age.

Despite fears about protectionism, international trade has increased rapidly – much of it reflecting "intra-industry" trade as multinational companies in electronics, cars, pharmaceuticals and many other industries treat the whole world not only as their market-place, but also as their potential production site. There is a difference between the traditional approach of US capitalism – to treat the world as a *single* market – and that of the Japanese, who see it as a series of local markets, each of which requires special attention in product-development. Non-Japanese multi-nationals have followed the Japanese in this respect. One theory about the dynamic behind the rapid growth in overseas investment – so that, for instance, the North American, European and Japanese multinationals set up production facilities in South East Asia, while, within South East Asia, countries such as Taiwan may themselves branch out towards overseas production – is the theory of the product cycle. At first, those companies in the lead, as a result of innovation and techno-logical superiority, enjoy a predominance in domestic markets, and export overseas. Gradually, others catch them up, the new product becomes a standard one, made by rivals, and, in order to maintain their competitive position, the original innovators move production to low wage countries.[2] Another theory is that overseas investment and production of the original innovation is simply forced by trade barriers, or difficulties in arranging licensing agreements.[3] These theories are not mutually exclusive, and both highlight the importance of technological change and the competitive process in spreading production.

The high cost of research and development has led not only to governmental assistance in individual countries, but to collaborative agreements between ostensibly competing firms. Taken with an accelerating rate of technological obsolescence[4] this has reinforced the oligopolistic tendencies of capitalism, within countries, regions and worldwide. Hardly a day goes by without some announcement in the financial columns of collaborative research ventures between ostensible competitors, as well as financial deals involving stakes in rival companies, and interlocking shareholdings. Investment, trade and technology all interact in a bewildering matrix of multinational alliances, which render out of date the simple model of independent firms competing with one another.[5]

In the semi-conductor industry "US and Japanese companies have been able to make a series of bilateral agreements with firms in each of the European countries, thereby preventing the emergence of serious European competition and reducing much of the European industry to the role of licensing and second-sourcing US and Japanese technology."[6] Ironically, the OECD reckons that, by promoting national champions in semi-conductors and thereby raising barriers to entry for those firms not favoured by procurement policies, individual European countries made it difficult for a truly specialised competitor to the US and Japan to emerge at the European level.[7] With encouragement from Brussels, European companies are now trying a more strategic approach, aimed at closing the gap with the Japanese and US.[8]

Modern capitalism in practice has been epitomised as follows: "The name of the game is to co-operate with one's competitors over common components, yet maintain keen competition at the final product stage; to erect credible barriers against players likely to enter the market; to control the range of products and services likely to act as substitutes for one's own activity; to modify one's bargaining power vis-à-vis suppliers or purchasers by means of long-term contracts or control of upstream operations; and to influence the balance of forces by making strategic moves and anticipating change." Market structures are not there, like diagrams on the page of the economics textbook: "new forms of organisation, the opening up of new markets and the introduction of new products and production methods continually undermine the possible equilibria and modify the rules of the game."[9]

The so called Dynamic Asian Economies, or Asian Tigers, are at one level seen as a threat to more advanced capitalist economies and their jobs – but at another level, they are the recipients of investment and technology from those very countries. And, despite concern about Japanese investment in the US and the UK, the latter "Anglo-Saxon" economies are themselves major overseas investors, accounting respectively for 30.5 per cent and 16.2 per cent of the total stock of foreign direct investment in 1988, the next biggest owner of overseas investment being Germany, with 9.1 per cent.[10] Japan held only 9.8 per cent of the total stock of foreign direct investment in 1988 – but, in conformity with popular anecdotal impressions, this was double the proportion it held in 1980.[11]

The growing interdependence of the capitalist world is seen in trends such as the rise from an eighth to one fifth (over the last 25 years) in the proportion of world output that enters international trade. Two thirds of this trade is accounted for by manufactures, compared with only 5 per cent in raw materials (excluding fuel).[12]

The industrial countries account for 70 per cent of this output and trade, selling a quarter of their exports to developing countries, and acquiring half their oil and a fifth of their other basic materials from developing countries. The developing countries sell a third of their exports to one another (compared with a quarter in 1980) but rely on industrial countries for nearly two-thirds of their trade.

About half the exports of North America and Latin America are for destinations within the American hemisphere, and half outside. For Western Europe the proportions are roughly two thirds of export trade *within* Europe and one third outside, whereas for Japan and South East Asia the position is the obverse of Europe's – two thirds of these countries' exports go outside the region, and one third is traded within the region.[13]

The "globalisation" of trade and production is seen in the fact that the direct investment by industrial countries in developing countries was traditionally in raw materials, mining, plantations and public utilities, but has shifted dramatically in emphasis during recent years to manufacturing, notably textiles, clothing and electronics.[14] Computers, telecommunications and modern technology generally (including "miniaturisation" of the size of products, as well as their weight) have reduced transport costs and boosted the flexibility of international trade. Between 30 and 40 per cent of the international trade of countries such as the US, UK and Japan comprises "intra-firm" trade – that is, shipments from one country to another of goods belonging to the same firm.[15]

The world was always a market for capitalism, and the under-developed countries a source of raw materials. The world is now capitalism's market *and* its production base. Given the dominance of international capitalism both by successful trading countries and by a relatively small number of very large corporations, the logic of protectionism has altered; protectionism is not in the interests of the big multinationals, even though it might still be attractive to the small capitalist firm, or to the emerging economy.

One of the myriad examples of the inter-dependence and inter-connections of the modern industrialised world is provided by the way "semi-conductors manufactured in the United States are used to assemble printed circuit boards in several developing countries, including El Salvador, Indonesia, Malaysia, Mexico and the Philippines, and shipped back to California's Silicon Valley for further processing."[16] The World Bank has produced a chart of the interrelationships between car manufacturers and the countries of the United States, Japan, Asia and Western Europe which looks like a printed circuit in itself. Products today use so many different technologies that few companies can remain at the frontier of technological change without interfirm alliances that span countries and regions.

The OECD has pointed out that "competition itself is undergoing far-reaching changes. Whereas in the past it was predominantly price-driven, it has now become technology-driven. Moreover, competition is perceived as increasingly imperfect, as being conducted between giant oligopolists at the one extreme and regional low-cost competitors at the other, against a background of multiplying joint-ventures, liaisons, cross-licensing and other forms of inter-corporate co-operation."[17]

As a result, it is difficult to distinguish "competition" from what the OECD terms "worldwide market-sharing arrangements".

This does not necessarily mean that modern capitalist firms avoid taking risks; but they certainly spread the risks of research, development and new marketing ventures – just as their financial counterparts will spread the risks of lending money, with syndicated loans. Funnily enough, although most large firms have a diversified range of products, spreading risk can mean *reducing* the range offered in one geographical area, but spreading out worldwide in the search for markets for tried and tested core products.[18] Again: "a multiplication of strategic alliances among firms of different home nationalities makes protectionism in foreign markets less probable, given the high degree of interdependence resulting from such collaborations."[19]

One of the unresolved questions about the course of capitalism in the 1990s is whether the "globalisation" interests of the multinationals and the consumer will triumph over the fears held by many that "regionalisation" and the building up of trading blocs may lead to increasing protectionism. One hopeful observation from United Nations economists is that: "All three candidates for regional blocs – Europe, the Western hemisphere and Japan, plus South East Asia – depend too much on extra-regional markets to become self-contained 'Fortresses'." It is intriguing that both protectionists and free-traders see advantages, for their own reasons, in regional blocs. Globalisation and regionalisation are not mutually exclusive, and can in theory be "building blocks rather than stumbling blocks to freer multilateral trade". But it all depends whether barriers towards non-participants are reduced when new trading blocs are set up.[20] "A strong 'home' market and regional grouping offer the necessary platform for launching into world markets," an OECD study declares, "nonetheless, the spectre of protectionism is more easily raised where regional integration is perceived to be likely to discriminate against the economic interests of non-members of the regional grouping."[21]

This is a battle that is still being fought. The trade economist Jagdish Bhagwati has suggested that the "new, long-run pro-trade forces" – such as globalisation, and the strong campaigns waged by chief executives of corporations against protectionism, give grounds for "guarded optimism". Others see a scramble for business, and jobs, by competing governments, leading in the reverse direction. International law and competition policy lag behind in this area, and "policing" of international trade and investment requires, ideally, a multilateral approach, rather than the bilateral deals favoured by, for instance, certain protectionist US Congressmen.

We may have globalisation of financial markets and globalisation of production and product markets, but there is not yet "globalisation" of government, acting in the general interest to ensure that the notorious "playing field" is level.

The multilateral institutions set up after the Second World War, such as the IMF, the World Bank and the GATT – were designed to try to harmonise international economic and trading relations; regular meetings through such networks as the OECD were originally conceived to try to ensure that the excesses of the inter-war years could be avoided, and the deficiencies of the marketplace made up. Attempts at the co-ordination of economic policy were made at regular meetings of finance ministers and central bank governors, and, after the mid 1970s, by the Group of Seven "summit" process as well. These attempts still take place, but are most notable for the disinclination of participants to pursue anything other than their own short-term national interest.

For many years international economic policy was conducted on the (at least tacit) supposition that all would benefit from co-operation in – indeed, co-ordination of – economic policies.[22]

This spirit of co-operation had its ups and downs, and one seasoned official aptly commented: "History teaches us that it is only when the United States becomes convinced that there is something wrong with the international economic system that things actually begin to happen."[23] The US was worried about the state of Europe after 1945, and things began to happen. It was worried about the sluggishness of the world economy in the late 1970s, and persuaded West Germany to take expansionary measures (which the latter subsequently regretted). It was worried about the rise of protectionism in the mid 1980s within the US and abandoned the monetarist philosophy of leaving things to the market, in the interest of bringing the dollar down to a more competitive level. At the time of writing, the Bush administration seemed to be sufficiently stung by an accusation from former President Richard Nixon that it was missing an historic opportunity with the collapse of communism to be prepared to make at least some effort to produce a large package of assistance for Russia and the other former Soviet republics. There were also signs that the EC had finally accepted the case for reform of its Common Agricultural Policy; this was widely perceived to be necessary in itself, and a prerequisite for resolution of the long period of deadlock in the GATT trade negotiations between the EC and US. One paradox facing capitalism was that, while a renewed burst of trade liberalisation ought to provide a stimulus to output and employment, fears about "jobs" were themselves causing protectionist pressures. Another paradox was that the former communist bloc was crying for help at a time when competitive, but inter-dependent, capitalist countries were far from confident in themselves.

The problems faced by capitalism in the difficult 1970s and early 1980s had certainly not led to its demise – as Lord Desai has pointed out, it emerged instead in "a new globalised framework" with "an international division of labour" and profit rates restored. But while communism collapsed, capitalism, ironically, responded to its own difficulties "by throwing out the consensus of the previous quarter century and reneging on previous promises to its citizens".[24] Thus the Left could point to high unemployment and in one observer's words "a worldwide poker game of everyone looking for cheap labour". Capitalism could once again be accused of all sorts of familiar crimes – but now there were no alternative ideologies on offer. It was up to capitalism to heal itself.

10

'Social Capitalism'

We have seen that, as an economic system – let alone as a moral one – communism has failed. We have also seen that some forms of capitalism – the German model in Western Europe, the Japanese in the entire trading world – are widely perceived to have done better than others, although the collapse of communism has indubitably put strains on Germany. It is an open question whether "capitalism" really is a "system" – as opposed to the condition into which many countries have evolved historically. But the word "system" can certainly be applied to the communism which was imposed on the USSR and, later Eastern Europe, and perhaps to the form of extreme capitalism, or *laissez-faire*, which reigned for a time in Britain during the 19th century.

Whether capitalism, or the "market economy", has "succeeded" is a more complex question than that of assessing whether communism, USSR-style, failed. It is almost tantamount to asking whether history has succeeded. What seems reasonably clear is that market economies have been infinitely more successful in satisfying the wants of their consumers, or of most of them, but that this has taken decades, indeed centuries, to achieve, and the time taken to build successful market economies in the former communist bloc will be a lot longer than was assumed by some of the "bourgeois triumphalists" in the initial euphoria which followed the collapse of the Berlin Wall.

Moreover there must be serious questions raised both about the extent to which capitalism and market economies have benefited the world, as opposed to about a fifth of it, and the degree to which the countries of the more successful OECD "market economy" group can continue to consume the world's resources. (The US, for example, contains 5 per cent of the world's population but accounts for 25 per cent of annual resource depletion and pollution).[1] At the heart of "market economics" is the price mechanism, and the concept of "opportunity cost"; yet it is widely conceded that the capitalist economies have for years run their affairs with only scant regard for what many scientists and environmentalists regard as the biggest cost of all – namely the free use of the planet's non-renewable resources.

This is not to say that capitalism does not adapt: it most certainly does. Whether it was the threat from internal revolution, or external communism, capitalist countries certainly adapted – one point of the Keynesian Revolution was to make capitalism safe for capitalists; a main aim of the post-war economic order – the Pax Americana – was to ward off communism. Similarly, when the sharp rise in the price of oil signalled in the 1970s that the world's natural energy resources might be finite, the market economies adapted to some extent with energy conservation measures. The threat of pollution generally has also led to adaptation – so much so that it was the "people's paradise" of the USSR and Eastern Europe that turned out to be far more polluted than the "capitalist" West. Nevertheless, it is a slow, reluctant process, and the 1980s and early 1990s were characterised by many statements of goodwill from international conferences and Group of Seven "Summits", but sluggish adaptation. The low price of gasoline in the United States is a constant reminder of how resistant consumers, pressure groups and Governments are to dire warnings about the likely state of "non-renewable" energy resources in the year, say, 2050 AD. The still profligate attitude towards the exploitation of the forests and oceans suggests room for improvement if we are serious about bequeathing a workable inheritance to our grandchildren. And the problems of the ozone layer have generated whole libraries of scientific concern.

The 1980s – the years of capitalist triumphalism – were also characterised by often severe pain in the developing countries. Professor Ajit Singh has pointed out that, while during the 1970s the developing nations were vigorously demanding a "new international order" (encouraged by the oil producers' success in pushing up the price of oil) "today, most of them (particularly in Africa and Latin America) are severely constrained by their balance of payments, heavily in debt and in the position of being suppliants before the IMF and the World Bank."[2] According to Singh the policies which dominated the OECD countries during the 1980s saw a switch from "stagflation" (low growth and high inflation) to "low growth and low inflation", which adversely affected the commodity price earnings on which third world countries principally depend. Although there were certainly huge write-offs of third world debt in the Western banking system during the 1980s and early 1990s, the experience for many third world countries was one of low growth (often negative in per capita terms) and a net transfer of resources to the advanced industrial countries. (At one point in the early 1980s the more heavily indebted developing countries were devoting an average of over 50 per cent of their export earnings to the servicing of debt.)[3]

Smaller countries, and developing nations, tend to grow faster than the OECD average when world trade is booming, and, conversely, to do worse than average during a period of slowdown. The 1980s were bad years for Latin America and Sub-Saharan Africa, where on average primary commodities accounted for respectively 83 per cent and 98 per cent of export earnings, at a time when weak commodity prices hit their terms of trade (the ratio of export to import prices) and the volume of their exports was in any case sluggish. By contrast, the Asian "Newly Industrialising Countries" (known as NICs) received less than 40 per cent of their export earnings from primary products, and demand for their exports of cheap manufactures did well – as was evident from the most casual perusal of shops throughout the advanced industrial economies of the world.[4]

Although heavily lectured by Washington and the multilateral institutions over the need to drop restrictions and various protective devices, the Asian "tigers" in fact used all manner of devices to assist their passage into the markets of the rest of the world."[5] One of the economic themes of the 1980s preached by Washington was "structural adjustment" – i.e. adoption of "free market" policies that were the ideal (but not necessarily always practised, as in the restraints on Japanese imports) in the United States. One recent study shows that the "structures" the IMF and World Bank wished to remove "consisted of a mixture of protection for the inefficient, intervention with a perfectly good economic rationale (eg. infant industry tariffs) and intervention with a social rationale (eg. food subsidies)." The World Bank's "structural adjustment programmes" were actually found to have a negative effect on aggregate invest-ment, and "living standards of the poor have evidently fallen in many developing countries, including those which have undergone structural adjustment. This appears to be partly in response to cuts in public expenditure, for which both the Bank and the Fund bear responsibility, and partly due to the impact of price reforms advocated by the Bank."[6] Meanwhile, of course, formal aid was cut back in keeping with the spirit of the times.

Under the influence of the US, the World Bank and IMF have put the emphasis on "macro-economic balances", rather than on building up the material and human capital which help to form a macro-economy in the first place. In the early 1990s the position of a number of Latin American countries was generally considered by the US economic establishment to have "turned round", with debt less of a burden, and "market reforms" in fashion. But at the World Economic Forum in Davos there were some interesting exchanges between Chicago economists urging the "minimalist state" and a whole succession of Latin American finance and economics ministers emphasising that what they wanted was "capitalism with a human face", and that they could not necessarily attract the right private investment from abroad unless the public sector infrastructure was in reasonable shape. As one study found: "A policy of trade liberalisation works better if industry is already competitive on export markets; price incentives to commercial farmers work better if those farmers have access to credit, fertiliser and good roads; privatisation works better if there exists a private sector able and willing to take over the public sector's assets."[7]

Spurred on by the collapse of communism, triumphalists in the West have committed two fallacies. One is the argument that the failure of the "maximalist" state necessarily implies the victory of the "minimalist" state. The second is that, even if this is so (which it is not) the argument can be applied to countries at widely varying stages of development. In practice, in the widely admired cases of Japan, South Korea and Taiwan, state intervention and assistance to industry have tended to describe a "U" shape, rising initially, but falling as it becomes apparent that former "infant" industries are now able to compete in, even dominate, world markets. The building up of export sectors and the infrastructure to support them "may require more rather than less state intervention".[8]

Even the World Bank, whose economists preach the extreme free market doctrines of North American universities, acknowledged in its 1991 World Development Report: "Selective state intervention has figured prominently in two of the impressive success stories of development: Japan and the Republic of Korea. Both countries employed taxes and subsidies, directed credit, restrictions on firm entry and exit, and trade protection to encourage domestic industry."[9] The Bank would apparently have preferred that they had not, and points to studies showing the high cost of intervention. One thing is clear: we shall never know how Japan would appear now if it had *not* indulged in appreciable "indicative" planning in the decades immediately following the Second World War. But the balance of the argument must surely rest with the policies associated with their considerable achievements.

The problem with intervention to help industry is that it can be open-ended, go on too long, encourage the market in corruption, and – above all, from the economist's point of view – perpetuate inefficiency, which does not maximise welfare in the long run. But if it is the case, as seems to be well established both in theory and in practice, that the infant industry requires protection before it can stand on its own feet, let alone take part in the race, then the example of Japan is surely relevant. It is possible to help, or subsidise, for a time, and then allow the industry to participate in the trading race according to GATT rules. It was noteworthy that, at the World Economic Forum meeting referred to above, the Latin American ministers were putting the emphasis on public spending in the infrastructure and social sphere, rather than on industrial subsidies.

Bureaucratic corruption and excessive, or over-extensive industrial subsidies are examples of "government failure". But the case for public sector intervention in market economies rests on the manifest failure of the market, unaided, to produce a desirable outcome in terms of economic welfare and the satisfaction of citizens. The public sector can produce the roads, the railways, the bridges, the education system that it does not necessarily pay individual entrepreneurs to endow. Its regulations and tax and subsidy policies can also protect the environment (or not, in the case of the USSR and Eastern Europe). The social benefits of such public sector activities are greater than the private costs. They have a benign external impact on the activities of individuals and businesses – just as poisonous exhaust fumes, effluent released into rivers and other industrial activities are harmful "externalities" of industrial activity (whether capitalist or communist), and need to be controlled by legislation in the wider public interest. A "public good", such as a road, or even lamp-post, is something which it is difficult to prevent everybody else from using, but whose absence benefits nobody. As one writer has put it: "Successful growth normally depends on devising institutions to overcome market failure, and countries differ enormously in their capacity to construct such institutions."[10] Successful growth also requires policies of "market augmentation" – helping the market along by creating the institutions which support a market economy. The right wing argues that in the absence of intervention, economies would grow faster. In South Korea it was the Government that built the capital market, although it has been argued that it retained control for too long.[11]

A classic example of the need for greater public sector intervention is provided by the City of Bangkok, the capital of a country, Thailand, which is often cited as one of the more successful newly industrialised countries. The amount of roadspace per acre in central Bangkok is far lower than in most comparable cities; there is no underground system, and not much of a suburban railway network; and the traffic-signal technology leaves a lot to be desired – allowing remarkably long gaps between changes in the lights. The result is the kind of traffic jams which make the visitor inclined to say he will never complain again about the traffic back home – and the situation is hardly alleviated by the manifest pollution from the traffic.

Growth models, in both capitalist and communist countries, were all the rage in the 1960s and 1970s. Perhaps less emphasis was placed in those days on what the capital was for, and whether the output was wanted by consumers. Nikita Khrushchev had boasted in 1961 that, within 25 years or so, the USSR would be producing more industrial goods than the USA. Writing in 1986, the *Guardian's* Martin Walker pointed out: "The curious thing is that Khrushchev's economic targets have been met. The Soviet Union produces 80 per cent more steel than the USA, 78 per cent more cement, 42 per cent more oil, 55 per cent more fertiliser, more than twice as much pig-iron and six times as much iron ore. It produces five times as many tractors and almost twice as many metal-cutting lathes."

In 1961 such products represented "the sinews of industrial power and, had the world's economy stood still, the Soviet Union would be its industrial giant." But the *market* economies of the Western world had moved on, and micro-chips (and other inventions of the innovation-driven capitalist countries) had moved in. Among other things, there was the adjustment of demand to the oil shocks of the 1970s, and the energy-saving investment which was thereby encouraged.[12]

The Austrian/American economist Joseph Schumpeter had argued that capitalism "incessantly revolutionises the economic structure *from within*, incessantly destroying the old one, incessantly creating a new one. This process of Creative Destruction is the essential fact about capitalism. It is what capitalism consists in and what every capitalist concern has got to live in."[13]

Schumpeter maintains that it was the ordinary and the poor who had most to gain from capitalism. "There are no doubt some things available to the modern workman that Louis XIV himself would have been delighted to have yet was unable to have – modern dentistry for instance. On the whole, however, a budget on that level had little that really mattered to gain from capitalist achievement . . . Electric lighting is no great boon to anyone who has enough money to buy a sufficient number of candles and to pay servants to attend to them. It is the cheap cloth, the cheap cotton and rayon fabric, boots, motor cars and so on that are the typical achievements of capitalist production, and not as a rule improvements that would mean much to the rich man." For Schumpeter the capitalist achievement consists not in more silk stockings for the rich – "Queen Elizabeth owned silk stockings. The capitalist achievement does not typically consist in providing more silk stockings for queens but in bringing them within the reach of factory girls in return for steadily decreasing amounts of effort."[14]

Whether this is the achievement of capitalism or technological progress is a moot point. Communism also managed to produce cheap goods – too cheap, and too shoddy, on the whole – at Keynes's "low level of efficiency". What is clear is that capitalism and market economies harnessed the potential of industrial and scientific progress. So far, the fruits of capitalist development have been plucked by the bulk of the populations of the advanced industrial countries – with a significant rider about the impact on what appears to be a growing underclass – but only by a relatively small elite in the vast majority of the rest of the world. One of the big questions is whether developing nations are effectively several hundred years behind the West in history, and have to go through it all the hard way, or whether, as visionaries certainly hoped in the golden age of 1951 to 1973, a judicious combination of technique, knowledge and goodwill would somehow be able to short-circuit this historical process. Certainly, the impatience and frustration displayed by more vociferous members of the aid lobby would suggest there is a constituency which believes a better-behaved capitalism could do a lot better for less fortunate countries.

The Right, and neo-Liberals, are correct in questioning the efficacy of unlimited aid, and in the end the object of assistance - to those backward countries that seek it – must surely be to enable them to stand on their own two feet. But in societies where for centuries the concept of the tithe, or one tenth of one's earnings, was considered an appropriate subsidy to the church (if only as the purchase price of a peaceful mind about the afterlife), the low-level of the United Nations target for aid (0.7 per cent of GDP) and the failure of many rich countries to achieve even that, demonstrate a certain parsimony – and not too much peace of mind for those who care about poverty. It did not reflect too well on Anglo-Saxon capitalism that, early in 1992, the US administration was lagging behind in its contributions to the United Nations, and expressing doubts about its ability to persuade Congress to fulfil its share of the basic commitment to increase the resources of the IMF by the G7 countries, in order to lend to Russia and other former Soviet Republics. This atmosphere was coloured by the protectionist tone of much of the debate in the US during Presidential election year, and the mood of a country which had won the Cold War but felt it was losing out to the Japanese in the capitalist race. The aid performance of the UK in the 1980s was also deplorable.

American capitalism in the 1950s had been supremely complacent. It had played a vital role in winning the Second World War;

it had long since established its supremacy over a diminishing British Empire and a British economy that was in relative decline; the works of economists such as J. K. Galbraith and even the Marxists Paul A. Baran and Paul M. Sweezy might have been critical, but delineated a system of Cosy Capitalism, under which oligopolistic competition ruled (Baran and Sweezy preferred the phrase "Monopoly Capital"). It seemed that, despite the existence of anti-trust legislation that had been conceived to control the monopolistic excesses of the earlier generation of "Robber Barons", corporations were comfortably organised, competing in such matters as advertising, but not too disruptive of one another's necessarily long-term plans when it came to pricing policy. American capitalism, as Galbraith never tired of pointing out, was far from the highly competitive and atomistic model favoured by the classical economists. Power had passed to the "technostructure" of specialists and corporate bureaucrats who ran the large corporations that accounted for the bulk of industrial production. "High technology and heavy capital use cannot be subordinate to the ebb and flow of market demand. They require planning; it is the essence of planning that public behaviour be made predictable – that it be subject to control."[15]

Galbraith saw the Keynesian commitment to support aggregate demand in the economy as part of the deal by which American capitalists led a relatively cosy life. Baran and Sweezy, from a Marxist standpoint, saw a similar form of capitalism in the US; but the atomistic form of competition which led Marx to predict crisis for capitalism via a declining rate of profit had given way to "monopoly capitalism", and there was no problem of a declining rate of profit under Cosy Capitalism. With Galbraith, they argued: "The corporation has a longer time horizon than the individual capitalist, and it is a more rational calculator. Both differences are fundamentally related to the incomparably larger scale of the corporation's operations."[16] The analysis pointed to US corporations as being systematic avoiders of risk-taking, and organisations with a "live and let live" attitude towards other corporations.[17]

What Galbraith and Baran and Sweezy diagnosed in the US capitalism of the 1960s was what Schumpeter had feared: the removal of a certain spark from capitalism as a result of the bureaucratisation of decision-making. Schumpeter's concerns stretched further than that, however: he thought this could mean that capitalism would evolve into what he dreaded most of all – namely socialism.

One can detect early warnings of the apprehensiveness being felt in the 1990s about Japanese competition from the complacency apparent in the "Cosy Capitalism" form of US big business in the

1960s. The assumption was that corporations had great freedom over their pricing policies – in the oligopolistic world they were "price makers" rather than "price takers", introducing innovations "not under the compulsion of competitive pressures but in accordance with careful calculations of the profit-maximizing course".[18] Thus, under monopoly or Cosy Capitalism new innovations were carefully controlled so as not to undermine the overall profitability of the firm, or industry. As Baran and Sweezy put it: "This means that in general there will be a slower rate of introduction of innovations than under competitive criteria." It pays the system not to make its capital equipment obsolete too soon; on the other hand consumer demand is manipulated so as to keep sales going – what Galbraith, in *The Affluent Society*, called "planned obsolescence" (such as the phasing in and out of those large tail-fins on US automobiles in the 1950s).

We have seen how, under the communist system, the incentive of profit or competition was distinguished by its relative absence. The "dynamic" of US capitalism was undoubtedly there, but it was a carefully controlled one. It is here that Japan found its opportunity. Ironically, not only did the United States go to great lengths to assist the post-war reconstruction of Japan. It also, in reaction to its isolationist phase of the inter-war years, and to the Great Depression, invested time, effort and faith in the various trade negotiations and tariff rounds (The Kennedy Round, the Tokyo Round, the Uruguay Round) which were aimed at opening up the world's trading system. "Competition" and "free enterprise" were very much the catchwords of these efforts – especially under President Reagan in the 1980s. But the US forms of competition and free enterprise were more subtle than the propaganda suggested, and the net result of the "globalisation" of trade was that the Cosy Capitalism of the United States discovered severe competition from the Japanese model.

What the "Japan bashing" of the early 1990s demonstrated was that the Cosy Capitalism model was only invulnerable up to a point. Serious competition from Japan – undoubtedly buttressed by a certain degree of protectionism *within* Japan – could unsettle the almighty United States economy. The effect of such competition can be exaggerated – the most publicised aspects of trade are not necessarily the most important ones, and there were many areas, computers, pharmaceuticals and a number of high tech industries, where the US continued to have an impressive share of world export trade, notwithstanding its prominent "bilateral" deficit with Japan. But it is at the margin that so many economic developments are important; and at the margin the US was almost universally considered to be losing out to Japan.

What Schumpeter had referred to as the "creative destruction" of capitalism was even beginning to worry Japan. Perhaps the best news US and European capitalism had received for a long time was the request, in February 1992, by Japan's Ministry of International Trade, for Japanese manufacturers to stop competing so intensely. MITI asked the Japanese electronics industry to make less frequent design changes. "Specifically, it was requested not to make changes to a product for at least a year after it was introduced."[19]

It is the devotion of the Japanese to working on improvements to products that worries some Western economists even more than their efforts at research. One Chicago University professor commented: "It's not so much their original inventions, or their research: it's that they just beaver away until they're the best."

The MITI decisions coincided with a spate of announcements about drastic falls in profits among the leading Japanese electronics firms – and even forecasts of an operating loss at Sony. Even Japan is not insulated from a slowdown in the general world economy – indeed, as we have seen, it is as dependent as any exporting country not just on the openness of world markets, but on a continuing high level of demand at home and abroad. There were worries in 1992 that Japan Inc. might have "over-invested".

What Japan achieved in the 1980s and early 1990s was a raising of the stakes of competitive capitalism. Those US car manufacturers who mouthed allegiance to the virtues of free enterprise and competition shouted "foul" when they felt its winds (even if the competitive aspect of the Japanese economy was more evident than the free enterprise side). But even Japan was now feeling the pinch.

The menacing tone of international economic relations in 1991–92 – with more and more sober observers talking openly of a retreat into protectionism, trading blocs and isolationism – inevitably revived thoughts of where we came in: the fundamental problems of capitalism, which may not have disappeared simply because communism as an economic system has collapsed in the former USSR and its satellites. Under the golden age the debate about business cycles had retreated to an ante-chamber. Much had been written about the way the vagaries of businessmen's psychology, unevenness in technological development and the financial system had contributed to the ups and downs of the traditional business cycle. Until the oil shocks of the 1970s the cycle was considered to be under reasonable control; and, after the shocks to the system in the mid 1970s and early 1980s, there had been much rejoicing in the Anglo-Saxon world about the rediscovery of sustained economic growth – "the recovery is now in its 44th month, the longest of any post-war recovery" was a typical boast. Businessmen were encouraged to believe their own business cycle had been conquered, and invested accordingly.

Capitalism celebrated the collapse of communism in the early 1990s with a remarkably severe recession of its own. This hardly put the "market economies" in the best of spirits to sort out their own mounting disputes over international trade – let alone to assist the former communist bloc, or step up their efforts to help the rest of the developing world. These two groups were in any case now competing for aid.

The recession of the early 1990s was a classic reaction to the financial excesses of the 1980s. Even Japan suffered from financial excesses – notably inflated values for real estate and quoted stocks. By 1991–92 it was evident that the capitalist business cycle was very much alive and kicking, and that ideas about "economic miracles" in the Anglo-Saxon economies had been fantasies. In the US the accumulated budget deficits of the 1980s limited the room for manoeuvre in traditional Keynesian fashion; in the UK inflation and balance of payments problems were also constraints, even in the depths of recession; in both countries the bad experiences of so many firms and individuals who had borrowed too much during the previous boom stirred severe inhibitions about spending for both investment and consumption. There was a crisis of confidence, which provoked some politicians and commentators to evoke memories of the 1920s and 1930s, and to forecast dire things for the rest of the decade. In particular, at the time of writing, fears were being expressed about a continuing stalemate in the GATT trade negotiations. Capitalist technological progress had led to a position where in the leading industrial economies agriculture only absorbed a few per cent of the labour force; pragmatic government intervention to encourage the "Green Revolution" in developing countries had transformed the agricultural situation in many developing countries. If there was one area of production where the East European economies could perform well in Western European markets, it was agriculture – provided that they were allowed sufficient access. But Brussels in general and France in particular, was being extremely difficult about this, despite an apparent resolve finally to reform the Common Agricultural Policy. The economic atmosphere in Europe was not improved by the almost slavish adherence shown by France and Britain towards exchange rates within the European Monetary System which appeared to be hampering their chances of stronger economic growth, and contributing to socially dangerous levels of unemployment. The two countries seemed to be more interested in how economic and monetary union would operate in the year 2000 than in the damage that was being caused by unemployment levels of around 10 per cent meanwhile. Indeed, the traditional goals of economic policy appeared to be out of perspective: Keynesian policymakers had attempted to balance the sometimes conflicting objectives of economic growth, full unemployment, low inflation and balance of payments equilibrium. The emphasis of both EMU and the approach to it was overridingly on the "convergence" of various indicators associated with low inflation. The rise of ominously demagogic politicians in France and Austria, to say nothing of the social harm done to the unemployed themselves, was being quietly ignored. The very phrase "full employment" was deemed by policy-makers to have a quaintly old-fashioned ring to it.

Economists sometimes gently deride businessmen for failing to distinguish between cyclical and secular trends. As the British commentator Samuel Brittan once observed: "Businessmen have a tendency to think that any point on the cycle is unique." Thus both in the USA and the UK, the belief in the growth spurt of the late 1980s was such that many people behaved as if the economic philosopher's stone had finally been discovered: the boom would continue for ever; property, or "real estate" prices would go on rising – or certainly hold their value; and weren't the "commies" lucky to have finally discovered capitalism. . .

Baran and Sweezy pointed out that the business cycle theories which pre-dated the Keynesian Revolution stressed three factors: "the monetary and credit system, the volatility of businessmen's psychology, and the unevenness of technological change." On the whole capitalism since the Second World War has shown no shortage of technological prowess – as a former chairman of ICI once said: "When the need is identified, we can more or less arrange the invention." – the problem has lain with harnessing it properly.

In the end, businessmen and consumers can indeed make the present point on the cycle look dangerously unique if they suffer a serious crisis of confidence. At what point does a cyclical recession become a prolonged depression? The lack of confidence in 1991–92 persisted sufficiently long for there to be a revival of "long wave" theories, with people arguing that capitalism had run out of inventive steam. Such heretical thoughts were voiced not by Marxists, who understandably felt it was time to keep themselves to themselves, but by passionate believers in the capitalist system, such as former editor of *The Times*, Lord Rees-Mogg.[20]

But even if the 1980s and early 1990s have seen less faith in Keynesian economic policies and international economic co-operation, one lesson of the 1920s and 1930s has most certainly not been forgotten: the central banks, while being functionally more inclined towards deflationary policies than other arms of public service, have never forgotten the way the inter-war slump was aggravated by excessive contraction of money and credit.

Thus in the early 1990s it became evident that the Chairman of the US Federal Reserve Alan Greenspan was more concerned about real economic activity and the health of the banking system than by uttering pious thoughts about the need for further progress towards zero inflation. In this respect, as in the general approach of Congress and the US administration, the monetarist experiment proved very short lived, and in the bias towards expansionary policies – via budget deficits, easier monetary policy and a relaxed attitude towards the exchange rate – US capitalism continues to be overseen by expansionists.

"Too much so," many would say about the expansionist tendencies of US economic policy. The US "Democratic Capitalism" model of the 1980s managed to combine widening gaps between rich and poor, and negligible increases in average real wages, with huge gains for the rich and veritably profligate central government deficits. One of the key mistakes made by Washington during the 1980s was to desist from using appropriate Keynesian policies at all phases of the cycle. Thus, as Galbraith has said: "What was politically possible against deflation and depression was not politically possible or feasible against inflation." Hence we reached the position under Anglo-Saxon capitalism (because the Conservative Party in Britain under Mrs Thatcher and John Major behaved in the same way) where a new law was effectively enunciated: "Income tax can only go down – it must never rise." Hence George Bush's infamous campaign remark: "Read my lips – no new taxes."

Having emerged from their respective recessions of the early years of the 1980s, both leading Anglo-Saxon economies employed Keynesian stimuli at inappropriate phases of the cycle, on top of the huge boost to credit that was inaugurated by the fashionable "deregulation" of the financial markets. It is by now a commonplace that under the deregulation phase, caution was thrown to the winds by both borrowers and lenders, asset prices were bid up, new borrowing took place on the basis of dubiously inflated asset prices, and people deluded themselves that the process could continue indefinitely. Meanwhile, despite the rhetoric of so called "supply-side" economics, the preponderance of new business investment for the future was taking place not in these deregulated paradises of Anglo-Saxon capitalism, but in the more pragmatic and regulated economies of Japan, South East Asia generally, and export-led Germany.

The net result of bad loans to the third world being supplemented by bad loans on their own doorsteps produced a situation in the US – the fount of the preaching of free market economics to the rest of the world – where, in the private opinion of senior officials, the capitalist banks (the very heart of the capitalist development process) were themselves for a time technically bankrupt.

The essence of capitalism is "making money". It is the indiscriminate way that raw capitalists go about this process that makes one question the wisdom of Dr Johnson's dictum that "A man is seldom more innocently employed than when making money." Since the inter-war slump, the financial system and the real economy have usually been in harmony under modern capitalism. But the "financial revolution" of the 1980s threw this harmonious relationship into jeopardy. Professor Alexandre Lamfalussy, General Manager of the Bank for International Settlements in Basle (known as "the central bankers' bank") has questioned whether the financial system itself needs the kind of "creative destruction" which Schumpeter regarded as the essence of capitalist progress in the field of industry, business and the innovation process.

"Is there not something about the financial system which would imply that 'destruction' carries a greater systemic risk than in other industries? In particular: do not globalisation and the speed with which shocks are transmitted create fertile ground for full-blown crises?"[21] Banking was developed to finance trade, but the number and speed of purely financial transactions during the 1980s – particularly in the US and UK – was out of all proportion to the real needs of trade and industry. Indeed, the word "trader" took on the connotation of one who specialised purely in financial transactions with other "traders".

We have seen how the United States developed a form of "cosy capitalism" which tried to minimise the damaging effects of the "creative destruction" process. This in turn has exposed its industry to the challenge from Japan's competitive planning process. It was the "free market" philosophy of the Reagan/Thatcher era which drove deregulation and banking and financial competition to its limits in the 1980s, and it was noteworthy that Japan and Germany felt it less necessary to compete so frantically. (The Japanese financial system was of course well endowed with deposits it could lend to New York, reflecting both its industrial earnings and the high propensity to save in Japan.) If German banks overextended themselves at the end of the 1980s and in the early 1990s, it was because of the political imperative to help the USSR and Eastern Europe. But in general the excesses of both lending and borrowing were led by Anglo-Saxon capitalism.

Excessively zealous competition in the financial markets can lead to low profit margins and bad debts. Excessive obeisance to market forces in the foreign exchanges can lead to disruptive over- or under-valuations of the exchange rate on which countries involved in competitive capitalism ultimately depend to balance their books with their trading rivals.

Lamfalussy notes that, despite his concern about the potential fragility of the all-important capitalist financial system during the 1980s, "crisis management" got the "monetary authorities" through. The system managed to survive the Latin American and East European debt crisis, the stock market crash of 1987, the collapse of the US "Savings & Loans" institutions, and various banking and financial failures such as that of Drexell Burnham Lambert in the US. "Crisis management" involved everything from the sharp reduction in interest rates early in the decade after the onset of the Mexican debt crisis in 1982, through the Plaza Agreement of 1985 (under which the dollar was deliberately brought down to improve US competitiveness and stem protectionist pressures) to probably the most important single sentence uttered in the financial world in the 1980s – when Federal Reserve chairman Alan Greenspan said the Fed stood ready to provide liquidity to the financial markets after the New York stock market crash of October 1987.

But is crisis management enough? Does not Competitive Capitalism require better rules for itself, perhaps incorporating the best lessons from the experience of individual countries, and a commitment to an international code of practice in economic policy which attempts to minimise risks to the system?

The central banks made a start with moves to strengthen the capital base of the commercial banks after the excesses of the 1980s, and the basic message from Basle was for the banks to put their own houses in order. This was necessary, but not necessarily good news for would-be borrowers, or the many previous borrowers who were forced, particularly in the Anglo-Saxon countries, into bankruptcy. The obvious victims of the new prudence being practised by Anglo-Saxon banks were the small businesses, and the potential entre-preneurs – the hero figures of the champions of the New Right, and Democratic Capitalism, during the 1980s. For, although modern capitalism is essentially dominated by big business, the tendency of the people surrounding, for example, Mrs Thatcher in the early 1980s was to laud small businesses above all.

At the best of times a very small proportion of new businesses finally makes the grade. But the rate at which such businesses were collapsing in the early 1990s heightened the contrast between the close relationship of banks and companies in Germany and Japan and the distant, and often difficult, one in the Anglo-Saxon economies.

As noted, if one thing was learned by the central banks from the inter-war years it was that liquidity should be pumped into the banking network, not drained out of it, in times of potential financial crisis. It is of paramount importance to all forms of capitalism to keep the banking system in tolerable shape; but it is unfortunate for the East Europeans and the members of the CIS that their first calls on capitalism for many years coincide with a contraction of a banking system that had simply carried capitalist competition to excess when extreme free market orthodoxy ruled during the 1980s.

Capitalism has entered the last decade of the millennium with business and consumers suffering from a crisis of confidence, and politicians and government officials from a crisis of competence. The former has been exacerbated by the latter, because the mishandling of economic policy has compounded the crisis of confidence. Pushing democratic licence to extremes, politicians in the US, UK and even Germany have produced what one senior official has called "the appalling paralysis of fiscal policy".[22] One of the most important Keynesian legacies to the capitalist system was the knowledge that the vicissitudes of the business cycle could be ironed out by the ability to *raise* as well as lower taxes. By the practice of fiscal profligacy in the pursuit of votes, Western politicians have made the running of their own capitalist system more difficult. Combined with the profligacy of credit creation under the deregulation free-for-all, the new law of taxation – that income tax can only fall, never rise – succeeded in exacerbating the business cycle, not ironing it out.

The excessive deflation under the monetarist regimes of the UK and US early 1980s was damaging; so was the excessive encouragement of expansion in the late 1980s. The US administration did not raise taxes to control the boom – wanting to believe in its immortality; the British Government actually lowered income taxes further in 1988, on top of a credit boom which had already extended the capacity of the system. In both of these Anglo-Saxon economies the industrial base was suffering from the slings and arrows of outrageous policies, although industrial production fared a lot better in the US than in the UK.

The fiscal profligacy of the US during the 1980s became notorious. The result was that the whole weight of macro-economic policy fell on monetary policy – monetary stimulation via lower interest rates being notorious among Keynesians as being akin to "pushing on a string". Even that model economy, Germany, fell into bad ways by largely eschewing fiscal means to pay the bill for unification, thereby throwing the weight of restrictive, anti-inflationary action on monetary policy. And the rest of capitalist Europe was voluntarily binding itself to the special circumstances of Germany's deflationary position via a refusal to realign exchange rates within the European exchange rate mechanism.

It is hardly surprising that, with business and consumer confidence so low, and economic policymakers seemingly paralysed, 1991–92 saw a revival of fears that recession might deepen into outright depression. In 1990–91 the German reunification boom had counteracted, to some extent, the contractionary effects on world trade of the recession in the Anglo-Saxon countries. But if the latter did not now emerge, and protectionist pressures in the US mounted, there could well be a threat of the worst scenario for international capitalism since the 1930s. As Professor Lamfalussy said: "The hard fact is that the resilience of our new financial environment has not yet been tested by a genuine worldwide recession."

It is worth noting that the ominous crisis of confidence in the "market economies" of the world in the early 1990s could certainly not be blamed on the price of oil, which by 1992 was, in real terms, back to the levels prevailing before the second oil shock of 1979–80. In the end the third world (in which category one has to include large segments of the former communist countries) is dependent on the buoyancy of the major capitalist countries – both for demand for its products, and financial and other assistance with its development. Informed estimates suggest the greater part of the US foreign aid budget (itself well below the UN target of 0.8 per cent of GDP) was geared one way or another (after the large flow to Israel) to the fight against communism. The "America First" movement during Presidential Election year was hardly conducive to great hopes in this respect.

Capitalism had triumphed over Communism, but the tools of economic management which had helped it to manage itself, and the spirit of international co-operation which had prevented competitive capitalism from endangering itself, were both looking worn.

The fashion for, and actuality of, the minimum of economic management during the 1980s – except at moments of potential systemic crisis – has been seen to bring with it severe costs. There are enough needs and wants in the world to show, without much argument, that the potential demands on technology and for further economic progress are still enormous. Even if the leading trading blocs do not resort to protectionism, the mere fact that the possibility, or probability, is so openly talked about and forecast is itself alarming. Not only is the Keynesian/international economic co-operation consensus of the post-war years at risk; not only do the excessively-free-market-orientated US and UK economies end up, ironically, *impeding* the function of their "market" economies – so that they live in terror of Japan and Germany; as if this were not enough, and the potential crisis of confidence among businessmen and consumers so disturbing (given the perceived incompetence of their own policy-makers) – as if this were not sufficiently formidable a challenge to the system in itself, we also encounter the problem of the transition from the Cold War, via the distribution of the Peace Dividend.

In theory the Peace Dividend should do nothing but good. Just as the post Second World War transition from the full scale production of armaments to (largely) civilian goods was an enormous benefit to the populations of the former adversaries, so the transfer of resources from armaments production to civilian requirements ought to be a considerable benefit – a true dividend.

On the other hand, just as the collapse of communism in Eastern Bloc countries is being followed by appreciation of the magnitude of the problems of constructing a successful market economy, so the Peace Dividend does not magically appear by itself. Indeed, the danger is that, if the present crisis of capitalist confidence persists, and previous "leave it to the free market" philosophies prevail, it is not inconceivable that we could witness all the bad news – closures of naval shipyards, and military aircraft production lines, without much in the way of good news from redeployment of resources to more productive ends.

The irony of the triumphalism surrounding the collapse of communism is that it coincides with the urgent need for capitalism itself to be better co-ordinated. The post-war consensus involved more planning than the subsequent revivalists of primitive capitalism acknowledged – and was more successful than they would ever have conceded – while still leaving large pockets of relative deprivation in the advanced countries, and vast areas begging for further help outside them. Japanese industrial capitalism has been stunningly successful internationally – too much so if it leads to serious recriminations from other countries – but anybody who has visited Japan, let alone the Japanese themselves, knows that there is still scope in Japan for aspects of the "social capitalism" of countries such as Germany and Sweden. US "democratic capitalism" fails not only a significant proportion of its racial minorities; it also fails the simple test that the visitor from outer space would be advised not to walk a large proportion of its urban streets.

There may be a long-term tendency towards convergence of economic performance – so that Japan's "competitive planning" version of industrial capitalism becomes more prevalent. Equally, there may be continued divergence, with Japan getting better and better, and others not nearly catching up. But all will suffer if the present crisis of confidence leads competitive capitalists to draw in their horns and put up the barriers.

There was much derisory talk, usually on the part of the left, about the "capitalist system" when communism was still being taken as a serious threat. But capitalism is not so much a system as a way of life that has evolved historically, and been harnessed to the Industrial Revolution – and so-called Post Industrial Society. One essential difference between communism and capitalism is that the former *was* a system, whereas the latter, by inclination, is not. Left to itself – possibly encouraged to be so by extreme free marketeers – capitalism embraces a Darwinian power struggle within society. Left to itself, capitalism brings out the anarchic tendencies of a certain side of human nature (witness the "Wild West" style capitalism at present flourishing in the former USSR). Left to itself, capitalism appeals to narrow private interest which, allied with power, luck and successful lobbying, tries to secure a partial set of rules which suits interested parties only. Under competitive capitalism a similar struggle occurs between countries as within them. Hence the need for the management of capitalism, by means of a clear set of rules, within countries and from without. It is true that international co-ordination broke down in the past. But, if we accept that the extreme free-market approach is a disaster, it is time once again to make the effort to manage capitalism more effectively.

Communism has indeed left capitalism to itself. Communism lost the competitive struggle. Now capitalism, to be successful, requires a system to be imposed on it. The threat of communism and socialism imposed a makeshift, quasi-system of rules on capitalism. But the collapse of communism, and the consequent (possibly temporary) abeyance of Western socialist movements, encourages, via bourgeois triumphalism, the anarchic tendencies of capitalism – both within and between capitalist countries. It will have become evident that "social capitalism" is the preferred form of this book; but, in the end, social capitalism is dependent on a successfully functioning "market economy". The problems of the global environment are almost certain to force a system on capitalism in the next century. What is needed meanwhile is the rescue of the world trading order, and the reinvigoration of the commitment to an orderly working of the international economic and financial "system" that characterised much of the 1945–73 period. Only by putting its own house in order and restoring its own confidence is capitalism likely to help the former communist countries now staring the spectre of capitalism in the face.

Conclusion

The problem facing the entire capitalist world is that similar accommodations of public and private interest have to be made on a global scale and a national scale. Just as there are failures of the marketplace within a national economy, so there are failures in economic relations between countries. Just as motivation based on self-interest can cause havoc with one national economy, and requires rules and regulations laid down by enlightened public intervention, so the self-interest of nations conflicts if they, collectively, are gobbling up the finite resources of the world faster than they are being replaced.

This book has been harsh on communism, but not laudatory of the capitalism in vogue when communism collapsed. This is not to suggest that there is a serious alternative to capitalism. But it seems desirable (from a humanitarian point of view) and judicious (from capitalism's point of view) that the emphasis should be on "social capitalism" at the national and international level. Traditionally, the prime motivation of capitalists is self-interest. With the demise of communism the main motive for capitalism to assist the Third World has gone. But at an international level, the new factors militating against the extreme free-market capitalism of the 1980s are likely to be the environment and the threat of large-scale migration. The argument that greater co-ordination has been tried before and failed comes up against the charge that the extreme free-market approach has itself been tried again and found seriously defective.

An approach based on simple faith in "markets" is inadequate for the problems now confronting a world economy that is also known by the label "the capitalist system". Scientists may disagree about the extent of the dangers to the environment from the emission of CO_2; and extrapolations about the rate at which energy resources will be used up can easily be ridiculed – thus the Club of Rome and Massachusetts Institute of Technology forecasts in the early 1970s about future oil consumption did not make enough allowance for the effect of conservation and substitution – nevertheless there is hardly any disagreement on one basic point: the world cannot go on with the familiar pattern of economic development, let alone adding to demand with a desirable improvement in the performance of the underdeveloped countries.

Simple mathematics demonstrates that the world will pollute itself beyond return, or run out of natural resources, if it does not take account of this prospect in its collective economic, industrial and trade policies. One suggestion is that economic development should be based on the requirement that the *natural* stock of capital – the earth's resources of minerals, trees, raw materials etc – should not be diminished over time.[1] This may not be wholly logical: but the desirable outcome must lie closer to this end of the spectrum than to a situation where resources are used up regardless, and economic activity takes place with no account of the environment on which it depends.

The earth and its atmosphere constitute a process whereby a continuous recycling of certain resources goes on – the most obvious being the way water eventually returns in the form of rain. The problem posed by recent economic and population growth has been that the rate at which resources such as forests can be renewed has run behind the rate at which they are being used up. This is an important area where the interests of the capitalist or market economies converge with those of the developing countries (the South).

One of the big concerns of the developing countries is that they will lose from the collapse of communism because of the way the attention of the West has been diverted. "Capitalist" involvement with the developing countries before the collapse of communism was characterised by a number of motives and historical accidents. There were the links of empire and colonialism; there was the desire, much emphasised by Marxists, for markets, sources of raw materials and cheap labour; there was also a certain ethical motivation, however minor a part this latter might have played (as expressed in the targets, not achieved for long, for development aid, and the responses to famines and other natural disasters); there was also the fear of the spread of communism.

Although there are still strong trading links between developed and developing countries, these are in some ways weaker than before. We have seen that, with the exception of oil, the developing countries are more dependent on the markets of the industrial economies than the latter are on the former. The industrial countries are rich in agriculture and in the use of synthetic materials for what they once imported from the South. Ethical motivation for helping the South took a blow during the Reagan/Thatcher years – indeed, the increase in destitution and inequality of income *within* industrial countries demonstrated that charity was not beginning at home.

These things go in cycles, and the response of the younger generation to Ethiopian famine – "Band Aid" and "Live Aid" – showed that ethical considerations were not entirely dormant.

The relationship between ethics and economics has been disputed since Aristotle. Niebuhr observed that "Society . . . makes justice rather than unselfishness its highest moral ideal."[2] Christ, Kant and (in the present day) Rawls have all offered different versions of the ideal of treating others the way one would wish to be treated oneself. Raw power and hard politics, however, provide a limit to the degree of economic equality within any society. Most redistribution of income and wealth in the 20th century has taken place during, or immediately after, world wars, when the sense of collective national effort has permeated into public policy. Despite the efforts of liberal, left wing and reformist parties generally, Pareto's observation that the distribution of income and wealth tends to remain skewed in an obvious pattern has stood the test of time. If anything, the weight of "redistributive" reform has been needed to prevent the rich from getting richer and the poor poorer. It was a singular achievement of the Reagan and Thatcher era that redistribution of income towards the rich was tolerated in two democracies. The ultimate revulsion of the British electorate towards such a policy was seen in the overthrow of Mrs Thatcher, because of the universal unpopularity of her poll tax, in 1990. Yet the British electorate voted resoundingly in its own self- interest in April 1992 when rejecting a Labour Party platform which offered help for the poor via higher taxes for middle and upper income groups.

There are (often unspoken) ethical assumptions, and ethical limits, to economic policy in a modern democracy. When homelessness reached the point in the London of the early 1990s where residents and visitors found themselves almost stepping over the homeless, huddled in doorways, on the way to the theatre, there was a widespread reaction that "something must be done". The author knows of no survey which distinguished between the proportion of passers-by whose revulsion was motivated by natural charity, or by self-interest (there might come a point where people would donate their taxes to the homeless in order to make life easier for themselves, if for no other reason). Nevertheless, there was a groundswell of political opinion against the policies which led to such hardship.

While the ethical debate has continued in capitalist societies over the years, ideas about total economic equality have gradually receded from the debate. Such equality was only achieved up to a point in the former Soviet Bloc. In Britain a Labour Party intellectual, Anthony Crosland, acknowledged in the 1950s that socialist ideals would have to be achieved by economic growth, not by redistribution. The slogan which unites most moderates of left and right is "equality of opportunity", which in the 1980s invited the riposte "opportunity to be unequal".

It is the proximity of social hardship that tends to prick consciences. There are to this day paternalist landlords and employers who see it as their duty to look after employees and tenants – some oppose the role of the state because they feel it is not needed; but not all employers and owners are so paternalistic, and even the best motivated paternalists can end up, if not prompted, employing their staff in a way which has not caught up with the times. (How many domestic staff wages are adjusted automatically for inflation? How many of the modern rich think their staff are entitled to as long holidays as they have themselves?)

But even the criterion of the "proximity" of hardship was sorely tested by the conditions, in the early 1990s, in such "enlightened" societies as Britain. One had to be a unique combination of saint and multi-millionaire to be able to claim, in London, that one had never refused to give alms to a beggar – indeed, that one had given more often than one had refused. Such a development in society was a classic case of the need for government, acting on behalf of society, to redistribute money in a way which would assess genuine need. The state is better equipped to make such an assessment than is the passing individual, who on a hurried journey meets a beggar. This argument applies to the broader areas of education, health and housing. It is a game of chance if the allocation of such resources to the poor has to depend on charity, as the New Right would prefer. But the real tragedy in the 1980s was that the problem of poverty was aggravated by economic policies biased, in the US and UK, towards redistribution of income and wealth towards the rich.

As has been noted, the "proximity" of hardship can, via the television screen, provoke charitable efforts such as Band Aid and Live Aid. But when the disasters mount, and leap out at people night after night, people are numbed – rather as they were said to be by the Vietnam War's prominence on television news bulletins.

There are limits to which historical leaps can be made, and we have seen how long it took the more successful capitalist economies to achieve their present standards of living. Nevertheless, whether the motive was post-colonial guilt, self-interest or altruism associated with the post-war golden age, there was at least a desire to give aid to the developing nations for much of the post-war period. The self-interest was motivated by the desire to prevent the spread of communism, and the theme of such discussions at the 1991 Bangkok IMF meeting that were not preoccupied with the problems of the G7 and the former Soviet Union was precisely that the collapse of communism and the problems of the east would divert attention from the South – as well as sapping the "self-interest" motive of the capitalist nations. Countries that received aid as a bulwark against the spread of communism would obviously slip down the list; countries that were indeed Soviet satellites would also lose money from the collapse of a donor that no longer had an economic model to export.

On top of which the entire aid effort had run into a combination of hostility in the capitalist countries to the amount of waste on military spending, prestige projects and corruption. During the 1980s the anti-aid philosophy had coincided with the shift to the right in the major Anglo-Saxon economies, and the spread of the antagonism towards the "dependency culture" from welfare spending at home to aid abroad.

Given the perennial political constraints on public spending, a move back towards "social capitalism" within the industrial countries would not necessarily, of itself, connote good news for the developing world. Indeed, just as the end of communism may be bad news for a developing world that could in the past play off one side against another, a reversal of the move to the right in the capitalist countries might lead to more welfare spending at home, but not abroad. With pent-up demand for better public services in many of the industrial countries, it is easy to see how once again there could be pretexts for failing to fulfil aid commitments.

The irony is that, at a time when most developing countries (including parts of China) have accepted the principle of market economics, their interests are being neglected and their role in global decision-making has been diluted by the way the Group of Seven has usurped such co-ordination of policy as there is. It has already been observed that the 1980s were bad years for most of the LDCs – outside the Asian NICs, India and China – with falls in living standards, low earnings from commodity prices and net outflows of capital. The principal way in which the G7 came to the assistance of the LDCs in the 1980s was through debt relief, where a prominent motive was the desire to protect the Western banking system.

Arguments on Christian/Kantian/Rawlian lines would imply a massive redistribution of income towards the third world. But any idea that such an ethical approach is practicable comes up against the fact that even against the background of the minimal generosity shown so far, with aid commitment targets of 0.7 per cent of GDP annually, such targets have nowhere near been met; and when such aid *is* granted, much of it is on a tied basis – that is, tied to the donor country's export shipments.

The potential global environmental crisis offers a long-term reason for the capitalist economies to pay more attention to the needs of the developing world out of self-interest, just as the sheer scale of the problems confronting the former communist bloc offers the scope for a modern Marshall Plan from which the recession-hit capitalist countries would benefit by supplying capital goods.[3] The future of the entire global economic system requires adaptation by advanced and developing countries in their use of natural resources and their pollution of the environment. It is in the interests of the developed capitalist economies that the South is helped to help the planet. The problems to be faced are intricate. On some calculations, natural resources that were taken for granted in the past will be used up; on others, the depletion of the ozone layer could cause such damage to plant life that the very process by which the sun provides the most fundamental form of growth would be threatened.

Adapting to the challenges of the environment could provide a major stimulus to the technological development of what we call capitalism. One expert has declared: "The 'good news', as we move into the last decade of the century, is that a new generation of technology is appearing, driven by government regulation and pulled by the market demands of the rapidly emerging 'green consumer'." The emphasis is on low inputs of raw material and fuel, efficiency of use, and minimum noxious emission.[4]

But "progress" has to be carefully monitored, and appropriate regulations properly designed and rigorously enforced. Thus, despite the phenomenon of "dematerialisation", under which the capitalist countries are tending to use less energy or material weight per new unit of output, total energy use has certainly not declined. The expansion of world population, and the growth of real incomes, after the first oil shock of 1973, meant that "over this period hailed for its growing 'energy efficiency' 125 countries increased their overall energy consumption, and world energy use expanded by 20 per cent."[5]

Successive World Economic Summits, and the 1990 World Climate Conference, have produced discussion and grand aims (including some OECD measures "agreed in principle" for the achievement of energy efficiency, and help to the LDCs in fighting pollution, by the year 2010), but, as the June 1992 Rio Earth Summit showed, world leaders were finding it difficult to get down to brass tacks. The attitude behind the slogan "America First" meant that President Bush only reluctantly took the Road to Rio. Market economies may have triumphed over communism, and communism may have produced more pollution, for a given output, than any other system. But, as one scientist observed: "It is becoming increasingly clear that a simplistic, market led energy policy does almost nothing to protect the environment . . . and ironic that, as the centrally planned economies crumble and switch to privatisation, a global energy strategy becomes imperative."[6]

In fact, the survival of the world as we know it depends on close co-operation between North and South in tackling the problems of global warming, the ozone layer, deforestation and the pollution of the sea and rivers. It has been demonstrated in the advanced economies that, notwithstanding the initial complaints of industrialists, "regulation" and the application of pollution controls are not obstacles to economic growth: they are both necessary in the long term and a contribution to growth in the short term – the move to the production of cars with catalytic converters was, for example, a boost to the German car industry in the late 1980s and early 1990s. The concept of relief for debt in Latin America in return for "good" environmental measures, such as the preservation of forests, is a start. But it has been well pointed out that the South's ability to co-operate with the North is a function of its economic development. Similarly, the population explosion which threatens to engulf the entire planet can eventually be reduced, to some extent automatically (in addition to the effect of family planning), by more rapid economic development: there is strong evidence that high real incomes correlate with smaller families.

The extreme free market philosophy is riven with holes, at both a national and global level. It soon became apparent to the US State Department in 1992 that an influx of Soviet nuclear scientists onto the market, prepared to sell their talents at the highest market price, would not be in the interest of the capitalist economies. Civilised society would break down if lawyers in the possession of confidential information about their clients simply sold this to the highest bidder in the tabloid press. Most people have a deep-seated objection to "profiteering", as opposed to the accepted concept of normal profit, in a market economy. It was the way the nomenclatura took to profiteering in the former communist bloc which appealed to Chicago economists, but not to the people at large. Earning money is a more fundamentally economic concept than making it.

The pursuit of profit, and the dictates of extreme market forces, can make it in the interests of developing countries to cultivate the basic drug plants. And why, since extreme market philosophies dictate that "capital" should be able to move wherever it will, should not "labour" do the same?

In the end, just as early capitalism had to adapt and make concessions to trades unionists, it is going to be in the interest of capitalist countries to develop a more harmonious and far-sighted relationship with the developing world. And this does not mean just the former communist bloc.

Believers in classical economics, free markets, and pure capitalism are at something of a loss when it comes to migration and the mobility of labour. There was much talk in Britain during the 1980s about the need to "free up" labour markets, and increase the mobility of labour. But in practice such mobility is welcomed only up to a point. Within a country it does not make sense for all labour to be attracted to a capital city – hence the importance of regional policies to maintain a balance, and a spread of investment and employment. Internationally, since the Second World War, the (often unspoken) consensus has been that the pursuit of free trade and freedom in the movement of capital would keep international labour mobility under reasonable control. The United States economy itself might have been born of large-scale migration from Europe; but large-scale immigration constitutes a hot political and social potato, and is best avoided, according to the unspoken assumption.

There were exceptions to this rule, when it suited host countries: thus certain jobs were filled in Germany by Turkish "guest workers", in the UK by West Indians and Asians, and in France by Algerians. So concerned were other members of the original European Economic Community, however, about a possible wave of Italian immigrants that free labour mobility was deliberately postponed until the late 1960s. In theory, with ageing populations and lower birth rates, EC countries stand to benefit in the 1990s, and after, from further migration. But the theory does not sit too comfortably with the social pressures already being caused, and reflected in election results in 1992, by high unemployment. Immigrant labour was much easier to absorb when unemployment was between 1 and 2 per cent in the 1950s, as opposed to 10 per cent and over in the early 1990s.

The obvious pressures coming in the 1990s are a vast wave of immigrants from Eastern Europe and the former Soviet Union, if economic progress in the east is not sufficient. Migration is the traditional economic response to hardship, or to the kind of atrocities suffered in the former Yugoslavia. And, as was becoming apparent in Italy in the early 1990s, there is also the chance that immigration pressures may step up from the third world – North Africa being one neighbouring source. The encouragement of the North American Free Trade Area has, to some extent, reflected a desire to stem migration of Hispanics across the US border by improving Mexican living standards via freer trade.

We have seen that the flow of migrants into West Germany was an important factor behind the terms on which German Monetary

Union was conducted. But the statistics early in 1992 indicated that there were still strong flows into Western Germany from the east. A "tolerable" flow of migration can bring economic benefits all round – indeed remittances by home migrant workers are estimated to total more than the actual flow of overseas aid from the OECD countries to the third world.[7] But the threat of migration – the free flow of labour getting out of hand – is an unexploded weapon in the hands of those developing countries whose peoples are not already so crippled by starvation as to be physically unable to migrate. It becomes in the self-interest of the capitalist and market economies to do a lot more to even out the economic inequalities between nations. At one extreme one could even imagine the "free market" in labour operating internationally to flood the advanced "market" economies to the point where the right wing ideal of dirt cheap labour is indeed achieved – but at the price of social discontent and sedition calculated to restore all the revolutionary fervour which capitalism, after the events of 1989, thinks it has finally quashed.

At a national level the demise of communism rather rules out the threat of "revolution" as a salutary constraint on the excesses of capitalism. Galbraith has drawn attention to the limits on more enlightened capitalism posed by the complacency of the majority – "the culture of contentment". But it may be that the social *dis*content of prolonged high unemployment could yet disturb this complacency.

The capitalist world has been suffering from too great a faith in the virtues of the free market, and from the excesses to which that faith led in the 1980s. With Keynesian techniques, with renewed international co-ordination and with the prodigious scope offered by continuous scientific and technological progress, there is no need to retreat into a despairing world of Kondratieff-style "long-wave" theories, or to bow to the spectre of prolonged Depression. Appropriate economic policy may not suffice to promote economic growth; but inappropriate economic policy certainly prolongs recession.

Communism was an inappropriate economic policy, and central planning caused poor economic performance. Communists put politics above economics. Extreme free-marketeers put economics above politics. Economics and politics have a symbiotic relationship. The problems now facing capitalists and former communists require acknowledgement of past mistakes, and careful, pragm̶   ̶ ̶
ordination. If people's lives are left to the vagaries of the fre̶
capitalism is indeed a dangerous spectre.

8 Au

Notes

INTRODUCTION

1. Francis Fukuyama, *The End of History and the Last Man*, Hamish Hamilton, London, 1992
2. Francis Fukuyama, *The Guardian*, London, 15 December 1989
3. Interview with George Blake, *The Guardian*, London, 19 September 1990
4. Abel Aganbegyan, *The Challenge: Economics of Perestroika*, London, 1988
5. Martin Malia, *International Herald Tribune*, London, 1 September 1990
6. William Keegan, *Sheffield Papers in International Studies*, no. 9, England, 1991, pp. 24–6
7. J K Galbraith, *The Affluent Society*, 1958
8. Winston S Churchill, Speech to House of Commons, London, 25 March 1954

CHAPTER ONE

1. J M Keynes, *Essays in Persuasion*, Macmillan, Cambridge University Press (CUP), 1984, p. 262
2. Ibid., p. 293
3. Ibid., p. 261
4. Ibid., p. 263
5. Ibid., p. 262
6. Ibid., p. 258
7. Ibid., pp. 267–8
8. Ibid., p. 306
9. Ibid., pp. 304–5
10. Ibid., p. 294
11. Ibid., p. 268
12. William L Shirer, *The Rise and Fall of the Third Reich*, Secker and Warburg, London, 1963, p. 185
13. Alan Bullock, *Hitler and Stalin: Parallel Lives*, Harper Collins, London, 1991. Also, interview with Lord Bullock, Channel Four Television, London, June 1991
14. J M Keynes, op. cit., pp. 292–3
15. J K Galbraith, *A History of Economics*, Penguin, London, 1987, p. 253
16. Correlli Barnett, *The Audit of War*, Macmillan, London, 1986
17. J K Galbraith, *A History of Economics*, Penguin, London, 1987, p. 255
18. Denis Healey, *The Time of My Life*, Michael Joseph, London, 1989, pp. 34–7
19. Robert Marjolin, *Architect of European Unity*, Weidenfeld and Nicolson, London, 1989, p. 48
20. Ibid.
21. Ibid., p. 49
22. J M Keynes, op. cit., p. 299

23. D E Moggridge, *Maynard Keynes: An Economist's Biography*, Routledge, London and New York, 1992

24. Lord Robbins, *Autobiography of an Economist*, Macmillan, London, 1971, pp. 154–5, p. 188

25. Angus Maddison, *The World Economy in the 20th Century*, Organisation for Economic Cooperation and Development (OECD), Paris, 1989, p. 63

26. Robert Marjolin, op. cit., p. 157

27. Robert Fraser, *The World Financial System* (A Keesing's Reference Publication), Longman, London, 1987, p. 13

28. *International Monetary Fund Articles of Agreement*, Bretton Woods, New Hampshire, 22 July 1944, Article 1, quoted in Fraser, op. cit., pp. 19 and 315

29. Robert Marjolin, op. cit., p. 231

30. Robert Fraser, op. cit., p. 13

31. Robert Marjolin, op. cit., p. 230

32. United Nations Economic Commission for Europe, *Economic Survey of Europe in 1989–90*, New York, 1989, Ch. 1: 10

33. Sir Alec Cairncross, *Years of Recovery*, Methuen, London and New York, 1985, p. 137

34. Sir Richard "Otto" Clarke, *Anglo-American Economic Collaboration in War and Peace*, 1942–9, ed. Sir Alec Cairncross, Clarendon Press, Oxford, 1982, p. 191

35. Ibid., p. 209

36. Alan S Milward, *The Reconstruction of Western Europe 1945–1951*, Methuen, London, 1984, p. 3

37. Ibid.

38. Angus Maddison, op. cit., p. 32

39. Ibid., p. 34

40. Ibid., p. 69

41. Ibid.

42. Ibid.

43. Ibid., p. 35

CHAPTER TWO

1. Arthur Seldon, *Capitalism*, Basil Blackwell, Oxford, 1990, p. 152

2. Reinhold Niebuhr, *Moral Man and Immoral Society*, Charles Scribner's Sons, New York, 1932

3. Adam Raphael, *The Guardian*, London, March 1973

4. OECD, *The Transition to a Market Economy*, Vol. 1, Paris, 1991, p. 108

5. Andrew Shonfield, *The Use of Public Power*, Oxford University Press (OUP), England, 1982, p. 25

6. *OECD Economic Surveys*, "Japan 1990/91", Paris, November 1991, p. 131

7. Irwin Stelzer, *Sunday Times*, London, 8 March 1992

8. Geoffrey Lean, *The Observer*, London, September 1989

9. Octavio Paz, *New York Times*, 8 December 1991

10. Peter Nolan, *The Chinese Economy and its Future*, Polity Press and Basil Blackwell, Oxford, 1990, p. 116

11. Ibid., p. 117

12. Gerhard Colm, quoted by Kurt Schmidt, in Peacock and Willgerodt (eds.), *Germany's Social Market Economy: Origins and Evolution*, Macmillan, London, 1989, p. 197

13. Michael P Fogarty, *Christian Democracy in Western Europe 1820–1953*, Routledge and Kegan Paul, London, 1966, p. 133

14. Ibid., p. 27

15. Hans Otto Lenel, "Evolution of the Social Market Economy" (quoting Röpke, and Eucken), in Peacock and Willgerodt (eds.), *German Neo-Liberals and the Social Market Economy*, Macmillan, London, 1989, p. 22

16. I am indebted to Neal Ascherson for this information.

17. Alfred Müller-Armack, "The Meaning of the Social Market Economy", in Peacock and Willgerodt (eds.), *Germany's Social Market Economy: Origins and Evolution*, Macmillan, London, 1989, pp. 82–6

18. Alan Peacock and Hans Willgerodt, *German Neo-Liberals and the Social Market Economy*, Macmillan, London, 1989, p. 4

19. Charles Feinstein (and others), *Historical Precedents for Economic Change in Central Europe and the USSR*, Credit Suisse First Boston/Oxford Analytica, England, October 1990, p. 32

20. Adam Przeworski, *Democracy and the Market – Political and Economic Reforms in Eastern Europe and Latin America*, CUP, Cambridge, 1991, p. 66

21. Mark Frankland, *Observer* Foreign News Service, London, 15 April 1992

22. Geoff Hodgson, *The Democratic Economy*, Penguin, London, 1984, p. 114

23. Jacques Attali, President, European Bank for Reconstruction and Development (EBRD), speech to Overseas Bankers Club, London, 3 February 1992

24. Ian Gilmour, *Inside Right*, Hutchinson, London, 1977, p. 235

25. OECD, *The Transition to a Market Economy*, Vol. 1, Paris, 1991, p. 291

26. Ibid., p. 292, and Hodgson, op. cit., p. 110

27. Angus Maddison, *Phases of Capitalist Development*, OUP, Oxford, 1989, pp. 11–13

28. Adam Smith, *An Inquiry into the Nature and Causes of the Wealth of Nations*, George Routledge, London, 1893 (edn.), p. 8

29. Ibid., p. 8

30. Angus Maddison, op. cit., Oxford, 1989, p. 16

31. Adam Smith, op. cit., p. 594

32. *Scientific American*, November 1990

33. E J Hobsbawm, *Industry and Empire*, Penguin, London, 1979, p. 77

34. Ibid., p. 94

35. Joseph A Schumpeter, *Capitalism, Socialism and Democracy*, George Allen & Unwin, London, 1976, p. 132

36. Frederic Austin Ogg and Walter Rice Sharp, *Economic*

Development of Modern Europe, Macmillan, New York, 1930, p. 462

37. Karl Polanyi, *The Great Transformation*, Beacon Press, Boston, USA, 1944, p. 139

38. Ibid.

39. Charles Gide and Charles Rist, *A History of Economic Doctrines* (2nd edition), George C Harrap, London, 1950, p. 30

40. Taussig, *Principles of Economics*, Vol. 2, p. 455

41. Ogg and Sharp, op. cit., p. 465

42. Ibid., p. 498

43. Polanyi, op. cit., p. 141

44. Ogg and Sharp, op. cit., p. 291

45. Friedrich List, *The National System of Political Economy*, 1841

46. Gide and Rist, op. cit., p. 290

47. Adam Smith, op. cit., p. 287

48. Ibid., p. 262

49. Ibid., p. 266

50. Ibid., p. 289

51. C R Fay, *Great Britain from Adam Smith to the Present Day* (3rd edition), Longmans, London, 1932, p. 315

52. Ibid., p. 127

53. Charles P Kindleberger, *A Financial History of Western Europe*, George Allen and Unwin, Boston and Sydney, 1984, pp. 191–3, and Edwin Green, *Banking*, Phaidon, Oxford, 1989, p. 55

54. Fay, op. cit., p. 385

55. Viscount Goschen, *Essays and Addresses*, p. 23

56. Fay, op. cit., p. 385

57. James Joll, *Europe Since 1870*, Harper & Row, New York, 1973, p. 474

58. Ibid., p. 442

59. V I Lenin, *Imperialism: The Highest Stage of Capitalism*

60. Robert Lekachman and Borin Van Loon, *Capitalism for Beginners*, Writers and Readers Publishing Cooperative, London, 1981, and Robert Fraser, op. cit.

61. Robert Fraser, op. cit., p. 59

62. Ibid., pp. 65 and 73

63. Ibid., p. 78

64. Ibid., p. 83

65. Ibid., p. 81

66. Maddison, op. cit. (Oxford), p. 140

67. Ibid., p. 267

68. Ibid., p. 149

69. Paul McCracken and others, *Towards Full Employment and Price Stability*, OECD, Paris, 1977

70. Maddison, op. cit. (Paris), p. 88

71. A J C Britton, *Macroeconomic Policy in Britain 1974–1987*, National Institute of Economic and Social Research, Cambridge, 1991, p. 133

72. Philip Armstrong et al., *Capitalism Since World War II*, Fontana, London, 1984, p. 237

73. Britton, op. cit., p. 133

CHAPTER THREE

1. Maddison, op. cit. (Oxford), p. 152

2. Milton Friedman and Anna J Schwartz, *Monetary Trends in the United States and the United Kingdom: their relation to income, prices and interest rates, 1867–1975*, University of Chicago Press, Chicago and London, 1982,

and Milton Friedman,
*Inflation, Causes,
Consequences, Cures*,
Institute of Economic Affairs,
London, 1974

3. Milton and Rose Friedman,
Free to Choose, Secker &
Warburg, London, 1980,
p. 253

4. Ibid., p. 254
5. Ibid., p. 262
6. Ibid.
7. *OECD Economic Outlook
48*, OECD, Paris, December
1990, p. 185
8. Friedman, 1980, op. cit.,
p. 265
9. Ibid., p. 266
10. Ibid.
11. Noted by Lekachman, 1981,
op. cit., p. 153
12. Lekachman, 1982, op. cit.
13. Sidney Blumenthal, *The Rise
and Fall of the Counter-
Establishment*, Times Books,
New York, 1986
14. Ibid., p. 4
15. Ibid.
16. Ibid., p. 66
17. Ibid., p. 153
18. Ibid., p. 55
19. Ibid., pp. 56–7
20. Ibid., p. 63
21. Ibid., pp. 182–3, and Jude
Wanniski, *The Public
Interest*, New York, 1975
22. Frank Ackerman,
*Reaganomics – Rhetoric vs
Reality*, Pluto Press, London,
1982, p. 16
23. Ibid., pp. 42–3
24. C A R Crosland, *The Future
of Socialism*, London, 1956
25. Robert Nozick, *Anarchy,
State & Utopia*, Blackwell,
Oxford, 1975, p. 163
26. Lekachman, op. cit., 1982,
p. 11

27. Ibid., p. 12
28. Ibid., p. 17
29. *OECD Economic Outlook
48*, OECD, Paris, December
1990, p. 175
30. David A Stockman, *The
Triumph of Politics*, Harper
& Row, New York, 1986,
p. 267
31. *Reaganomics & After*,
Institute of Economic Affairs,
London, 1989
32. *OECD Economic Surveys*,
"United States 1989–90",
Paris, November 1990, p. 65
33. Stockman, op. cit., p. 366
34. Ibid., p. 369
35. Ibid., p. 367
36. Ibid., p. 371
37. *OECD Economic Surveys*,
"United States 1989–90",
Paris, November 1990, p. 21

CHAPTER FOUR

1. Feinstein, op. cit., p. 26
2. Ibid., pp. 22 and 26, quoting
O Crisp, in R Cameron (ed.),
*Banking in the Early Stages of
Industrialization*, 1967, and P
Gatrell, *The Tsarist Economy
1850–1917* (1986)
3. Maurice Dobb, *Economic
Growth and Underdeveloped
Countries*, Lawrence &
Wishart, London, 1963
(reprinted 1973), p. 29
4. Ibid., p. 30
5. Ibid., p. 32
6. Maddison, op. cit. (Paris,
1989), p. 62
7. Ibid., and G D H Cole, *The
Intelligent Man's Guide to the
Post-War World*, Victor
Gollancz, London, 1948,
p. 792

8. Maurice Dobb, *Soviet Economic Development Since 1917*, Routledge & Kegan Paul, London, 1972, p. 297
9. Ibid., pp. 298–9
10. Ibid., p. 301
11. V M Molotov, Foreign Minister, 2 July 1947, quoted in Fraser, op. cit., p. 13
12. Fraser, op. cit., p. 19
13. Dobb, op. cit. (1972), p. 312
14. Cole, op. cit., p. 795
15. Ibid., pp. 804–5
16. Dobb, op. cit. (1963), p. 33
17. Ibid., p. 62
18. J M Keynes, *The General Theory of Employment, Interest and Money*, New York, 1936, p. 381
19. Maddison, op. cit. (Paris, 1989), p. 35
20. Alec Nove, *The Soviet Economic System*, George Allen & Unwin, London, 1977, p. 379
21. A N Kosygin, in Alec Nove and D M Nuti (eds.), *Socialist Economics*, Penguin, England, 1974, p. 319
22. Ibid.
23. Ibid., p. 323
24. Ibid., p. 329
25. Alec Nove, in Nove and Nuti, p. 360
26. Ibid., p. 361
27. Ibid.
28. Ibid., p. 362
29. Ibid., p. 361
30. Maddison, op. cit. (Paris, 1989), p. 100
31. Ibid.
32. Ibid., p. 101
33. Raymond G H Seitz, US Ambassador to the Court of St James's, speech in Birmingham, England, 11 May 1992
34. Maddison, op. cit. (Paris, 1989), p. 101

CHAPTER FIVE

1. Britton, op. cit., p. 298
2. Maddison, op. cit. (Paris, 1989), p. 101
3. F A Hayek, *The Road to Serfdom*, Routledge & Kegan Paul, London, 1944, p. 26
4. F A Hayek, *American Economic Review*, September 1945, quoted in Subroto Roy, *Philosophy of Economics*, Routledge, London, 1989
5. John F Helliwell, OECD, *The Transition to a Market Economy*, Vol. 1, Paris, 1991, p. 119
6. Andrew Shonfield, *Modern Capitalism*, Oxford, 1965, pp. 126 and 192
7. Jean-Charles Asselain, *Planning and Profits in Socialist Economies*, Routledge & Kegan Paul, London, 1981, pp. 14–15
8. Ibid., p. 14
9. Janos Kornai, *Economics of Shortage*, Amsterdam, 1980
10. UN Economic Commission for Europe (UNECE), *Economic Survey of Europe in 1989–90*, New York, 1990, Chapter 1.14
11. Maddison, op. cit. (Paris, 1989), p. 100, and Aganbegyan, op. cit., *passim*
12. UNECE (New York, 1990), op. cit., Ch. 1.6
13. Ota Sik, quoted Asselain, op. cit., p. 105
14. *A Study of the Soviet Economy*, International Monetary Fund, The World Bank, Organisation for Economic Cooperation and Development, European Bank for Reconstruction and Development, Vol. 3, Paris,

February 1991, pp. 68 and 323. (Henceforth referred to as the "Joint Study".)

15. Janos Kornai, *Anti-Equilibrium*, North-Holland, Amsterdam, 1971, p. 254
16. Ibid., pp. 295 and 298
17. Ibid., pp. 287–8
18. Ibid., p. 289
19. J Llewellyn and S Potter, in *Economic Policies for the 1990s*, Blackwell, Oxford, 1991, pp. 14 and 18
20. Joint Study, Vol. 1, p. 12
21. Joint Study, Vol. 3, p. 353
22. Aganbegyan, op. cit., p. 8
23. Ibid., p. 7
24. Ibid., p. 37
25. Ibid., pp. 36–9
26. Joint Study, Vol. 3, p. 220
27. Ibid., p. 213
28. Ibid., p. 183
29. Ibid., p. 9
30. Ibid., p. 10
31. Ibid., p. 7
32. Ibid., p. 8
33. Ibid., p. 109
34. Aganbegyan, op. cit., p. 128
35. Ibid., p. 136
36. Ibid., p. 226
37. Joint Study (Summary), p. 7
38. Joint Study, Vol. 3, p. 15
39. Ibid., p. 14
40. Kindleberger, op. cit., p. 202
41. Joan Robinson, *Freedom & Necessity*, George Allen & Unwin, London, 1970, p. 79
42. Aldous Huxley, *Ends and Means*, Chatto & Windus, London, 1938
43. Schumpeter, op. cit., p. 189
44. Joint Study, Vol. 3, p. 303

CHAPTER SIX

1. Sir John Harvey-Jones, *The Observer*, London, 25 August 1991
2. Feinstein, op. cit., p. 1
3. Joint Study, Vol. 3, pp. 304–5
4. Feinstein, op. cit., p. 30
5. Ibid.
6. Ibid., p. 31
7. Marvin J Wolf, *The Japanese Conspiracy*, New English Library, England, 1984, pp. 287–8
8. Feinstein, op. cit., p. 32
9. Ibid.
10. Przeworski, op. cit., p. 182
11. European Bank for Reconstruction and Development (EBRD), *A Changing Europe*, Annual Report 1991, London, 1992
12. Milward, op. cit., p. 94
13. Ibid., p. 97, and Feinstein, op. cit., p. 27
14. Feinstein, op. cit., p. 19
15. Dr Hannes Androsch, speech, Vienna, May 1991
16. Ibid.
17. Y Park, in OECD, *The Transition to a Market Economy*, Vol. 1, Paris, 1991, p. 151
18. Robert B Reich, *The Work of Nations*, Simon & Schuster, London, 1991, pp. 196–207
19. Alistair Cooke, *Financial Times*, London, 10 October 1991
20. Michael Ignatieff, *The Observer*, London, 15 September 1991
21. Przeworski, op. cit., p. 189
22. UNECE, 1991–92, (op. cit.)
23. Przeworski, op. cit., p. 183
24. UNECE, 1990–91 (op. cit.)
25. Ibid., p. 139
26. Ibid., p. 126
27. Ibid., p. 139
28. John M Starrels, *Assisting Reform in Eastern Europe*, IMF, Washington DC, 1991, p. 5

29. UNECE, 1990–91, p. 43
30. Ibid., p. 139
31. UNECE, 1991–92, p. 57
32. Richard Portes, *European Economy: The Path of Reform in Central and Eastern Europe*, Special Edition no. 2, 1991, Directorate-General for Economic and Financial Affairs, Brussels, 1991, p. 4
33. Ibid., p. 5
34. Dr Hannes Androsch, op. cit.
35. Portes, op. cit. (*European Economy*, 1991), p. 12
36. *OECD Economic Surveys: Hungary*, OECD, Paris, July 1991
37. Joint Study, Vol. 3, p. 339
38. Anthony R Boote and Janos Somogyi, "Economic Reform in Hungary Since 1968", IMF Occasional Paper 83, Washington DC, July 1991, pp. 1–3
39. *OECD Economic Surveys: Hungary* (op. cit.), p. 71
40. Hungarian National Bank President, quoted in *Financial Times*, 11 September 1991, *OECD Economic Surveys: Hungary*, (op. cit.), p. 23
41. *OECD Economic Surveys: Hungary* (op. cit.), p. 128, UNECE 1991–92, and EBRD, April 1992 (op. cit.)
42. *OECD Economic Surveys: Hungary* (op. cit.), p. 113
43. Ibid., p. 128, and EBRD, April 1992 (op. cit.), p. 81
44. *OECD Economic Surveys: Hungary* (op. cit.), p. 20
45. Boote and Somogyi, op. cit., p. 33, and *OECD Economic Surveys: Hungary* (op. cit.), p. 23
46. UNECE, 1990–91, p. 266 (table)

47. David Begg, "Economic Reform in Czechoslovakia: should we believe in Santa Claus?" in *Economic Policy*, 13, CUP, England, October 1991, p. 247 (quoting Ehrlich, 1987)
48. Ibid., p. 260, (quoting Hare and Hughes, 1989)
49. Cathy Savage, *Euroview*, Nomura Research Institute, London, October 1991, p. 6
50. Begg, op. cit., p. 270
51. Ibid., pp. 263 and 275, and *European Economy* (op. cit.), p. 105
52. *European Economy* (op. cit.), p. 105, and Begg, p. 279 (op. cit.)
53. *Privatisation, Restructuring & Defence Conversion*, EBRD, April 1982, p. 3
54. UNECE 1991–92, p. 51
55. Ibid.
56. *The Wall Street Journal Europe*, 14 April 1992
57. Jacques Attali, speech to First Annual Meeting, EBRD Board of Governors, Budapest, 13 April 1992
58. Anatole Lieven, *The Tablet*, London, April 1992
59. UNECE, 1991–92, p. 135
60. John Lloyd, *Financial Times*, 5 August 1992

CHAPTER SEVEN

1. Leslie Lipschitz, "German Unification, Economic Issues" (eds. Leslie Lipschitz and Donogh McDonald), Occasional Paper 75, IMF, Washington DC, December 1990, p. 16
2. *World Financial Markets*, Morgan Guaranty Trust, October 1991, p. 13

3. Ibid., p. 1
4. Berlin Economic Institute Bulletin, 1 March 1991, p. 16
5. Sir Donald MacDougall and others, *Report of the Study Group on the Role of Public Finance in European Integration*, Commission of the EC, Brussels, 1977
6. *OECD Economic Outlook, 50*, Paris, December 1991, p. 81
7. *German View of the Social Market Economy*, German Embassy, London, 24 July 1991
8. Helmut Kohl, West German Chancellor, speech to Bundestag, 17 June 1992

CHAPTER EIGHT

1. Michael D Stephens, *Japan and Education*, Macmillan, London, 1991, pp. 83 and 87
2. Dr Raymond Vernon, *International Economic Insights*, Vol. 2, no. 6, Institute for International Economics, Washington DC, November/December 1991, p. 2
3. G C Allen, *The Japanese Economy*, Weidenfeld and Nicolson, London, 1981, pp. 19–21
4. Ibid., p. 31
5. Cf. G. C. Allen, pp. 91 and 129
6. Ibid., p. 89
7. Ibid., p. 87
8. Ibid., p. 161
9. Ibid., p. 175
10. *Japan 1992: An International Comparison*, Keizai Koho Centre, Tokyo, Tables 1.1 and 1.6, and *OECD Economic Outlook*, Paris, December 1992, p. 123
11. *Japan 1992*, op. cit., Table 3.4
12. "OECD In Figures, Statistics on the Member Countries", Supplement to *The OECD Observer*, No. 170, Paris, June/July 1991, p. 27
13. Ibid., pp. 56–7
14. Kiichi Miyazawa, Japanese Prime Minister, reported in *The Guardian*, London, 10 January 1992, p. 9
15. "OECD In Figures", 1991, op. cit., p. 61
16. Ronald Dore, in *Improving Britain's Industrial Performance*, Employment Institute, London, May 1991, pp. 38–9
17. Alan S Blinder, "Profit Maximisation and International Competition", in *Finance and the International Economy: 5*, Richard O'Brien (ed.), OUP for The AMEX Bank Review, 1991, p. 47
18. Seiichi Masuyama, National Economic Development Office Conference Paper, "Capital Markets and Company Success", London, 21/22 November 1991
19. Ibid.
20. Akio Morita and Sony, *Made in Japan*, Collins, London, 1987, p. 225
21. Japanese banker, in private conversation
22. Morita, op. cit., p. 244
23. Ibid.
24. Michael E Porter, *The Competitive Advantage of Nations*, Macmillan, London, 1991, p. 398
25. Hiroyuki Odagiri, *Growth Through Competition,*

Competition Through Growth, Clarendon Press, Oxford, 1992, p. 313

26. Ibid., p. 317
27. Ibid., p. 316
28. Jacques J Polak, in *International Economic Insights*, November/ December 1991 (op. cit.), pp. 29–30
29. Seminar at World Economic Forum, Davos, January 1992
30. Odagiri, op. cit., p. 316
31. Morita, op. cit., p. 253
32. Lawrence B Krause, "Japanese Capitalism: A Model for Others?", *International Economic Insights*, November/ December 1991 (op. cit.), p. 7
33. Ibid., p. 10
34. *International Herald Tribune*, Paris, 21 January 1992
35. Ibid.
36. George Fields, *Wall Street Journal* (Europe), 30 January 1992
37. Will Hutton, *The Guardian*, London, 28 January 1992
38. Jagdish Bhagwati, *Protectionism*, the MIT Press, Cambridge, Mass., 1988
39. Adrian Hamilton, *The Financial Revolution*, Viking, England, 1986
40. *International Herald Tribune*, 8 February 1992
41. *OECD Economic Surveys, Japan, 1990–91*, OECD, Paris, 20 November 1991, p. 131
42. Alan Blinder, op. cit., p. 48
43. *International Herald Tribune*, 23 June 1992
44. Adrian Hamilton, op. cit., p. 167
45. *International Herald Tribune*, 11 January 1992
46. T McCarthy, *The Independent*, 15 February 1992
47. S G Warburg, *International Asset Allocation*, 1992 *Outlook*, London, p. 8
48. Odagiri, op. cit., p. 337

CHAPTER NINE

1. Morita, op. cit., p. 225
2. Gee San, "Technology, Investment and Trade under Economic Globalisation: The Case of Taiwan", citing Vernon (1966), in *Trade, Investment and Technology in the 1990s*, OECD, Paris, p. 59
3. Ibid., citing Hymer (1976)
4. Barrie Stevens and Michel Andrieu, "Trade, Investment and Technology in a Changing International Environment", in OECD, 1991, *Trade, Investment* etc, p. 115
5. Wolfgang Michalski, "Trends and Developments in the Globalisation of Production, Investment and Trade", in OECD, 1991, *Trade, Investment* etc, p. 7
6. Alexis Jacquemin, "Strategic Competition in a Global Environment", in OECD, 1991, *Trade, Investment* etc, p. 28
7. Ibid.
8. Ibid.
9. Ibid., p. 13
10. *Global Economic Policies and the Developing Countries*, World Bank, Washington DC, May 1991, p. 11
11. Ibid., p. 10
12. Ibid., p. 8

13. *Trade and Development Report, 1991*, United Nations Conference on Trade and Development (UNCTAD), New York, 16 September 1991, p. 72

14. World Bank 1991, *Global Economic Policies* etc, p. 11

15. Ibid.

16. Ibid., p. 12

17. Stevens and Andrieu, op. cit., p. 116

18. Jacquemin, op. cit., p. 17

19. Ibid., p. 19

20. UNCTAD, 1991, op. cit., p. 71

21. Stevens and Andrieu, op. cit., p. 117

22. John Llewellyn, Stephen Potter and Lec Samuelson, *Economic forecasting and policy – the international dimension*, Routledge & Kegan Paul, London, 1985, *passim*

23. Stephen Marris, in Willem H Buiter and Richard C Marston (eds.), *International Economic Policy Coordination*, Cambridge, 1985, p. 383

24. Meghnad Desai, "The Transition from Socialism to Capitalism", in Mann and Halliday (eds.), *Transition in World Systems*, Blackwell, Oxford, 1991; and "Is Socialism Dead?", Public Lecture in Ahmedabad, India, December 1991

CHAPTER TEN

1. *International Herald Tribune*, 29 April 1992

2. Ajit Singh, in Jonathan Michie (ed.), *The Economic Legacy 1979–1992*, Academic Press, London, 1992, p. 34

3. John Toye, "Britain, the United States and the World Debt Crisis", in Michie (ed.), op. cit., pp. 27–8

4. World Bank, 1991, *Global Economic Policies* etc, op. cit., p. 16

5. Robert Wade, *Governing the Market*, Princeton, 1991

6. Paul Mosley, Jane Harrigan and John Toye, *Aid and Power*, Routledge, London and New York, 1991, Vol. 1, p. 300

7. Ibid., pp. 303–4

8. Ibid., p. 304

9. World Development Report 1991, *The Challenge of Development*, OUP, p. 102

10. Nolan and Furens, op. cit., p. 114

11. Yung Chul Park, in OECD, 1991, *The Transition to a Market Economy*, op. cit., Vol. 1, pp, 150–2

12. Martin Walker, *The Waking Giant*, Michael Joseph, London, 1986, p. 53

13. Schumpeter, op. cit., p. 83

14. Ibid., p. 67

15. J K Galbraith. *The New Industrial State*, Hamish Hamilton, London, 1967, p. 319

16. Paul A Baran and Paul M Sweezy, *Monopoly Capital*, Penguin, London, 1975 edn., p. 58

17. Ibid., p. 59

18. Ibid., p. 100

19. *The Independent*, London, 18 February 1992

20. Cf. James Dale Davidson and William Rees-Mogg, *The Great Reckoning: How the*

World will change in the depression of the Nineties, Sidgwick, London, 1992
21. Alexandre Lamfalussy, Lecture to City University, London, 5 March 1992
22. Ibid.

CONCLUSION

1 Cf. David Pearce, Edward Barbier and Anil Markandya, *Sustainable Development*, Earthscan, London, 1990, *passim*
2 Niebuhr, op. cit., p. 258
3 Robert Skidelsky, *Financial Times*, 4 April 1992

4 Bill L Long, "Policies for the Environment", in Llewellyn and Potter, 1991, op. cit., p. 361
5 Paul Harrison, *The Third Revolution*, I B Tauris, London, 1992, p. 277
6 Professor Ian Fells, "Energy Strategy & the Environment", lecture at City University, London, 18 March 1992
7 Philip L Martin, "International Migration: A New Challenge", *International Economic Insights*, Institute for International Economics, Washington DC, March/ April 1992, p. 4

Bibliography

Ackerman, Frank, *Reaganomics – Rhetoric vs Reality*, London, 1982

Aganbegyan, Abel, *The Challenge: Economics of Perestroika*, London, 1988

Allen, G. C., *The Japanese Economy*, London, 1981

Armstrong, Philip, Glyn, Andrew & Harrison, John, *Capitalism since World War II*, London, 1984

Asselain, Jean-Charles, *Planning and Profits in Socialist Economics*, London, 1981

Baran, Paul A. & Sweezy, Paul M., *Monopoly Capital*, England, 1975

Begg, David, "Economic Reform in Czechoslovakia: Should we believe in Santa Claus?", *Economic Policy*, eds Georges Menil & Richard Portes, October 1991, Vol. 6, No. 2

Bhagwati, Jagdish, *Protectionism*, Massachusetts & London, 1988

Blumenthal, Sidney, *The Rise and Fall of the Counter-Establishment*, New York, 1986

Boote, Anthony R. & Somogyi, Janos, "Economic Reform in Hungary since 1968", *Occasional Paper 83*, Washington DC, July 1991

Brittan, Samuel, *The Role and Limits of Government*, Aldershot, 1987

Britton, A. J. C., *Macroeconomic Policy in Britain 1974–1987*, Cambridge, 1991

Buchanan, James M. & others, *The Consequences of Mr Keynes*, London, 1978
Reaganomics and After, London, 1989

Buiter, Willem H. & Marston, Richard C. (eds.), *International Economic Policy Coordination*, Cambridge, 1985

Cairncross, Sir Alec, *Years of Recovery*, London & New York, 1985

Cairncross, Frances, *Costing the Earth*, London, 1991

Clarke, Peter, *The Keynesian Revolution in the Making, 1925–1936*, Oxford, 1990

Clarke, Sir Richard, *Anglo-American Economic Collaboration in War and Peace 1942–1949*, ed. Sir Alec Cairncross, Oxford, 1982

Cole, G. D. H., *The Intelligent Man's Guide to the Post-War World*, London, 1948

Crawshaw, Steve, *Goodbye to the USSR*, London, 1992

Crook, Clive & Franklin, Daniel, *Eastern Europe in Transition*, London, 1990

Davidson, James Dale & Rees-Mogg, William, *The Great Reckoning: How the world will change in the depression of the Nineties*, London, 1992

De Menil, Georges & Portes, Richard (eds.), *Economic Policy*, CUP, October 1991

Directorate-General for Economic and Financial Affairs, "European Economy", *The Path of Reform in Central Eastern Europe*, Brussels, 1991, Special Edition No. 2

Dobb, Maurice, *Economic Growth and Underdeveloped Countries*, London, 1963
Argument on Socialism, London, 1966
Soviet Economic Development since 1917, London, 1972

Economic Commission for Europe, Secretariat of (Geneva), *Economic Survey of Europe in 1989–90*, UN, New York, 1990
Economic Survey of Europe in 1990–91, UN, New York, 1991
Economic Survey of Europe in 1991–92, UN, New York, 1992

Employment Institute, *Improving Britain's Industrial Performance*, London, 1991

European Bank for Reconstruction and Development, "A Changing Europe", *Annual Report 1991*, London, 1992

Fay, C. R., *Great Britain from Adam Smith to the Present Day* (3rd edition), London, 1932

Feinstein, Charles & others, *Historical Precedents for Economic Change in Central Europe and the USSR*, Oxford & London, 1990

Fogarty, Michael P., *Christian Democracy in Western Europe 1820–1953*, London, 1966

Fraser, Robert, *The World Financial System*, (Keesing's), London, 1987

Friedman, Milton & Rose, *Free to Choose*, London, 1980

Fukuyama, Francis, *The End of History and the Last Man*, London, 1992

Galbraith, John Kenneth, *A History of Economics*, London, 1987
The New Industrial State, London, 1967

Gerschenkron, Alexander, *Economic Backwardness in Historical Perspective*, New York, Washington & London, 1965

Gide, Charles & Rist, Charles, *A History of Economic Doctrines* (2nd edition), London, 1950

Gilder, George, *Wealth and Poverty*, New York, 1981

Gilmour, Ian, *Inside Right*, London, 1977

Graham, David & Clarke, Peter, *The New Enlightenment*, London, 1986

Green, Edwin, *Banking*, Oxford, 1989

Griffiths, Brian, *The Creation of Wealth*, London, 1984

Hamilton, Adrian, *The Financial Revolution*, England, 1986

Harrison, Paul, *The Third Revolution: Environment, Population and a Sustainable World*, London & New York, 1992

Heilbroner, Robert L., *Between Capitalism and Socialism*, New York, 1970

Hobsbawm, E. J., "Industry and Empire", *Pelican Economic History of Britain Vol. 3*, London, 1979

Hodgson, Geoff, *The Democratic Economy*, England, 1984

Huxley, Aldous, *Ends and Means*, London, 1938

Hyams, Edward, *The Millennium Postponed*, London, 1974

International Institute for Economics, "International Economic Insights", *The Great Migrations of the 1990s*, Washington DC, March/April 1992

"International Economic Insights", *The Many Flavours of Capitalism*, Washington DC, November/December 1991

International Monetary Fund, The World Bank, Organisation for Economic Cooperation and Development, European Bank for Reconstruction and Development (joint study), *A Study of the Soviet Economy* (3 vols.), Paris, February 1991

Johnson, Christopher (ed.), "The Market on Trial", *Lloyds Bank Annual Review Vol. 2*, London & New York, 1989

Joll, James, *Europe since 1870*, New York, 1973

Keegan, William, "Two Cheers for Capitalism", *Sheffield Papers in International Studies*, 1991, No. 9

Keizai Koho Centre, Japan. Institute for Social and Economic Affairs, *Japan 1991: An International Comparison* & *Japan 1992: An International Comparison*

Kemp, Tom, *The Climax of Capitalism*, London, 1990

Kennedy, Paul, *The Rise and Fall of the Great Powers*, London & Sydney, 1988

Keynes, John Maynard, "Essays in Persuasion", *The Collected Writings of John Maynard Keynes, Vol. IX*, London, 1984

Kindleberger Charles P., *A Financial History of Western Europe*, London, 1984

Kornai, Janos, *Anti-equilibrium*, Amsterdam, 1971

Lekachman, Robert & Van Loon, Borin, *Capitalism for Beginners*, London, 1981

Lekachman, Robert, *Greed is Not Enough: Reaganomics*, New York, 1982

Lenin, V. I., *What is to be Done?* Progress Publishers, Moscow, 1947

Lipschitz, Leslie & McDonald, Donogh, "German Unification. Economic Issues", *Occasional Paper No. 75*, Washington DC, 1990

Llewellyn, John & Potter, Stephen J. (eds.), *Economic Policies for the 1990s*, Oxford, 1991

Maddison, Angus, *Phases of Capitalist Development*, Oxford, 1989
The World Economy in the 20th Century, Paris, 1989

Marer, Paul & Zecchini, Salvatore (eds.), *The Transition to a Market Economy* (2 vols.), Paris, 1991

Marjolin, Robert, "Architect of European Unity", *Memoirs 1911–1986*, London, 1989

Michie, Jonathan (ed.), *The Economic Legacy 1979–1992*, London, 1992

Milward, Alan S., *The Reconstruction of Western Europe 1945–1951*, London, 1984

Moggridge, D. E., *Maynard Keynes: An Economist's Biography*, London & New York, 1992

Morita, Akio & Sony, *Made in Japan*, London, 1987

Mosley, Paul, Harrigan, Jane & Toye, John, *Aid and Power Vols. 1 & 2*, London & New York, 1991

Niebuhr, Reinhold, *Moral Man and Immoral Society*, New York, 1932

Nolan, Peter & Furens, Douglas, *The Chinese Economy and its Future*, Oxford, 1990

Nove, Alec, *The Economics of Feasible Socialism*, London, 1983
Socialist Economics, England, 1974
The Soviet Economic System, London, 1977

O'Brien, Richard (ed.), *Finance and the International Economy: 5*, Oxford, 1991

Odagiri, Hiroyuki, *Growth Through Competition, Competition Through Growth*, Oxford, 1992

"OECD In Figures", Statistics on the Member Countries, Supplement to *The OECD Observer*, June/July 1989, No. 158, June/July 1991, No. 170, June/July 1992, No. 176

OECD, "Industrial Policy in OECD Countries", *Annual Review 1991*, Paris, 1991
OECD Economic Outlook, Paris, December 1991, No. 50
OECD Economic Surveys: Germany, Paris, July 1991
OECD Economic Surveys: Hungary, Paris, July 1991
OECD Economic Surveys: Japan, Paris, November 1991
OECD Economic Surveys: United States, Paris, November 1990

Trade Investment and Technology in the 1990s, Paris, 1991

Ogg, Frederic Austin & Sharp, Walter Rice, *Economic Development of Modern Europe*, New York, 1930

Peacock, Alan & Willgerodt, Hans (eds.), *German Neo-Liberals and the Social Market Economy*, London, 1989

Germany's Social Market Economy, London, 1989

Pearce, David, Barbier, Edward & Markandya, Anil, *Sustainable Development: Economics and Environment in the Third World*, London, 1990

Peck, Merton J. & Richardson, Thomas J. (eds.), *What is to be done?*, New Haven, 1991

Polanyi, Karl, *The Great Transformation*, Boston, 1944

Porter, Michael E., *The Competitive Advantage of Nations*, London, 1991

Portes, Richard & others, *The Economic Consequences of the East*, London, 1992

Prust, Jim & an IMF staff team, "The Czech and Slovak Federal Republic: An Economy in Transition", *IMF Occasional Paper 72*, Washington DC, October 1990

Przeworski, Adam, *Democracy and the Market: Political and Economic Reforms in Eastern Europe and Latin America*, Cambridge, 1991

Readman, Peter & others, *The European Money Puzzle*, London, 1974

Robinson, Joan, *Freedom & Necessity*, London, 1970

Rollo, J. M. C. & others, *The New Eastern Europe: Western, Responses*, London, 1990

Rosenberg, Nathan & Birdzell L. E. Jr, "Science, Technology and the Western Miracle", *Scientific American*, November 1990, Vol. 263, No. 5

Roy, Subroto, *Philosophy of Economics*, London, 1989

Schumpeter, Joseph A., *Capitalism, Socialism and Democracy*, London, 1976

Seabrook, Jeremy, *The Myth of the Market*, London, 1989

Seldon, Arthur, *Capitalism*, Oxford, 1990

Sen, Amartya, *On Ethics and Economics*, Oxford, 1987

Siebert, Horst, "German Unification: The Economics of Transition", *Economic Policy*, eds. Georges Menil & Richard Portes, October 1991, Vol. 6, No. 2

Shirer, William L., *The Rise and Fall of the Third Reich*, London, 1963

Shonfield, Andrew, *In Defence of the Mixed Economy*, Oxford, 1984

Modern Capitalism, Oxford, 1965

The Use of Public Power, Oxford, 1982

Smith, Adam, *An Inquiry into the Nature and Causes of the Wealth of Nations*, London, 1893 edition

Stalin, Joseph, *Leninism*, London, 1940

Starrels, John M., *Assisting Reform in Eastern Europe*, Washington DC, 1991

Stephens, Michael D., *Japan and Education*, London, 1991
Education and the Future of Japan, England, 1991

Stockman, David A., *The Triumph of Politics*, New York, 1986

Tomlinson, Jim, *Hayek and the Market*, London, Winchester, Massachusetts, 1990

United Nations Conference on Trade and Development, *Trade and Development Report 1991*, New York, 1991
"The Least Developed Countries", *1991 Report*, New York, 1992

Wade, Robert, *Governing the Market*, London, 1992

Walker, Martin, *The Waking Giant*, London, 1986

Winckler, Georg (moderator), *Central and Eastern Europe Roads to Growth*, Washington, 1992

Wolf, Marvin J., *The Japanese Conspiracy*, England, 1984

The World Bank, *Global Economic Prospects and the Developing Countries*, May 1991
World Development Report 1991, Oxford 1991
"Development and the Environment", *World Development Report 1992*

Index